# Infectious Disease Ethics

Michael J. Selgelid · Angela R. McLean · Nimalan Arinaminpathy · Julian Savulescu

Editors

# Infectious Disease Ethics

Limiting Liberty in Contexts of Contagion

Previouly published in: Archivum Immunologiae et Therapiae Experimentalis 56: 147–152, 2008
Health Care Analysis 10: 29–35, 2002
Health Care Analysis 10: 67–85, 2002
Journal of Bioethicial Inquiry, 6:2, various articles, 2009
NanoEthics 3: 175–183, 2009
Poiesis and Praxis 3: 229–241, 2005

Springer

*Editors*
Michael J. Selgelid
Monash University
Centre for Human Bioethics
Clayton, Australia

Angela McLean
University of Oxford
Institute for Emerging Infections
Oxford, UK

Nimalan Arinaminpathy
University of Oxford
Institute for Emerging Infections
Oxford, UK

Julian Savulescu
Oxford Uehiro Centre for Practical Ethics
Oxford, UK

ISBN: 978-94-007-0563-0



Printed on acid-free paper

Springer is part of Springer+Business Media (www.springer.com)

# Contents

# Preface

This volume is an expansion of a Special Issue of *Journal of Bioethical Inquiry* (Volume 6, Number 2, June 2009) which was produced from a conference—on "Infectious Disease Ethics: Limiting Liberty in Contexts of Contagion"—at the University of Oxford on 4 July 2007. This conference was jointly organised by Julian Savulescu, Michael Selgelid, and Angela McLean and was jointly held by the James Martin 21$^{st}$ Century School (Program on Ethics of the New Biosciences and Institute for Emergent Infections) of the University of Oxford, and the Centre for Applied Philosophy and Public Ethics (CAPPE) of the Australian National University. In addition to conference proceedings, this volume includes a number of reprints of what we consider the most important relevant articles published in Springer and/or Kluwer journals during recent years.

Michael Selgelid thanks the Brocher Foundation (www.brocher.ch) in Hermance (Switzerland) for hosting him as a visiting researcher in 2009 (during the period when the majority of the editorial work on this volume took place) and in 2007 (when the majority of the organisation for the relevant conference at Oxford took place). Production of this volume was also partly supported by an Australian Research Council Discovery Project Grant on "Infectious Diseases, Security and Ethics". We thank Michal Dick for research assistance.

**Michael J. Selgelid, Angela R. McLean, Nimalan Arinaminpathy, and Julian Savulescu**

# Introduction

**Michael J. Selgelid, Angela R. McLean,**
**Nimalan Arinaminpathy, Julian Savulescu**

## Infectious Disease History and Status Quo

Infectious diseases are among humankind's worst enemies. They have historically caused more morbidity and mortality than any other cause, including war (Price-Smith 2001). Killing roughly 15 million people each year, they are currently the biggest killers of children and young adults worldwide.

Public health and medical progress—most notably with regard to improvements in sanitation, hygiene, and nutrition; and the development of vaccines and antibiotics—led to dramatic improvements in infectious disease control during the past two centuries, especially in developed countries. Early in the second half of the twentieth century, modern medicine's power over infectious diseases appeared to be so great that it was commonly believed that it was "time to close the book on infectious disease" (Sassetti and Rubin 2007, 279).[1]

During recent decades, however, it has become clear that infectious diseases remain a major threat to humankind. Their continued danger is partly revealed by the phenomenon of "emerging and re-emerging infectious diseases", whereby many new diseases (such as AIDS, Ebola, and SARS, to name just a few) have come into existence (or started spreading in humans, while transmission was formerly limited to other animals) and "old" diseases have been making strong comebacks. Related to this is the growing problem of drug resistance, for example the serious problems posed by new forms of tuberculosis (TB). Extensively drug resistant tuberculosis (XDR-TB) is resistant to so many classes of drugs that half of XDR-TB patients cannot be successfully treated. In the context of TB, therefore, it may soon be as though we have returned to a situation analogous to the pre-antibiotic era (Selgelid 2008). Unlike AIDS (which is only transmissible via exchange of bodily fluids), TB is an airborne disease that can readily be transmitted from person to person via casual contact: by coughing, sneezing, and even talking. In 2007 an American lawyer thought to be infected with XDRTB was subjected to the first US federal quarantine restriction since 1963.

One of the worst pandemics (i.e., widespread global epidemics) in history was the great Spanish Flu, which killed somewhere between 20 and 100 million people in 1918-19. Experts have for many years warned that it is not a matter of if, but when, the next major flu pandemic will strike. Although flu pandemics are not regularly cyclical, there were three pandemics in the last century; and with 40 years passed since the last pandemic of 1968, it has been widely believed that the next major pandemic is overdue. After several years of concern that a pandemic would arise from H5N1 avian influenza—which kills over 60% of humans it infects but has not, to date, led to sustained human-to-human transmission—a pandemic of H1N1 swine influenza, originating with a human epidemic in Mexico, was declared by WHO in June 2009. Although this particular pandemic did not turn out to be very severe (in terms of morbidity and mortality), the danger that a more severe pandemic arising from another strain of influenza (e.g., H5N1)—or another disease altogether—still remains.

In some ways we are now better prepared for a major pandemic than our predecessors were in 1918-19. Global surveillance for potentially pandemic-causing diseases is greater today than ever before. Moreover, antiviral drugs, vaccines, and antibiotics may allow us to fight the next severe pandemic more effectively than was possible in 1918-19 (when such effective pharmaceutical interventions were not yet available). In the case of a severe flu pandemic, however, the supply of antivirals will likely not meet demand; it takes 6 months before large-scale production of vaccine against a new strain of influenza is possible and several years before world population demand can be met (WHO 2009). Meanwhile, other aspects of the contemporary world

[1] Though this quote is routinely attributed to former US Surgeon General William Stewart, there appears to be no evidence that he ever actually said this. Whether or not Stewart himself said this, according to Sassetti and Rubin, "the sentiment was certainly widely shared".

may exacerbate dangers in comparison with the situation in 1918-19. Increased population densities, particularly in megacities, and the increase in trade and travel associated with globalisation, for example, may facilitate the speed at which the next major pandemic will spread (Arinaminpathy et al. 2009; Brockmann et al. 2005).

## IDE: Infectious Disease Ethics

Though ethical issues associated with infectious disease have not been a traditional focus of discussion within the discipline of bioethics—and though it has been argued that the topic of infectious disease was for a long time grossly neglected by bioethicists (Selgelid 2005; Francis et al. 2005)—this has started to change. AIDS was perhaps an exception all along; it, at least, received substantial discussion among bioethicists since its emergence was first recognized in the early 1980s. More recently, the SARS crisis of 2003 and fears over influenza and bioterrorism (especially following the events of 11 September 2001 and the subsequent anthrax attacks in the US) have attracted additional attention to ethical problems posed by infectious disease. The growing literature on ethics and infectious disease is partly related to the emergence of public health ethics as a rapidly growing subdiscipline of bioethics; and a number of recent books have focused on ethical issues associated with infectious disease in particular (Selgelid et al. 2006; Balint et al. 2006; Lemon et al. 2007; Battin et al. 2009). We call this new field Infectious Disease Ethics (IDE).

Infectious diseases raise a relatively unique constellation of ethical problems. Because (in most cases) infectious diseases are spread from person to person, innocent individuals can present a threat to other innocent individuals. Issues of respect for liberty, responsibility, prioritization, discrimination, equality, and distributive justice arise acutely. Restrictions of liberty and incursions of privacy and confidentiality may be necessary to promote the public good.

Even allowing or inflicting risk of harm on individuals may be morally required in extreme circumstances. Depending on the disease, imposition of quarantine may sometimes be necessary to prevent a major epidemic. However, in cases where an airplane, cruise ship, building, or region is quarantined, uninfected individuals held in (possibly close) confinement with infected individuals may themselves end up becoming infected—and perhaps die—as a result. Though this would be unfortunate, unintentional imposition of such harms may be justified (just as we tolerate killing of innocent individuals in times of war) if the stakes for public health are sufficiently high.

Part of the ethical importance of infectious diseases relates to the fact that their consequences can be so severe. Naturally-occurring epidemics have constituted some of the most devastating events in human history. For example, the Black Death eliminated one-third of the European population over the course of a few years in the middle of the fourteenth century.

The Astronomer Royal and President of the Royal Society, Martin Rees estimates that "the odds are no better than fifty-fifty that our present civilisation on Earth will survive to the end of the present century" (Rees 2003). One of the most significant threats to civilization this century will be the use of bioweapons and bioterrorism. Such dangers are exacerbated by recent advances in the life sciences which may facilitate development of a new generation of biological weapons (of mass destruction). Much recent debate has focused on the "dual-use" aspect of biotechnological research: the same discoveries which may lead to scientific and/or medical progress may also facilitate aspiring bioterrorists. We will thus require an ethics of infectious disease to deal not only with naturally occurring pandemics but also with those which will almost inevitably be caused by evil human beings. It has perhaps never been more urgent in the last 100 years to develop an ethical as well as a medical approach to dealing with widespread outbreaks of infectious disease.

Finally, we should recall that the topic of infectious disease is closely connected to the topic of international justice. The infectious disease burden (at present, anyway) is by far the highest in poor countries. For example, 95% of TB cases and 98% of TB deaths occur in developing countries. This is partly because things like malnutrition, lack of sanitation and hygiene, poor education, and crowded living and working conditions are factors which increase chances of becoming infected with such diseases. Furthermore, the poor are more likely to suffer bad outcomes when infection occurs because they cannot afford medicines for which they must pay out-of-pocket, and healthcare systems in poor countries are usually weak. The fact that many poverty-stricken patients in poor countries cannot afford to finish courses of treatment they have started is part of the explanation for the rise of drug resistant disease. When drug resistant strains of disease emerge and spread, these pose increased risks to rich and poor countries alike. There are thus self-interested as well as moral reasons why wealthy nations should do more to help improve the healthcare situation in poor countries.

## Oxford Conference

This volume is one step towards supporting the development of IDE. It is largely a product of an interdisciplinary conference that took place at University of Oxford in 2007. This conference strengthened our conviction that the interdisciplinary space between philosophers and scientists, where it exists, can offer fertile ground for collaborative efforts. Nonetheless, a lively discourse between both groups was lost in translation from the conference and review process to this edited volume—which is an expansion of a Special Issue of *Journal of Bioethical Inquiry* produced from the conference proceedings (but also contains a number of additional papers). A recurring critique from philosopher reviewers during the journal review process was that papers by scientists were "naive" in their treatment of the ethical issues raised. The common riposte from scientists was "we are not ethicists, we're just describing an ethical issue we have observed". Furthermore, especially during the conference, scientists sometimes complained that the philosophers were not sufficiently informed about empirical matters and thus not realistic. This creative tension clearly points towards a rich potential for deeper, longer collaborations producing joint papers that can move these questions on from a cross-disciplinary discourse to a truly interdisciplinary one.

## This Volume

As our subtitle—Limiting Liberty in Contexts of Contagion—suggests, paramount among ethical issues associated with infectious disease are those that arise with conflict between the goal to promote individual liberty, on the one hand, and the goal to promote other legitimate social goals such as (equality or) utility in the way of public health, on the other. The papers in this volume focus on such conflicts and, *inter alia*, illustrate the diversity of ways in which such conflicts can arise and offer carefully argued, creative solutions for addressing them.

Part I addresses ethical issues associated with Pandemic Planning. In Chapter 1 Marcel Verweij explores the question of how scarce medical resources should be allocated in the context of a severe flu pandemic. Though ethical principles appealing to values such as utility and equity may sometimes conflict, he argues that there may be convergence among principles with regard to the goal of allocating resources in order to save the most lives. In Chapter 2 Arinaminpathy et al. demonstrate ways in which mathematical modelling may be used to inform allocation decisions regarding a limited stockpile of antiviral drugs—which may be efficacious in both alleviating symptoms of treated individuals and reducing disease transmission in the community—in the context of a flu pandemic. They conclude that modelling reveals that strategies which optimally minimise morbidity and mortality are often not intuitively obvious, and that they may conflict with popular theories of justice.

The papers in Part II consider Health Workers' Rights and Duties in the context of infectious diseases. In Chapter 3, Lawrence Gostin objects to policy that requires healthcare workers infected with HIV or HBV to be reviewed by expert panels and inform patients of their serological status—because recent evidence demonstrates that risks of disease transmission to patients are low. He proposes an alternative policy that, he argues, "would achieve high levels of patient safety without discrimination and invasion of privacy". In Chapter 4, Carl Coleman challenges the argument that a driving factor behind the emergence of drug resistance is that doctors face legal pressure to provide inappropriate prescriptions to patients. When prescription decisions are based on sound public health principles, according to Coleman, it is unlikely that doctors would be held liable for malpractice (even in cases where they refuse to prescribe drugs that would benefit patients).

Part III turns to ethical issues associated with Vaccination Policy. In Chapter 5, Angus Dawson questions the extent to which public health policy makers should be influenced by public perceptions regarding vaccination dangers. He concludes that policy decisions should be "primarily concerned with the creation and maintenance of public goods"—and that they should thus be primarily based upon scientific evidence rather than public perceptions (which should, nonetheless, be taken into consideration). In Chapter 6, Helen Fletcher et al. identify ethical challenges that would arise with the development of a new, improved TB vaccine. They argue that the development and deployment of such a vaccine would "reduce the occurrence of conflict between the rights and liberties of infected individuals versus those of society".

The papers in Part IV consider questions about Coercion and Compensation. Søren Holm, in Chapter 7, defends the idea that those who are subjected to liberty restrictions in the name of public health protection should be compensated in return. He addresses numerous arguments that might be offered in opposition to this idea, and he argues that they are unpersuasive. In Chapter 8, A. M. Viens et al. aim to show how compensation may be grounded in a moral principle of reciprocity. They argue that policy based on such a principle could morally legitimise and increase trust in—and thus motivate compliance with—restrictive public health policies.

Part V examines ethical questions about Opt-Out HIV testing. Harold Jaffe offers arguments in support of opt-out testing in Chapter 9. Though he admits that this approach raises "issues concerning 'voluntariness', access to care, and stigma", he argues that "the potential benefits of opt-out testing far outweigh its potential adverse effects". In Chapter 10's commentary on Jaffe's analysis, Dominic Wilkinson demonstrates ways in which debates about opt-out HIV testing parallel those concerned with organ donation.

The papers in Part VI analyse emerging ethical issues associated with public health Surveillance. In Chapter 11, Ronald Bayer and Amy Fairchild question the legitimacy of name-based HIV reporting. While the policy in question raises questions about conflicts between privacy and public health, they aim to show how an understanding of history should inform debates about HIV reporting and surveillance ethics more generally. Leslie Francis et al., in Chapter 12, draw attention to ethical issues associated with "syndromic surveillance" in particular. While this kind of surveillance may allow early detection of disease patterns, they argue, it may pose "novel problems for informed consent, patient privacy and confidentiality, and risks of stigmatization".

Part VII, finally, explores ethical issues associated with Dual-Use Research with implications for biological weapons making. In Chapter 13, Michael Selgelid analyses the concept of "dual use" and identifies benefits and limitations of implementation of science codes of conduct as a means to reduce risks associated with dual-use research. Though codes of conduct are often considered to be voluntary science governance instruments, he argues that they could and/or should form part of a broader regulatory oversight system. In Chapter 14, Hans-Jörg Ehni questions the extent of scientists' duties and responsibilities in contexts involving dual-use research. He argues that the scientific community and (other) relevant institutions, rather than individual scientists, should bear primary responsibility for preventing harmful applications of research.

We hope that this volume stimulates the reader to appreciate just how urgent and significant IDE is. Though this collection of papers demonstrates recent rapid progress in public health ethics discourse, there is still much work to be done.


**Acknowledgement**

An earlier version of this Introduction was published as the Editorial of the Special Edition of *Journal of Bioethical Inquiry* on "Infectious Disease Ethics: Limiting Liberty in Contexts of Contagion" (Volume 6, Number 2, 2009, pp. 149–152).


**References**


Arinaminpathy, N., A.R. McLean, and H.C. Godfray. 2009. Land use change and infectious disease. Forthcoming.

Balint, J., S. Philpott, R. Baker, and M. Strosberg, eds. 2006. *Ethics and epidemics*. Oxford, UK: Elsevier.

Battin, M.P., L.P. Francis, J.A. Jacobson, and C.B. Smith. 2009. *The patient as victim and vector: Ethics and infectious disease*. Oxford, UK: Oxford University Press.

Brockmann, D., L. Hufnagel, and T. Geisel. 2005. Dynamics of modern epidemics. In *SARS: A case study in emerging infections*, McLean A.R., May R.M., Pattison J and Weiss R. A (eds). Oxford, UK: Oxford University Press.

Francis, L.P., M. Battin, J.A. Jacobson, C.B. Smith, and J. Botkin. 2005. How infectious diseases got left out—and what this omission might have meant for bioethics. *Bioethics* 19(4): 307–322.

Lemon, S.M., M.A. Hamburg, P.F. Sparling, E.R. Choffnes, A. Mack, and Rapporteurs, Forum on Microbial Threats. 2007. *Ethical and legal considerations in mitigating pandemic disease: Workshop summary.* Washington, DC: The National Academies Press.

Price-Smith, A.T. 2001. *The health of nations: Infectious disease, environmental change, and their effects on national security and development.* Cambridge, MA: MIT Press.

Sassetti, C.M., and E.J. Rubin. 2007. The open book of infectious diseases. *Nature Medicine* 13(3): 279–280.

Rees, M. 2003. *Our final century.* London: William Heinemann.

Selgelid, M.J. 2005. Ethics and infectious disease. *Bioethics* 19(3): 272–289.

Selgelid, M.J. 2008. Ethics, tuberculosis and globalization. *Public Health Ethics* 1(1): 10–20.

Selgelid, M.J., M.P. Battin, and C.B. Smith, eds. 2006. Ethics and infectious disease. Oxford, UK: Blackwell.

Stop TB Partnership. 2007. Extensively drug-resistant tuberculosis (XDR-TB): The facts http://www.stoptb.org/events/world_tb_day/2007/assets/documents/5.5%20XDR%20TB.pdf (accessed 19 May 2009)

WHO. 2009. Vaccines for the new influenza A (H1N1) http://www.who.int/csr/disease/swineflu/frequently_asked_questions/vaccine_preparedness/en/index.html (accessed 19 May 2009)

# Part I: Pandemic Planning

Bioethical Inquiry (2009) 6:159–169
DOI 10.1007/s11673-009-9161-6

# Moral Principles for Allocating Scarce Medical Resources in an Influenza Pandemic

**Marcel Verweij**

Received: 13 November 2008 / Accepted: 7 May 2009 / Published online: 26 May 2009


**Abstract** One of the societal problems in a new influenza pandemic will be how to use the scarce medical resources that are available for prevention and treatment, and what medical, epidemiological and ethical justifications can be given for the choices that have to be made. Many things may become scarce: personal protective equipment, antiviral drugs, hospital beds, mechanical ventilation, vaccination, etc. In this paper I discuss two general ethical principles for priority setting (utility and equity) and explain how these principles will often point in diverging directions. Moreover, each of these principles can be understood in different, again often competing, ways. Notwithstanding these controversies and conflicts, in the context of pandemic response there are at least some points of convergence: several policies can be justified by appeal to different ethical principles and theories. Convergence may be found with respect to a focus on saving the most lives (instead of other aggregative accounts); giving priority antiviral prophylaxis and therapy for life-saving pandemic responders; and, partly depending on epidemiology of the pandemic, to prioritise vaccination of children. Although decision-making about access to intensive care will involve choices with immediate tragic implications, the ethical complexity of these choices is relatively modest (although decisions will not be easy): there are persuasive moral reasons for giving priority to patients who are expected to benefit most within the shortest time. Finally, in the last section I tentatively argue that constraints on people's freedom, as necessary for an effective public health approach, may support giving somewhat more weight to saving the most lives, than to concerns of equity.

**Keywords** Ethics · Justice · Influenza · Pandemic · Priority-setting · Rationing · Triage · Efficiency · Equity · Fairness · Equitable access · Vaccination · Antiviral drugs · Neuraminidase inhibitors · Intensive care · Mechanical ventilation · Harm principle

This paper is largely based upon a background report I wrote for the World Health Organization (Verweij 2008). The report was used as input for a WHO consultation process that lead to ethical guidance for influenza pandemic preparedness and response plans (WHO 2007). In preparing my report I benefited from comments from numerous persons at the WHO and members of a working group of whom I would like to mention especially Andreas Reis, Dan Brock, Iwao Hirose, and Clement Adebamowo. I am also grateful to Michael Selgelid for some very fruitful comments on my tentative argument in the last section of this paper.

M. Verweij (✉)
Ethics Institute, Utrecht University,
Heidelberglaan 8,
3584 CS Utrecht, The Netherlands
e-mail: m.f.verweij@uu.nl

## Ethics and Pandemic Influenza

It is generally expected that sooner or later a novel influenza A virus sub-type easily transmissible from person-to-person will emerge and cause pandemic disease. Humans will then have little or no immunity against this virus, which could spread as easily as common seasonal influenza, infect many people worldwide and may potentially result in very high mortality and morbidity rates. In the 20$^{th}$ century three such pandemics occurred, with the 1918–1920 "Spanish Flu" as the most devastating epidemic. It is estimated that the Spanish Flu caused 50 million deaths worldwide, but experts emphasise that these figures are uncertain, and that the death toll could even be up to 100 million (Johnson and Mueller 2002). Nowadays the world population is much larger and a comparable toll in our times could be between 175 and 350 million (Barry 2005). There are also many reasons for thinking that a new pandemic would be less disastrous. Compared to 1918, people in most parts of the world today live in conditions that are much better in terms of hygiene. Moreover, at least in high-income countries, far fewer people have shortages of necessary nutrition. Today's state of medical knowledge and the possibilities for treating patients with all kinds of illnesses and symptoms are far more advanced in comparison with the limited medical possibilities 90 years ago. Antiviral drugs (neuraminidase inhibitors like oseltamivir) may possibly help to avoid some of the worst complications of influenza; antibiotics will play a role in the treatment of secondary bacterial infections; and mechanical ventilation can help patients who develop respiratory failure as a result of influenza. On the other hand, modern mobility seems to create ideal conditions for a new virus to spread over the world within a matter of days or weeks. Vaccination offers reasonable protection against seasonal influenza, but in a pandemic mass production of an effective vaccine will not start for several months. Moreover, the basic as well as sophisticated medical resources we have now may become extremely scarce if the population is overwhelmed by a pandemic. Certainly, such resources are not commonly available in many low-income countries. And last but not least, it is unknown what sort of antigenic shift in the virus will cause the next pandemic and, hence, there is uncertainty to what extent, for example, antiviral drugs will be effective in reducing morbidity and mortality during a pandemic. All expectations and predictions about the magnitude and impact of a new influenza pandemic are filled with uncertainty. Some scenarios assume attack rates of up to 35 percent and lethal disease in 1–2 percent of all persons who develop symptoms, yet such assumptions may be a gross overestimation or underestimation of the crisis (LCI 2006). Even in less extreme scenarios, drastic public health interventions will be necessary to contain or mitigate the pandemic. Policies that aim at "social distancing" will be important, such as the closure of schools and workplaces, and the quarantine of persons who may be exposed to the virus. Moreover, examination, isolation and treatment of patients will be necessary. Obviously, vaccination will play a major role as soon as an effective and safe vaccine is available. People may need to be compelled to comply with such interventions, and this clearly raises ethical and legal concerns (Kotalik 2005; Gostin and Berkman 2007).

In this paper I will not focus on such measures, but on the moral problems that arise due to scarcity of medical resources. Even if a pandemic were not as severe as the darkest scenarios suggest, one can reasonably expect that, both on local and global scales, the demand for medical care and protection will exceed (affordable) supplies. Countries are now creating stockpiles of neuraminidase inhibitors like oseltamivir (*Tamiflu*), which may be used both as prophylactic as a therapeutic means against influenza. The Netherlands has a stockpile which should be sufficient for treating 5 million citizens (30 percent of the population) who it is projected would develop influenza symptoms. However, even with such a stockpile, there may be insufficient drugs available for large-scale (post-exposure) prophylaxis. The more drugs are used for prevention of infection in persons who *might* get infected, the less will be available for treating persons who are having symptoms of influenza.

Many patients who get ill may develop respiratory failure and require mechanical ventilation. The need for such intensive care will go far beyond available resources.

Moreover, the disease will hit health care professionals and related personnel as well: working in the frontline they may even run greater risks of infection than other citizens. This only reinforces pressure on the health care system, where much more must be done with fewer staff. Triage decisions for allocating scarce possibilities for treatment will be inevitable. These decisions need to be made about supportive medical care (e.g. ventilators), antibiotics, antiviral drugs, and vaccines, as well as access to healthcare facilities in general. Two very general ethical principles for such decisions are utility and equity. In this paper I explore different interpretations of these two principles, and discuss how these can conflict but also converge in general policies as well as in choices concerning allocation of specific resources.

## Resource Allocation in a Pandemic

Throughout the last decades it has been very difficult to establish consensus-based or well-justified principles for priority setting in health care (Daniels 2008, 105-117). In times of an influenza pandemic the same controversies arise, but in extraordinary circumstances. The demand and need for health care will be much higher than is normally the case and simultaneously the health care system will be weakened as a result of ill or absent staff. If only relatively few persons can be treated, and most others are left without the care they need, this may raise distrust in professionals, institutions and governments. Moreover, fear of the disease may paralyse societal life or lead to panic and further distrust in governments and institutions. In such circumstances, the objective of developing principles for priority setting seems even more controversial than in "normal" health care settings. Finally, important factual issues that are more or less known in normal circumstances (the effectiveness of the various medical options; which groups are most at risk; which patients most urgently need treatment; and how many there are) are not known in advance.

However, these extraordinary features do not necessarily render any attempt to priority setting impossible, and to some extent they might even facilitate the development of some principles for priority setting. First, a pandemic is to be considered as a world-wide emergency situation where all or almost all individuals are susceptible and therefore threatened. Policies should focus, then, on protection of all members of the population at large. This is an objective that few will reject. Second, the uncertainties about *who* will be most at risk for severe illness and death in a pandemic might necessitate that decision-makers focus on general principles and arguments, instead of on specific groups or persons who should be given priority. If all are uncertain about who would benefit from certain proposals and who would not, this might help generate some agreement on principles—the unknown dimensions and characteristics of a future influenza pandemic create, as it were, an inevitable "veil ignorance" similar to the "original position" in Rawls's theory of justice (Rawls 1971).

Two further complexities need to be mentioned at this stage. Priorities need to be set for medical resources that differ in many relevant respects, with vaccination, patient care, and antiviral drugs being the most notable. Vaccination is meant purely for preventive purposes and is aimed at those who have not yet been infected; (hospital) medical care involves therapy aimed at the (very) ill; and antiviral treatment can be used as an early treatment for patients, and as post-exposure or pre-exposure prophylaxis. There are also differences in the dynamics of scarcity. Production of vaccines will not start within several months after the onset of the pandemic, and vaccines may then become available in increasing quantities. The availability of antiviral drugs and access to hospital care, on the other hand, will decrease rapidly during the first weeks of the pandemic. These differences in resource availability over time justify having distinct approaches for priority setting.

An additional complexity is that the differences between high-income countries and middle- and low-income countries will be immense. Some high-income countries expect to have sufficient stockpiles of antiviral drugs for treating all persons who develop symptoms of influenza. Low-income countries will probably have little or no stockpiles at all. Something similar applies to vaccination. Many high-income countries are signing contracts with pharmaceutical companies, in order to reserve production capacity and get pandemic vaccine as soon as it becomes available. Low-income countries will not have such contracts, and hence might have nothing to distribute. Some dilemmas that are seen as perplexing in hospitals in the developed world, such as priority setting in critical-care departments, may be completely absent in many regions in Africa, where no intensive care units might be available at all. Low-income countries must balance their efforts in pandemic preparedness with regular health care needs, given that such needs often remain unmet even in "normal circumstances". Any adequate response to a pandemic requires infrastructures for primary care and prevention. Hence, for many low-income countries the first priority for pandemic preparedness may involve strengthening their basic health care facilities and infrastructure.

In the following sections I will discus two general principles for priority setting: utility and equity. In major disasters where many lives are at stake, there are strong moral reasons to protect the population and save as many as possible with available resources. On the other hand, distribution of scarce medical resources should also be equitable and fair. Arguably, these general principles are relevant in any situation of allocation of scarce medical resources. In the context of a pandemic, however, these principles may be given different weight and interpretation.

## Efficiency and Utility: Saving Most Lives With Available Resources?

A common assumption in health care is that patients who are most ill and urgently require treatment, should be treated first. In an influenza pandemic a different approach might be justified and necessary. Pandemic influenza will spread rapidly, potentially affecting or killing many people, and it will put the health care system under very heavy pressure. All persons run the risk of being infected, many (if not all) are at some risk of fatal illness, and clearly not all can be saved. Moreover, during an epidemic, one should not only focus on the beneficial effects of prophylaxis or therapy for the persons who are treated. Vaccination of a person will not only protect this person, but also prevent this person becoming contagious and infecting others. The same applies to other forms of protection, including prophylactic uses of antiviral drugs. In these circumstances it makes sense to depart from the common medical ethos of prioritising the most needy and urgent, and to allocate health care resources in such a way that maximum protection of the population at large will be realised. Efficient application of scarce medical resources then becomes a central concern. A principle of mere efficiency however is silent with regard to *which* goods are to be maximised. Likewise, a consequentialist ethical theory, endorsing the idea that one should maximise expected value, must have a clear account of which values are to be promoted.

Epidemiological modeling studies and government action plans for pandemic planning and response often focus on *saving the most lives*. This objective probably fits many people's common sense moral beliefs about how to act in a disaster, yet a focus on saving the most lives is not the only reasonable option. Utilitarians and other consequentialists may argue that a broader account of health benefits is preferable. For example, allocation of medical resources could be done in such a way to maximise life-years, or quality-adjusted life-years (QALYs) or disability-adjusted life years gained.

More broadly, public health interventions could aim at maximizing expected utility, in which goods as diverse as life, health, happiness, economic flourishing, etc are combined. As a result, utilitarianism can sometimes prioritise protecting societal institutions or essential economic functions instead of saving the most lives (Kass et al. 2008).

Such a broad conception of aggregate value has implications that are rejected by many non-consequentialist theories. After all, if it is acceptable in moral argument to aggregate benefits and harms over people, then one must sometimes accept that to save one person in real need is not required if this would lead to a small inconvenience for a great number of persons. In this way, the stronger claim of the individual is given less weight than the much smaller claims of the many, which is considered unacceptable in a theory where persons are of central concern (cf. Scanlon 1998). A non-consequentialist theory like Scanlon's however can accept the principle to save the greater number of lives, starting from the assumption that all persons have a strong and equal claim to have their lives saved. In a pandemic many persons will get ill and may die, and not all can be saved. In those circumstances it is reasonable for all to accept a principle that supports saving the largest number of lives. Such a principle seems to involve aggregation of the claims or lives of individuals. However, if the focus is on saving lives (and not on less weighty values), and if each life counts equally, this will not allow sacrificing someone's life in order to secure smaller benefits for the greater number.[1]

[1] Hirose (2001) shows that in a contractualist framework it is even possible to accept the principle to save the greater number, without relying on aggregation or combining the claims of individuals. Assuming that all persons whose lives are in danger have a equal claim to be saved, the Pareto principle and the requirement of universalisation are sufficient to argue for saving most lives.

There are also consequentialist and pragmatic reasons against policies that maximise general utility. Especially when society finds itself threatened by a lethal infectious disease, potentially raising panic and fear, it is important that the public feel they can trust health care institutions and government policies. Policies that aim to protect societal and economic functions may support giving governments and others in positions of leadership priority access to prevention and treatment. If governments and persons in power receive a level of protection that is inaccessible to large parts of the public, this will easily raise suspicion and distrust amongst the public. In contrast, a principle to *save as many lives as possible* is very simple and clear, and cannot be easily tailored to secure just the interests of groups who are in power. This further helps to avoid unfairness and to promote public acceptance.

These considerations support the adoption of an approach that distributes health care during the pandemic on the basis of maximizing health benefits, and saving lives in particular. The scope of concerns is restricted to concerns about health and disease, and non-health benefits should not determine rationing policies. Of course, protecting the economy and other sources of welfare are important considerations for pandemic preparedness, but these might especially play a role in determining the (extra) budget available for pandemic response. For example, building a stockpile will require large amounts of extra funds and deliberation about how many resources should be made available will depend on weighing the importance of non-health goods, such as welfare or education (Cf. Brock 2003).

If the focus is on health benefits, and saving lives in particular, a next issue is whether *indirect* benefits should be taken into account as well (Brock 2003). For example, treating a health care worker is not only beneficial because it might save her life, but if she recovers, she will contribute to saving the lives of further persons. Therefore, it makes sense to give health care workers priority access to treatment. In normal health care circumstances, such considerations are often considered inappropriate and unfair. In a pandemic, however, many persons will die from influenza, and the number will rapidly increase if essential health services cannot be sustained. A policy that gives some priority to protecting and treating persons who save lives will reduce overall mortality and hence increase each person's chance of survival. For that reason, the policy can be justified to anyone. This approach also mitigates an ethical dilemma by providing care to healthcare providers who are asked to assume an increased risk of disease because of their occupations and provides a practical incentive for them to come to work.

In conclusion, in response to a pandemic it is essential for governments to protect the population at large. Even though a pandemic will pose a threat to all values in societal life, there are consequentialist and non-consequentialist reasons for focusing on policies that maximise health benefits, and, more narrowly, on saving the most lives. Nevertheless, even though a focus on "saving lives" will be less unfair than a focus on broader health benefits, conflicts with equity are still inevitable.

## Equitable Access and Fairness

The second principle, equity, or fairness, involves giving equal weight to equal claims. This general idea already played a role in shaping the principle of saving the most lives. There are, however, further implications of equity (notably egalitarian concerns) that need to be clarified, not only because they may sometimes conflict with utility, but also because there are various conflicting implications between the different concerns of equity. In short, equity supports (1) a rejection of various forms of discrimination, (2) attempts to minimise unfairness, and (3) giving priority to groups who have a relatively strong claim to life-saving treatment, such as persons at high risk of severe disease and death, and persons who are relatively young. Moreover, (4) if certain groups of "pandemic responders", while working for the protection of all, are at increased risk to get infected themselves, it would be fair and reciprocal if they were given priority access to prevention and therapy as well.

### Discrimination and Group Favouritism

Some practices are inconsistent with any account of fairness. In the face of a pandemic there is a danger that authorities who have the power to set priorities and allocate resources will favour their own friends and families or ethnic group, or otherwise discriminate according to religion, gender, etc. For example, authorities might decide to use limited stockpiles of antivirals to prophylactically protect themselves and their groups, and leave others in a situation where no antivirals will be available for treating persons who become ill. Such discrimination is grossly unfair and violates basic human rights. If decisions about whom to save from a lethal disease, and who not, are just based upon personal characteristics of members in the population (kinship, friends, ethnicity, nationality, gender, etc), then such decisions obviously violate the equal worth of persons. Priority setting should be based upon criteria that are relevant and justifiable to all—not just to one's own group. If priorities are set on the basis of personal preferences of those in power, this will normally lead to a situation where groups who are suppressed or otherwise worse off will be neglected. Moreover such policies will probably not protect the health of the public in any efficient way.

### Minimizing Unfairness

Issues of fairness do not just arise in cases of explicit discrimination. A policy that aims to save the greater number of lives (or to maximise health benefits more generally) can be unfair as well. For example, focusing vaccination on urban areas might save more lives more efficiently than giving equal attention to rural areas, just because in urban areas there will be more people with more interaction and hence more transmission of the virus, compared with rural areas. Yet this policy could leave the rural areas unprotected. This might be unfair because, even if, with the same resources, more persons can be saved in urban areas, persons in rural areas could argue that their lives should be taken into account as well, and policies that disregard their interests completely would be unfair. If the sole principle were to save the most lives with given resources, such forms of unfairness may be inevitable. However, priorities should be devised in such a way that unfairness is minimised where possible. In the example above, this would support a more proportionate distribution of vaccines over urban and rural areas. This does not necessarily imply that the vaccine must be given to equal portions of both populations. Some modeling studies suggest that directing limited vaccine supplies to children (who are sometimes considered as "superspreaders") would reduce virus transmission in communities. Longini et al. (2004) claim that vaccinating 80% of the children aged less than 19 years is almost as effective as vaccinating 80% of the population. If this were true, such vaccination of all children in urban and rural areas would give both children and adults a reasonable prospect of protection and thus strike a reasonable balance between efficiency and equity.

### Priority to Worst-Off: Risks

These considerations however do not exhaust the implications of equity. Equity also supports giving priority to persons who are worst off (Arneson 2002; Cf. Parfit 1997). This idea is one of the basic principles in John Rawls's egalitarian theory of justice (Rawls 1971).

Yet which persons could rightly claim they are "worst off" and should therefore be given priority in pandemic rationing policies? If priorities are set with the aim of saving lives (and not, more broadly, maximizing welfare) then it makes sense to restrict evaluation of people's situations to issues that are relevant for the value that is at stake, that is, their life. Persons who are worst-off from an economic point of view do not just for that reason have a stronger claim to protection of their life compared to others. On the other hand, someone who is very ill has a stronger claim to care than someone who is and might remain healthy. This supports prioritizing therapeutic treatment over prophylaxis in many cases, which is especially relevant in decision-making about antiviral treatment. For the same reasons, one might argue that persons in high-risk groups have a stronger claim to protection—they run a greater risk of dying if they are infected—than other persons. Only during a pandemic will it become clear which groups are at highest risk.

### Priority to Worst-Off: The Fair Innings Argument

There is another sense in which certain persons have a stronger claim than others to have their lives protected. This has to do with their age and whether or not someone has been able to live up to a full lifespan. One might argue that death at 80 is not as bad as death at 40, and death at 5 is worse than at 40. This suggests a specific account of fairness, known as the *fair innings argument* (Daniels 1988; Williams 1997). The basic egalitarian principle is that institutions should promote equality of opportunity. Older persons will have had many more opportunities in their life than persons who die at young age. Therefore, when we can save some but not all, it is fair to save younger persons, who would be worse off if they died at their age, than the elderly (Kamm 1993). While the fair innings argument, as such, supports giving priority to saving the lives of the young above saving the elderly, it does not specify age groups or cut-off points for prioritisation. Decisions about where to draw the line will also be based on availability of resources.

It is clear that egalitarian approaches can point in completely different directions: some will give priority to saving the elderly, assuming they run a higher risk of severe disease and death than others, others will prioritise children, given that they have not had the many opportunities of life which the elderly have had. For that matter, there are also different (non-egalitarian) arguments for prioritizing children and young adults. Depending on the epidemiology of the pandemic, protecting the young might be the best way to maximise health benefits in terms of life years saved (or DALYs or QALYs). Moreover, if society at large is at risk, then from a utilitarian point of view it could make sense to protect those groups that will be most important for the sustaining and rebuilding of societal functions, now and in the future (Emanuel & Wertheimer 2006).[2]

## Reciprocity Towards Persons Who Accept Risk for the Common Good of Saving Lives

There are also different (non-egalitarian/non-prioritarian) reasons why some persons may have a relatively strong claim to life-saving treatment. Special consideration should be given to the circumstances of health care workers and others who play an essential role in fighting the pandemic and may do so in a situation in which they themselves run a greater risk of being infected than those in the general population (University of Toronto Joint Centre for Bioethics Pandemic Influenza Working Group 2005). If health care workers who treat influenza patients, but also persons who clean contaminated spaces, run significant risks in their work, they have a very strong claim to be protected against disease or be treated as well as possible when they get ill. Society needs them to accept risks and therefore it would be fair if society offers them protection that might compensate for the increased risk. This argument raises questions about scope: which groups should be given special treatment for reasons of fairness, but also, what level of protection can they reasonably claim? Is the provision of personal protective equipment (PPE) sufficient? Or should they also have priority access to vaccination or even pre-exposure prophylaxis? Certainly, priority treatment if they get ill is justifiable and also provides a practical incentive for individuals to accept increased risk of exposure.

This argument of reciprocity depends on whether, in the case of pandemic influenza, health care workers and other pandemic responders indeed do run a significantly greater risk of infection than other citizens. If there is an increased risk to health care workers, then reciprocity supports giving priority access to protection and treatment in such a way that their risk will be similar to that of other citizens. However, if influenza is spreading very easily within society, there may be little or no increased risk of exposure in hospitals. Moreover, if there is an increased risk of exposure in hospitals, consistent use of PPE may reduce that risk to health care workers to a level that is similar to that of other citizens. In such cases, the argument of reciprocity will not support further priority health care for health care workers.

However, there are also independent (consequentialist) arguments for prioritizing health care workers and other pandemic responders as a group to be protected. Protecting them will contribute to sustaining the health care system, preventing nosocomial spread of the infection, and otherwise save the lives of people. This supports priority access to PPE, post-exposure prophylaxis, and vaccination for health care workers. It may also support access to anti-viral treatment if

[2] Emanuel and Wertheimer (2006) suggest an approach to vaccine allocation that combines (a) the fair-innings argument with (b) (utilitarian) concerns about public order, but they also introduce (c) an "investment refinement". The latter element involves giving priority to people between early adolescence and middle age, because they invested more in their lives compared to, e.g. very young children. However, it is difficult to see why persons who have invested more in their lives have a stronger moral claim to life-saving interventions than others. It may be tragic if persons have been investing in their lives in vain, but why would that support giving them priority access to vaccination? Maybe the "investment refinement" is relevant if it protects especially persons who are necessary to sustain and rebuild society, but then Emanuel and Wertheimer do not need an additional principle next to their (utilitarian) "public order" principle.

they get ill as this would increase the chance that they will recover and be able to continue their (life-saving) work. These arguments however are not a matter of fairness or equity, and they also apply to a much broader group of persons who are important for saving the lives of others but do not run increased risk, including, for example, vaccine producers.

## Some Converging Implications (and the Questions They Raise...)

So far I have explored and discussed the various general implications of concerns of efficiency and equity with respect to allocation of scarce resources during a pandemic. Although these implications may often point in different directions, there are at least some points of convergence. The more a specific policy can be supported by appeal to different moral considerations—even theoretical accounts that are often considered as counterparts, such as consequentialist and non-consequentialist theories—the more the policy can be considered reasonable and justified. I have already argued that *saving the most lives* is a general policy aim that can be justified from such different theoretical approaches. Before discussing two more specific points of convergence (priority for specific health care works or pandemic responders, and triage criteria for critical care) let me briefly discuss some more general policies.

On a very general level, the policy strategies which the WHO recommends in the various stages of pandemic preparedness and response (WHO 2005a, 2005b), seem consistent with any of the ethical accounts I have discussed. In case of a first outbreak, rapid response is essential, aiming at containment at the source. By combining antiviral prophylaxis with strict non-medical public health strategies (isolation, social distancing) there might be a chance that the epidemic will be contained. If necessary, countries may even have good reason to donate part of their antiviral stockpiles if the country in which the outbreak occurs would not have enough resources to contain the epidemic. Such interventions may save the most lives and, hopefully, some regions might remain unaffected completely. If the outbreak cannot be contained, a next aim is to prevent, as long as possible, the introduction of the virus into non-affected populations, again by means of prophylactic use of antivirals and other, non-medical public health measures. This helps to gain time for more effective policies/interventions such as development and production of a pandemic vaccine. If the introduction of the pandemic virus in a new region cannot be prevented, policies will aim at reducing possibilities of transmission within the population using pharmaceutical and non-pharmaceutical interventions to the limits of availability. At this stage, however, trade-offs have already emerged between using antiviral drugs for prophylaxis to inhibit further spread of the virus and, on the other hand, "saving" drugs for treatment of patients who might depend on antiviral drugs to survive. One of the central strategies at this phase of the pandemic will then be to maintain essential public health services.

Indeed, this last strategy may be the best example of convergence between (often competing) ethical approaches in priority setting during a pandemic: to protect persons who are essential for public health services. I have argued in the previous section that health care workers and pandemic responders who fulfill essential jobs in the prevention of infection and the treatment of patients *and*, who by doing so, face increased risk of infection themselves, have a strong moral (reciprocity) claim towards society to receive adequate levels of protection. Moreover, for the protection of society as a whole it is essential that these groups are motivated to continue their work in the frontline. Priority access to prevention and treatment is therefore not just a matter of fairness; it can be supported on utilitarian grounds as well. This does not necessarily mean that these "frontline workers" should be given priority access to any form of medical treatment. It makes sense to offer pandemic responders who assume extra risk personal protective equipment and possibly antiviral prophylaxis (depending on availability); to vaccinate them as soon as vaccine is available; and to treat them with antiviral drugs if they get ill. The latter treatment may also enable them to go back to their work if they recover from the disease. It is less obvious that a pandemic responder, who becomes ill and develops respiratory failure, should also be given priority access to intensive care and mechanical ventilation—that is, to give her priority over other citizens who have the same respiratory problems. One might argue that these pandemic responders already received a relatively high level of protection compared to others, which makes it less clear why fairness would support prioritizing them for mechanical ventilation as well. The utilitarian argument—that the pandemic responder would go on saving lives after he will have recovered from respiratory problems—also seems less convincing. Full recovery might be uncertain and, moreover, take a long time.

The allocation of critical care, however, may be another example where ethical considerations do converge, even though the moral decisions to be made are difficult and painful. Marsh (2006) estimates that in the UK four to five times as many intensive care beds (than are currently available) would be needed to treat all persons who are in need of mechanical ventilation. In contrast to other allocation contexts, decisions in the critical care department will have immediate consequences for the lives of patients who are and who are not selected for treatment. Arguably patients should only be referred to critical care if they really need mechanical ventilation or other basic life support; hence, those who are referred but cannot be admitted due to scarce resources might die within a short time. Nevertheless, the ethical dimensions of allocation of mechanical ventilation are, in some respects, less complex than many other decisions—although this does not imply that decision-making is easy. First, all patients who are eligible for ventilation treatment are equally worse off in terms of their immediate risk of dying. Second, arguably the role of indirect benefits ("by saving this person's life we will also secure additional benefits") in intensive care is minor. Several commentators propose that, in a pandemic, critical care triage should be based upon the principle to help the greatest number of people survive the crisis (Marsh 2006; Hick and O'Laughlin 2006). Indeed, as argued above, the principle to save the most lives may be justified by appeal to consequentialist and non-consequentialist theories. This may involve prioritizing patients who have the best prospects of surviving with ventilation, but also to giving lower priority to patients who are expected to require a ventilator or intensive care bed for a relatively long time. Several proposals for medical criteria on this basis have been published (Hick and O'Laughlin 2006; Christian et al. 2006). One of the controversies in such triage criteria is whether age should be a factor to include. Age might be a predictor of the chance of survival in critical care, though possibly not a reliable one (Christian et al. 2006). However, there are also other reasons for giving priority to patients who are relatively young: the fair innings argument (a non-consequentialist argument) and also the expected life years saved (a consequentialist argument).

There will be more points of convergence with respect to allocation of scarce resources, but these will depend more strongly on the specific epidemiological characteristics of the pandemic. For example, if pandemic vaccine is available, different normative arguments could justify giving priority to vaccination of children. Such a policy could be supported again by appeal to the fair innings argument and possibly by appeal to the principle to maximise expected life years (or DALYs or QALYs) saved. But if children are "superspreaders", then vaccinating them might reduce the risks of many other members of society as well (Longini et al. 2004). On the other hand, it could be that vaccinating especially the highest risk groups would ultimately save more lives. Moreover, some suggest that public health measures that aim at social distancing (closing of schools, etc.) could diminish children's role as superspreaders, and then part of this justification would break down.

## Allocation of Medical Resources and Constraints on Liberty

Most of the papers in this special issue of the *Journal of Bioethical Inquiry* focus on infectious disease control interventions that set constraints on people's liberties. Isn't liberty also a relevant value with respect to rationing of scarce medical resources? In a fundamental sense, concerns about liberty are relevant indeed. Instead of reflecting on how the state and public health authorities should allocate scarce antiviral drugs or vaccines, a relevant question could have been whether such allocations should better be left to the market. Choosing for state control involves giving less weight to people's liberty than to the goals of public health. Although a general discussion of the role of liberty goes beyond the scope of this paper, it makes sense to briefly discuss a specific example where liberty is at stake, because it suggests some conclusions for the relative weight of the principles of saving the most lives and of equitable access.

Should individuals be allowed freedom to buy their own pharmaceutical protection—for example, a personal stockpile of antiviral drugs? One of the problems with personal stockpiles of oseltamivir is that the drugs may be used in insufficient doses or inadequate courses of therapy. This could lead to the emergence of oseltamivir-resistance in the influenza virus, and thus undermine the effectiveness of antiviral therapy worldwide (Moscona 2005). Assuming that the state is justified in constraining people's freedom if necessary to prevent harm to others—the harm principle (Mill 1859)—there are good reasons for not allowing personal stockpiling.

A different line of argument would be that allowing individuals and companies to build their own stockpiles (or allowing physicians to prescribe oseltamivir on demand) might undermine the attempts of governments to create a sufficient stockpile for public health purposes, and hence obstruct the distribution that was aimed for in the plans for pandemic preparedness and response (Cf. Brett and Zuger, 2005). Something similar might happen with the currently available H5N1 vaccine. Suppose that the H5N1 virus became easily transmissible from human to human, and the vaccine still offered protection against the new virus. It would then be rational for individuals to buy H5N1 vaccine (or get a prescription) but governments would simultaneously try to build a stockpile of vaccine for public health purposes. Given that vaccine supplies and production capacity are limited, free sale or prescription of vaccine would undermine public health goals (either by draining the supplies, or by raising the price), which could be a reason for the state not to allow individuals to buy vaccination for themselves.

However, this would imply that the state does not allow individuals to protect their own lives, which is a very basic infringement on personal freedom. Can such an infringement be justified by appeal to public health goals? This depends on what the goals are, and to what extent they can be attained. Following the argument in this paper, the public health goals would involve using resources in a way that saves the most lives but also promotes equitable access. A policy that constrains people's freedom and opportunities to protect their own lives can be more easily justified by arguing that this is necessary to save as many lives as possible, than by arguing that the policy will lead to a more equitable distribution of drugs or vaccine. For a consequentialist—focusing on maximising aggregative value—this will be obvious. Liberals and libertarians however may support this line of argument as well because the "saving the most lives" justification fits within the framework of the harm principle. On the other hand, to constrain people's freedom to protect themselves, in order *to secure a more equitable distribution* of protection, would be much more controversial, as it may neither find support in the harm principle, nor in consequentialist concerns. If this rather tentative analysis could be developed and strengthened, it will have implications for the relative weight of efficiency and equity in rationing policies. Where rationing policies require constraints on people's freedom to self-protection, governments would have reason to give more weight to *saving the most lives* than to securing *equitable access*.

## Conclusion

Throughout this paper I have argued that there is a reasonable ethical basis for rationing scarce medical resources during an influenza pandemic. Although the principles of utility and equity will often conflict and, moreover, both can be interpreted in different, often diverging ways, there are also converging lines of argument. On a general level, *saving the most lives with given resources* is a defensible interpretation of the principle of utility which can also find support from non-consequentialist approaches. On a practical level I have argued how utility and equity can jointly support policies that prioritise the protection of health care workers. Both principles will also allow allocating intensive care in a way that gives priority to patients who are expected to need mechanical ventilation for only a relatively short period. Finally, depending on the characteristics of the pandemic, there might be good reasons for prioritising protection of young children and young adults over older persons.

Obviously, in numerous situations and scenarios for pandemic planners moral conflict is inevitable. Policies for pandemic preparedness and response should therefore not only be based upon substantive moral principles like utility and equity, but also promote procedural fairness and accountability (Daniels 2008; Verweij 2008). Nevertheless, some policies can be supported by appeal to such diverging principles as utility and equity, and this conclusion may encourage bioethicists, influenza specialists and policy makers to seek and test more points of convergence.

## References


Arneson, R. 2002. Egalitarianism. In *The Stanford Encyclopedia of Philosophy (Fall 2002 Edition)*, ed. Edward N. Zalta. http://plato.stanford.edu/archives/fall2002/entries/egalitarianism.

Barry, J.M. 2005. The story of influenza. In *Institutes of Medicine: The threat of pandemic influenza: are we ready?*, ed. S.L. Knobler, A. Mack, et al., 57068. Washington: National Academic.

Brett, A.S. and A. Zuger. 2005. The run of Tamiflu—Should physicians precribe on demand? *New England Journal of Medicine* 353(25): 2636–2637.

Brock, D. 2003. Separate spheres and indirect benefits. *Cost Effectiveness and Resource Allocation* 1: 4. doi:10.1186/1478-7547-1-4.

Christian, M.D., L. Hawryluck, R.S. Was, N.M. Lazar, et al. 2006. Development of a triage protocol for critical care during an influenza pandemic. *Canadian Medical Association Journal* 175(11): 1377–1381. doi:10.1503/cmaj.060911.

Daniels, N. 1988. *Am I my parents' keeper? An essay on justice between the young and the old.* New York: Oxford University Press.

Daniels, N. 2008. *Just health.* Cambridge: Cambridge University Press.

Emanuel, E. and A. Wertheimer. 2006. Who should get influenza vaccine when not all can? *Science* 313: 854–855.

Gostin, L.O. and B.E. Berkman. 2007. Pandemic influenza: Ethics, law, and the public's health. *Administrative Law Review* 59(1): 121.

Hick, J.L. and D.T. O'Laughlin. 2006. Concept of operations for triage of mechanical ventilation in an epidemic. *Academic Emergency Medicine* 13(2): 223–9.

Hirose, I. 2001. Saving the greater number without combining claims. *Analysis* 61(4): 341–42.

Johnson, N.P.A.S. and J. Mueller. 2002. Updating the accounts: global mortality of the 1918–1920 "Spanish" influenza pandemic. *Bulletin of the History of Medicine* 76: 105–115.

Kamm, F.M. 1993. *Morality, mortality. Death and whom to save from it. Volume 1.* Oxford: Oxford University Press.

Kass, N.E., J. Otto, D. O'Brien, and M. Minson. 2008. Ethics and severe pandemic influenza: maintaining essential functions through a fair and considered response. *Biosecurity and Bioterrorism: Biodefense Strategy, Practice, and Science* 6(3): 227–236. doi:10.1089/bsp. 2008.0020.

Kotalik, J. 2005. Preparing for an influenza pandemic: ethical issues. *Bioethics* 19(4): 422–431.

Longini, I.M., E. Halloran, A. Nizam, and Y. Yang. 2004. Containing pandemic influenza with antiviral agents. *American Journal of Epidemiology* 159: 623–633.

Marsh, R. 2006. Hard decisions will have to be made: view from intensive care. *BMJ* 332: 790–791. doi:10.1136/bmj.332.7544.790.

Mill, J.S. 1859. *On liberty.* London: John W. Parker and Son.

Moscona, A. 2005. Oseltamivir resistance—Disabling our influenza defenses. *New England Journal of Medicine* 353(25): 2633–2636.

Parfit, D. 1997. Equality and priority. *Ratio* 10(3): 202–221.

Rawls, J. 1971. *Theory of justice.* Oxford: Oxford University Press.

Scanlon, T. 1998. *What we owe to each other.* Cambridge: Harvard University Press.

University of Toronto Joint Centre for Bioethics Pandemic Influenza Working Group. 2005. *Stand on guard for thee. Ethical considerations in preparedness planning for pandemic influenza.* Joint Centre for Biomedical Ethics: Toronto.

Verweij, M. F. 2008. Equitable access to therapeutic and prophylactic measures. In: Addressing ethical issues in pandemic influenza planning, : World Health Organization Discussion Papers. Geneva: WHO. WHO/HSE/EPR/GIP/2008.2

WHO. 2005a. *Global influenza preparedness plan. The role of WHO and recommendations for national measures before and during pandemics.* Geneva: WHO. WHO/CDS/CSR/GIP/2005.5.

WHO. 2005b. *Responding to the avian influenza pandemic threat. Recommended strategic actions.* Geneva: WHO. WHO/CDS/CSR/GIP/2005.8.

WHO. 2007. *Ethical considerations in developing a public health response to pandemic influenza.* Geneva: WHO. WHO/CDS/EPR/GIP/2007.2.

Williams, A. 1997. Intergenerational equity: An exploration of the "fair innings" argument. *Health Economics* 6: 117–132.

Bioethical Inquiry (2009) 6:171–179
DOI 10.1007/s11673-009-9164-3

# Effective use of a Limited Antiviral Stockpile for Pandemic Influenza

**Nimalan Arinaminpathy · J. Savulescu · Angela R. Mclean**

Received: 12 September 2008 / Accepted: 10 May 2009 / Published online: 26 May 2009


**Abstract** Just allocation of resources for control of infectious diseases can be profoundly influenced by the dynamics of those diseases. In this paper we discuss the use of antiviral drugs for treatment of pandemic influenza. While the primary effect of such drugs is to alleviate and shorten the duration of symptoms for treated individuals, they can have a secondary effect of reducing transmission in the community. However, existing stockpiles may be insufficient for all clinical cases. Here we use simple mathematical models to present scenarios where the optimum policies to minimise morbidity and mortality, with a limited drug stockpile, are not always the most intuitively obvious and may conflict with theories of justice. We discuss ethical implications of these findings.

**Keywords** Pandemic influenza · Antiviral drugs · Public health

N. Arinaminpathy (✉) · A. R. Mclean
Department of Zoology, University of Oxford,
Oxford OX1 3PS, UK
e-mail: nim.pathy@zoo.ox.ac.uk

J. Savulescu
Oxford Uehiro Centre for Practical Ethics,
Oxford OX1 1PT, UK

## Introduction

A pandemic influenza virus is one to which the great majority of the human population has no prior immunity. Past pandemics have ranged in disease severity, from the devastating "Spanish flu" of 1918 (Johnson and Müller 2002) to the comparatively mild "Hong Kong flu" of 1968 (Kilbourne 2006). Nonetheless, all pandemics have exerted a considerable and global impact on society, including a death rate exceeding those of seasonal influenza outbreaks. The SARS outbreaks of 2003 (Fan and the Asian Development Bank 2003) demonstrated the great potential for social and economic disruption caused by the spread of a lethal pathogen. There is every reason to expect that an influenza pandemic will have a very significant impact when it arises.

It is now widely accepted that we should be speaking of "when" and not "if" a pandemic happens (Taubenberger et al. 2007). There is, however, much uncertainty surrounding the subtype and strain that will be involved: H5N1 influenza is causing much concern (WHO 2008) because of its high case fatality rate in humans, but H7N7 and H9N2 are equally plausible pandemic candidates, having also caused many human cases (Centers for Disease Control and Prevention 2003; Wan et al. 2008). At the time of writing (May 2009) an H1N1 influenza A virus, closely related to viruses found in pigs (Swine Flu), is the latest variant to threaten a pandemic with official reports of over 1,000 cases in 21 countries. The

WHO's phase of pandemic alert stands at phase 5, awaiting a confirmed outbreak in a community outside the WHO-designated Americas region to rise to the top, "pandemic" level.

Because pandemic viruses cannot be predicted in advance it is not possible to protect humans with a vaccine of high efficacy before the pandemic spreads. In fact, it is unlikely that an effective vaccine will even be available during the first six months of a pandemic (Webby and Webster 2003). During this time antiviral drugs will be the first line of defence for pharmaceutical intervention, and several countries have been stockpiling such drugs, mainly oseltamivir (tradename Tamiflu) (Ward et al. 2005). These stockpiles are being widely used in the ongoing outbreaks of H1N1 both to treat known cases and to prevent the establishment of known outbreaks by treating the close contacts of cases. The currently circulating viral strain is mild making it hard to tell if the drugs are effective either in ameliorating symptoms or in reducing onward transmission. The widespread use of drugs for prophylaxis on a national scale would be prohibitively expensive, and so, in the UK and US pandemic plans, for example (US Dept of Health and Human Services 2005, UK Department of Health 2007), the primary role of oseltamivir is for therapeutic (post-symptomatic) treatment. Treatment by oseltamivir of *seasonal* influenza, taken within 48 h of symptoms, alleviates and shortens the duration of symptoms, as well as reducing the risk of mortality (McGeer et al. 2005), and it is hoped that the drug will have the same effect against a pandemic influenza virus.

Stated objectives for public health interventions are consistent across many countries: the Australian plan states that "antivirals will be used as part of a comprehensive public health intervention to reduce illness and death" (Australian Department of Health and Ageing 2006), while public health advisory committees in the US "considered the primary goal of a pandemic response to decrease health impacts including severe morbidity and death" (US Dept of Health and Human Services 2007). According to the UK plan, "The priority in an influenza pandemic is to reduce the impact on public health (i.e. reduce illness and save lives). Interventions will therefore be applied where they will achieve maximum health benefit" (UK Department of Health 2007).

The US and the UK currently have drug stockpiles sufficient to treat 25% of the population. However, what if this turns out to be insufficient? Specifically, if a stockpile is potentially insufficient for all clinical cases, should we treat only priority cases in an effort to preserve the drug supply, or should treatment continue to be dispensed to as many clinical cases as possible until the stockpile is exhausted? UK policy is in line with the former; at first all symptomatic cases will receive treatment and, if supplies run low, drugs will be prioritised for health care workers and those most at risk (UK Department of Health 2007). This policy makes sound intuitive sense, but is it the best way to minimise morbidity and mortality? Is it consistent with a principle of just allocation of limited resources?

In this paper we take these questions as starting points to argue that the problem of resource allocation goes deeper than merely the direct effects of treatment. Infectious disease dynamics are intrinsically "nonlinear", meaning, for example, that an epidemic started by two infectious individuals is not twice as large as one caused by a single individual. The fundamental issue here is that drug treatment protects those taking the medicine *and* gives some protection to people they might otherwise have gone on to infect. This preventive effect is clearly positive, but it can lead to complex balances between treatment strategies that are good for the individual versus strategies that are good for the community.

The first part of this paper is concerned with how best to minimise numbers of infections, with a limited stockpile. This objective has clear advantages for the general population, and for continuity of the economy. The second part of this paper addresses the situation where a subgroup in the population has a particularly high risk of mortality. For instance, young adults suffered a higher mortality rate than any other age group in the "Spanish flu" pandemic of 1918 (Jordan 1927). In such a scenario, we argue that prioritizing the treatment of those at most risk of death is not always in agreement with minimising infection and overall numbers of deaths. In both cases we first use mathematical models to explore rational strategies from a consequentialist approach, and then discuss ethical implications.

## Minimising Infection–the Basic Model

Here we present an outline of the basic mathematical model; further technical details are given in the appendix. We assume a well-mixed population, in which the overall rate of infection is a product of the number of infected cases, the rate of contact between members of the population, and the probability of infection per contact. This is expressed in equations given in the appendix.

$R_0$ is the basic reproductive number, the average number of secondary cases arising from a single clinical case, in an otherwise susceptible population, and in the absence of any treatment (Anderson and May 1992). Assuming a fixed amount of contact between members of the host population, we can take $R_0$ as a measure of the virus transmissibility. A pandemic-capable virus requires a value of $R_0$ greater than 1.

Now, consider a policy of dispensing treatment to a certain proportion of infected cases: that is, implementing a certain antiviral *coverage*. We make several simplifying assumptions. We assume a well-mixed population and neglect use of antiviral drugs for prophylaxis, assuming their dominant role is for post-symptomatic treatment. We also neglect drug resistance. Further, in the basic model we assume that the only effect of treatment is to reduce the duration of clinical symptoms, that there is no latent period of infection, and that all cases are symptomatic. Although seemingly strong assumptions, however, these do not change the qualitative nature of our results.

An aggressive (high coverage) antiviral programme will dispense treatment to all cases presenting with clinical symptoms, and a conservative (low coverage) programme will dispense treatment to only a limited number of those cases. Assume first that there is an unlimited supply of antiviral drugs. How many drugs would be used by the end of the epidemic?

Figure 1 shows the calculated drug usage for a range of coverage policies, for different plausible values of $R_0$. A notable feature of this graph is that aggressive policies are not always more drug-consuming than conservative ones. For example, in the case $R_0=1.5$, fewer drugs are dispensed overall if 90% of infected cases receive treatment than if only 60% do. This is because the potential benefits of treatment are not limited to those individuals receiving it; by accelerating their recovery, treatment also shortens their infectious period, and thus reduces the *spread* of disease, leading to fewer cases overall. If dispensed to sufficiently many cases, therefore, this effect can in fact reduce the overall number of drugs needed. In the extreme case of $R_0=1.2$ and with over 60% of cases receiving treatment, the treatment programme is

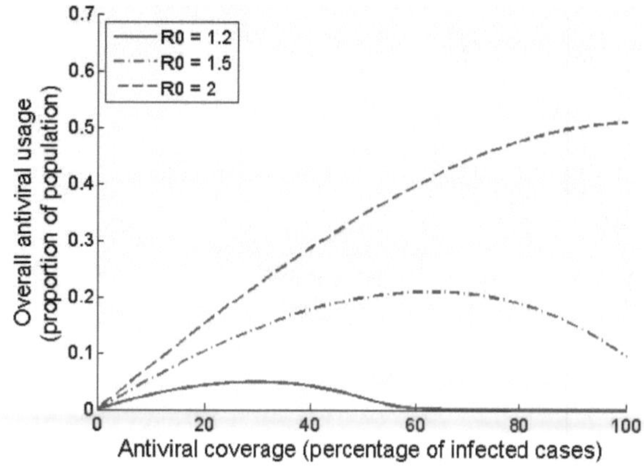


**Fig. 1** Predicted total antiviral usage for a range of disease transmissibility (R0). Assuming that infected cases recover in an average of 3.5 days and 5 days with and without treatment, respectively

effective in stamping out infection before it can spread widely and hence only a very small number of drugs are used. However, such an effect is, as one might expect, dependent on the viral transmissibility and on the drug efficacy. For a highly transmissible virus and/or a poorly effective drug, antiviral usage always increases with coverage, as in the example $R_0=2$ in the diagram.

The role of widespread treatment in reducing the spread of infection is an example of the fundamental role of infection dynamics in disease control. We can now consider how the picture might change if there were only a limited stockpile. This is implemented in the model by imposing zero antiviral coverage once the drug usage exceeds a given stockpile level. Say, for example, that there are enough drugs for a quarter of the population, as in the current US and UK stockpiles. Figure 2 shows how the epidemics would progress according to this model, for different coverage policies, assuming that $R_0$ is 1.7 (a moderate value). An aggressive 95% coverage exhausts the stockpile, but a conservative 30% coverage avoids doing so. On these grounds alone the latter might appear preferable. Nonetheless, the epidemic peak is significantly reduced and broadened by the aggressive policy. Analysis of this model, presented in detail elsewhere (Arinaminpathy and McLean 2008), also shows that although an aggressive policy exhausts the stockpile, it results in fewer cases overall than the conservative one.

These results are also valid in an extended model that includes more details, such as asymptomatic

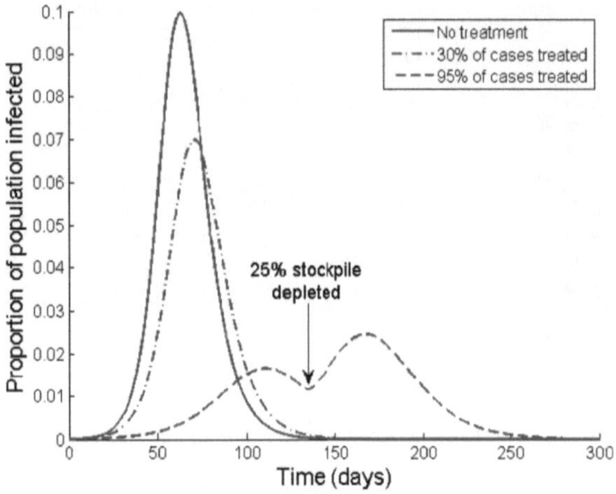


**Fig. 2** Predicted epidemic curves for different antiviral coverage policies, using same drug parameters as in Fig. 1, and assuming $R_0$=1.7. Note that the 'aggressive' policy of 95% coverage depletes the stockpile

cases, different stages in the course of illness and infectiousness, and a drug that reduces infectiousness as well as the infectious period: irrespective of whether or not an aggressive strategy depletes the stockpile prematurely, it leads ultimately to fewer cases, and a lower and broader epidemic peak than a conservative policy aiming to avoid runout. Here the public health planner, faced with the potential exhaustion of a stockpile, must choose between an assured supply of drugs, but a greater overall number of cases and pressure on health services, and on the other hand minimising the overall disease burden, but potentially denying treatment to those infected towards the end of the epidemic. This is particularly true if no vaccine, or alternative treatment, is available when the stockpile has been exhausted. This seems a likely scenario, given that it will take at least six months from the start of a pandemic for a effective vaccine to be available (Webby and Webster 2003). Any problem of resource allocation is burdened with a trade-off between the interests and welfare of individuals. In this case, however, the tension between the consequentialist approach (driving the aggressive coverage policy) and equitability (a key guiding principle in many pandemic plans) is amplified by the underlying disease dynamics.

Note that here we have deliberately limited ourselves to the simplest possible models, in order to highlight the dynamical effects of "aggressive" versus "conservative" antiviral deployment. More detailed models could include realistic inefficiencies in deployment, such as the delay between developing symptoms and receiving drugs, and the effect of non-pharmaceutical interventions such as social distancing. Nonetheless, this basic framework provides a useful method for focusing on the epidemiological effects of widespread antiviral treatment.

## Minimising Mortality

If the disease were to show specific targeting of mortality towards a sizeable subgroup of the population, such as young adults in 1918, then the overall priority may well be to minimise numbers of deaths. What is the best way to deploy a limited stockpile, to achieve this end?

In an extension of the basic model presented above, we now consider a twofold coverage policy: there is a certain antiviral coverage for the general population and another for the risk-group. The question now is how best to balance these two coverages, with respect to a limited stockpile. Here, there are two significant measures of the drug performance: its efficacy in reducing onward transmission, by speeding the recovery of treated cases, and its protection against mortality for individuals.

Figures 3 and 4 show plots of total mortality and total number infected, for two different scenarios for the drug effectiveness, and with a stockpile sufficient to treat 25% of the population. Further parameters are given in the figure legends. In the first scenario, depicted in Fig. 3, the drug is effective in both the general population and in the risk group, at reducing transmission and mortality. The ridges in the plotted surfaces correspond to policies under which the exhaustion of the stockpile coincides with the end of the epidemic. With any greater coverage in either group the stockpile would be prematurely exhausted. The first main point to note is that the policy for minimising mortality is not the same as that for minimising attack rate (numbers infected). For the former (see Fig. 3a), drugs should be prioritised for risk-group cases and any remaining stockpile used for the general population. For the latter (see Fig. 3b), the opposite is true and the general population instead takes priority. Despite this contradiction, most non-fatal infections of influenza do not result in lasting disability, and so many would argue that the policy to

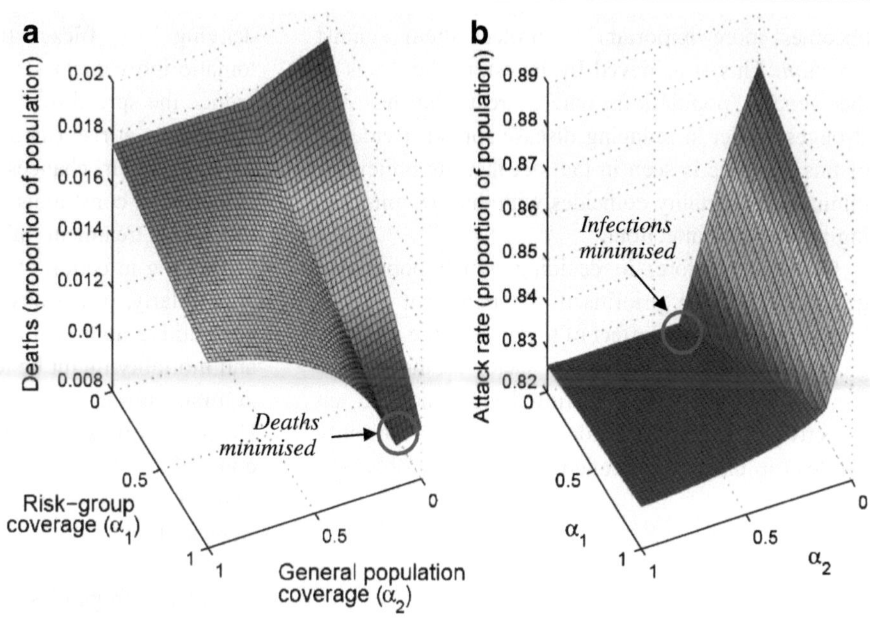


**Fig. 3** **a** Total deaths and **b** infections (attack rate) vs antiviral coverage policy, in a scenario where the drug is effective in both groups, in reducing infection and mortality. Red circles indicate where deaths are minimised (figure a) and numbers of infections are minimised (figure b). Assuming here that 20% of the population is 'at risk'. Further parameter details are given in the Appendix

minimise overall *mortality* should take precedence over the policy to minimise numbers *infected*.

Consider, however, the situation depicted in Fig. 4, where the drug works well at reducing transmission as well as mortality risk in the general population, but offers only very weak protection against mortality in the risk group. This situation is not implausible: clinical features of serious human cases of H5N1 have raised questions about the potential efficacy of oseltamivir for these cases (WHO 2007). Here, minimising mortality agrees with minimising overall numbers of infections: prioritise treatment for the general population, and spend any remaining drugs on the risk group cases. It must be stressed that this is not merely a matter of "abandoning" the risk group as a result of their poor response to treatment: this policy also offers indirect protection for risk group members. Specifically, because the drug performs so poorly in the risk group, rather than aiming to protect these cases against mortality through direct treatment, it

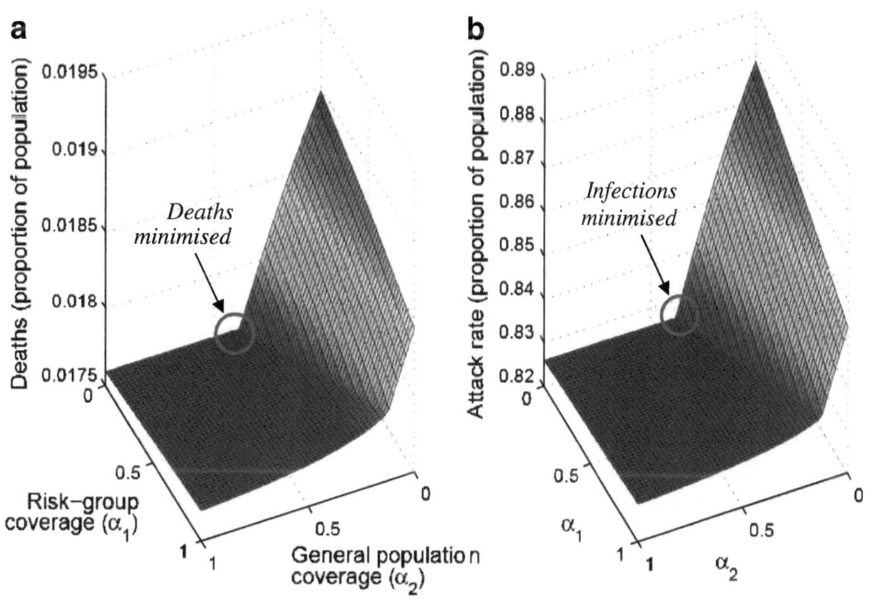


**Fig. 4** **a** Total deaths and **b** infections (attack rate) vs antiviral coverage policy. Here the drug has some effect in the general population, but very limited effect in the risk-group. Minimising mortality agrees with minimising numbers of infections

becomes more important to protect them against *infection*. This is achieved by investing the drugs in the general population, where treatment has the strongest effect in reducing disease spread. Evidence of this dynamic is seen in the fact that the policy for minimising mortality coincides with that for minimising numbers of infections.

Overall, therefore, in deciding which population groups should be prioritised for treatment with a limited stockpile, the effect of the drug in the different groups can be as significant a factor as the disease itself. Consequently, a rational approach to an objective as straightforward as minimising mortality can lead to unexpected conclusions.

## Discussion

The problem of resource allocation for control of infectious diseases has some subtle elements not observed in other healthcare settings. Rather than merely reacting to symptoms, antiviral drugs can in fact fundamentally affect the course of an epidemic. If treatment has any therapeutic effect on the individual level, it also reduces transmissibility, and thus can play a role in limiting the spread of disease in the community.

Take, for example, the objective of devoting resources to the worst off, a central tenet of the Rawlsian perspective of distributive justice (Rawls 1971). At first glance it seems clear that this favours prioritising symptomatic treatment for those most at risk. However, we have seen that a policy to minimise mortality should be guided not only by the effect of the disease itself, but also by the drug efficacy in different groups of the population. As we have shown, in cases in which antivirals have low efficacy in high risk populations, it is possible for the community-wide effect of treatment in the general population to offer more protection than direct treatment of high risk-group members. In this case, is it more "just" to prioritise the general population, if necessary even denying treatment to those hardest hit by a pandemic? There are two reasons to think that denial of treatment of the worst off is consistent with a Rawlsian "maximin" theory of justice of prioritizing the worst off. Firstly, control of infection spread might be regarded as being as much a "public good" as availability of the drugs themselves. Secondly, by denying low efficacy treatment of high risk symptomatic individuals, drugs can be used to maximally reduce the spread of disease and so *indirectly* benefit those most at risk (though not those symptomatic) by reducing their chances of contracting the disease. Under such constraints, justice paradoxically requires *denial* of treatment of the worst off, in favour of preventing infection of those most at risk.

Similarly, in the absence of a sizeable risk group, an intuitive approach aimed at minimising morbidity and mortality might be to dispense drugs aggressively at first, subsequently rationing if supplies run low. However, our simple model suggests, under certain constraints, that both consequentialism (aimed at reducing deaths to a minimum) and Rawlsian justice (aimed at benefitting the worst off, in this case, those most at risk) require maintaining an aggressive policy throughout (regardless of the risk of exhausting the stockpile). This would minimise the overall number of cases, and reduce spread, as well as broadening and delaying the epidemic peak.

Such policies based either on consequentialism or Rawlsian egalitarianism raise other ethical questions about the equity of drug distribution. Both policies would discriminate against infections late in the epidemic, probably including those who have been most compliant with infection-prevention measures and are least responsible for contracting the illness. Should some of the drug stockpile be preserved for these late cases, at the cost of greater numbers of cases, and the greater pressure on health services, that would otherwise result? Both consequentialism and egalitarian justice again seem to require denying some people the opportunity of a chance of treatment. Or should everyone have an equal chance of accessing treatment at all stages of the epidemic, regardless of their individual chance of benefit or the consequences for others?

The stated goal of distributors of antivirals is to reduce deaths. This may require denial of access to either symptomatic high risk individuals or those contracting the disease late in an epidemic.

Some notes of caution are in order. First, a problem with this analysis, as with many resource problems in healthcare, is uncertainty. The optimum strategy for antiviral deployment can only be known once we have the relevant data for drug efficacy in different parts of the population. However, until a pandemic-capable virus emerges, and starts to spread widely, we will not know which groups might be at risk, nor the drug parameters needed to guide these strategies. Nevertheless, if a virus should emerge in South-East Asia, effective and rapid case analysis during this time could well provide valuable data with which to guide antiviral deployment in other countries. Our discussion does not offer direct solutions for this uncertainty; nonetheless, it highlights the need for continuous, accurate surveillance, and illustrates how this information could usefully inform an antiviral deployment strategy.

Second, the models presented here are necessarily gross simplifications: in reality many other factors will play a role, including stochasticity, and heterogeneities in the population. Moreover, not all clinical cases will start the treatment on time, and not all will finish it, reducing the effective stockpile size and potentially increasing the chances of emergence of a drug-resistant strain. Nor have we considered the possibility of presymptomatic postexposure prophylaxis and its impact on spread and overall mortality. In any case, the strength of the modelling approach presented here lies not in its quantitative predictions, but its capacity for providing heuristic insights, and these are likely to remain valid in yet more detailed models. Moreover, the analysis presented here demonstrates the fundamental effect that disease dynamics can have, on traditional debates about ethical resource allocation.

Pandemic planning is continually under review, and we suggest here that it would be beneficial to move away from regarding drug treatment as a purely reactive strategy, to an appreciation that it can also shape the course of an epidemic. A closer understanding of this behaviour could well provide valuable input for informing strategic priorities and their ethical implications.

**Acknowledgements** The authors gratefully acknowledge funding from the James Martin 21st Century School.

## Appendix

### The Basic Model

We consider a single wave of infection in a closed population, neglecting births and deaths. The population is divided into 5 groups: a proportion S is susceptible to infection; a proportion $I_T$ is infected and receiving treatment; a proportion $I_N$ is infected without treatment; a proportion $R_T$ is removed through treatment, and a proportion $R_N$ is removed without having received treatment. ("Removed" applies here equally well to recovery, or death.) Moreover, assume that a proportion $\alpha$ of infected cases receive treatment.

Infected cases recover in an average of $1/\gamma_T$ days and $1/\gamma_N$ days with and without treatment, respectively. We denote $\beta$ as the rate of infection.

The governing equations are as follows:

$$\dot{S} = -\lambda S,$$
$$\dot{I}_T = \alpha\lambda S - \gamma_T I_T,$$
$$\dot{I}_N = (1-\alpha)\lambda S - \gamma_N I_N,$$
$$\dot{R}_T = \gamma_T I_T; \quad \dot{R}_N = \gamma_N I_N.$$

where $\lambda=\beta\ (I_T+I_N)$, and the dot denotes a time-derivative. Now, the total number of drugs that have been dispensed at any given time is $(I_T+R_T)$, a non-decreasing function of time. If there is a stockpile of drugs sufficient to treat a proportion $M$ of the population, then the stockpile is depleted when $(I_T+R_T)=M$, and we set $\alpha=0$ for all subsequent time in the calculation.

The following parameter values were used to prepare Figs. 1 and 2:

| Parameter | $\gamma_N$ | $\gamma_T$ | $M$ |
|---|---|---|---|
| Value | 1/5 | 1/3.5 | 0.25 |

Finally, the value of beta was chosen to give the correct value of $R_0$, according to the expression: $R_0=\beta/\gamma_N$.

### The Extended Model: Risk Group

Assume that a certain proportion $p$ of the population is "at-risk", that is suffering a higher case fatality rate than the general population. Denoting members of the general population with superscript (g) and the risk group with superscript (r). Write $C_T^{(r)}$ and $C_N^{(r)}$ for the case fatality rates in the risk group with and without treatment, respectively. Corresponding quantities in the general population are obtained by substituting superscripts (g) for (r). Hence, by assumption, we have $C_N^{(r)}>C_N^{(g)}$.

Now, adopt the notation of the basic model for the two population groups so that, for example, $S^{(r)}$ denotes the proportion of the total initial population that is susceptible, in the risk-group. To these classes we add $D^{(r)}$ and $D^{(g)}$, the numbers dead from the risk group and from the general population respectively, written as proportions of the total initial population. Then we have two sets of governing equations: for the risk-group,

$$\dot{S}^{(r)} = -\lambda^{(r)} S^{(r)},$$
$$\dot{I}_T^{(r)} = \alpha^{(r)}\lambda^{(r)} S^{(r)} - \left(\gamma_T + \mu_T^{(r)}\right) I_T^{(r)},$$
$$\dot{I}_N^{(r)} = (1-\alpha^{(r)})\lambda^{(r)} S^{(r)} - \left(\gamma_N + \mu_N^{(r)}\right) I_N^{(r)},$$
$$\dot{R}_T^{(r)} = \gamma_T I_T^{(r)}; \quad \dot{R}_N^{(r)} = \gamma_N I_N^{(r)},$$
$$\dot{D}_T^{(r)} = \mu_T^{(r)} I_T^{(r)}; \quad \dot{D}_N^{(r)} = \mu_N^{(r)} I_N^{(r)},$$

Where

$$\lambda^{(r)} = \beta^{(rr)}\left(I_T^{(r)} + I_N^{(r)}\right) + \beta^{(gr)}\left(I_T^{(g)} + I_N^{(g)}\right)$$

and $\beta^{(gr)}$ is defined as the numbers of secondary infections arising per day in a completely susceptible risk group, due to one infected member of the general population. Corresponding equations for the general population are obtained by interchanging superscripts (r) and (g). Note that this model involves a twofold coverage policy, where drugs are dispensed to a proportion $\alpha^{(r)}$ of risk-group cases and a proportion $\alpha^{(g)}$ of the general population.

The mortality terms $\mu^{(r)}$, $\mu^{(g)}$ are chosen to give the appropriate case fatality rates, according to the expressions

$$C_T^{(r)} = \frac{\mu_T^{(r)}}{\gamma_T + \mu_T^{(r)}}; \quad C_N^{(r)} = \frac{\mu_N^{(g)}}{\gamma_N + \mu_N^{(g)}},$$

and correspondingly for the general population.

The following parameter values were used to prepare Fig. 3:

| Parameter | $p$ | $\gamma_N$ | $\gamma_T$ | $C_N^{(r)}$ | $C_T^{(r)}$ | $C_N^{(g)}$ | $C_T^{(g)}$ | $M$ |
|---|---|---|---|---|---|---|---|---|
| Value | 0.2 | 1/5 | 1/3.5 | 0.1 | 0.05 | 0.001 | 0.002 | 0.25 |

The same values were used for Fig. 4, except for the risk-group case fatality rate with treatment $C_T^{(r)}$, which had the value 0.1.

All case fatality rates (terms in C) are given as proportions.

## References


Anderson, R.M. and R.M. May. 1992. *Infectious diseases of humans: dynamics and control.* Oxford: Oxford University Press.

Arinaminpathy, N. and A.R. McLean. 2008. Antiviral treatment for the control of pandemic influenza: some logistical constraints. *Journal of the Royal Society, Interface* 5(22): 545–553. doi:10.1098/rsif.2007.1152.

Australian Department of Health and Ageing. 2006. The Australian health management plan for pandemic influenza. http://www.health.gov.au/internet/main/publishing.nsf/content/phd-pandemic-plan.htm (accessed 8 May 2009).

Centers for Disease Control and Prevention. 2003. Human cases of Avian Influenza A (H7N7) infection – The Netherlands, 2003. http://www.cdc.gov/flu/avian/h7n7-netherlands.htm (accessed 8 May 2009).

Fan, E.X. and the Asian Development Bank. 2003. *SARS: Economic impacts and implications*. Singapore: ADB.

Johnson, N.P.A.S. and J. Müller. 2002. Updating the accounts: global mortality of the 1918–1920 "Spanish" influenza pandemic. *Bulletin of the History of Medicine* 76: 105–115. doi:10.1353/bhm.2002.0022.

Jordan, E.O. 1927. *Epidemic influenza: A survey.* Chicago: American Medical Association.

Kilbourne, E.D. 2006. Influenza pandemics of the 20th century. *Emerg.Infect.Dis.* http://www.cdc.gov/ncidod/EID/vol12no01/05-1254.htm (accessed 8 May 2009).

McGeer, A., et al. 2005. Clinical features of laboratory confirmed influenza illness requiring hospital admission in Ontario, Canada: Implications for treatment recommendations. Presented at the 2005 European Scientific Working Group on Influenza (ESWI) congress, Malta. *See also* Commentary in Roche investor update, http://www.roche.com/inv-update-2005-09-13b

Rawls, J. 1971. *A theory of justice.* Harvard: Harvard University Press.

Taubenberger, J.K., D.M. Morens, and A.S. Fauci. 2007. The next influenza pandemic: can it be predicted? *Journal of the American Medical Association* 297: 2025–2027. doi:10.1001/jama.297.18.2025.

UK Department of Health. 2007. Pandemic flu: a national framework for responding to an influenza pandemic. http://www.dh.gov.uk/en/Publicationsandstatistics/Publications/PublicationsPolicyAndGuidance/dh_080734 (accessed 8 May 2009).

U.S. Department of Health and Human Sevices. 2005. HHS strategic plan, appendix D. http://www.hhs.gov/pandemicflu/plan/#overview (accessed 8 May 2009).

Ward, P., I. Small, J. Smith, P. Suter, and R. Dutkowski. 2005. Oseltamivir (Tamiflu) and its potential for use in the event of an influenza pandemic. *The Journal of Antimicrobial Chemotherapy* 55(Suppl 1): i5–i21. doi:10.1093/jac/dki018.

Wan, H., et al. 2008. Replication and transmission of H9N2 influenza viruses in ferrets: Evaluation of pandemic potential. *PLoS ONE* 3(8): e2923. doi:10.1371/journal.pone.0002923.

Webby, R.J. and R.G. Webster. 2003. Are we ready for pandemic influenza? *Science* 302: 1519–1522. doi:10.1126/science.1090350.

World Health Organisation. 2007. Clinical management of human infection with avian influenza A (H5N1) virus. http://www.who.int/csr/disease/avian_influenza/guidelines/ClinicalManagement07.pdf (accessed 8 May 2009).

World Health Organisation. 2008. H5N1 Avian influenza: timeline of major events. http://www.who.int/csr/disease/avian_influenza/ai_timeline/en/index.html (accessed 8 May 2009)

# Part II: Health Workers' Rights and Duties

Health Care Analysis (2002) 10:67–85
DOI 10.1023/A:1015670414550

# Rights and Duties of HIV Infected Health Care Professionals

**Lawrence O. Gostin**



**Abstract** In 1991, the CDC recommended that health care workers (HCWs) infected with HIV or HBV (HbeAg positive) should be reviewed by an expert panel and should inform patients of their serologic status before engaging in exposure-prone procedures. The CDC, in light of the existing scientific uncertainty about the risk of transmission, issued cautious recommendations. However, considerable evidence has emerged since 1991 suggesting that we should reform national policy. The data demonstrates that risks of transmission of infection in the health care setting are exceedingly low. Current policy, moreover, does not improve patient safety. At the same time, implementation of current national policy at the local level poses significant human rights burdens on HCWs. Consequently, national policy should be changed to ensure patient safety while protecting the human rights of HCWs. This article proposes a new national policy, including: (1) a program to prevent bloodborne pathogen transmission; (2) a responsibility placed on infected HCWs to promote their own health and well-being and to assure patient safety; (3) a discontinuation of expert review panels and special restrictions for exposure-prone procedures; (4) a discontinuation of mandatory disclosure of a HCW's inflection status; and (5) the imposition of practice restrictions if a HCW is unable to practice safely because of a physical or mental impairment or failure to follow careful infection control techniques. A new national policy, focused on management of the workplace environment and injury prevention, would achieve high levels of patient safety without discrimination and invasion of privacy.

**Keywords** Health care professionals · HBV · HCV · HIV · Infected · Privacy · Rights · Risk

A decade ago the Centers for Disease Control and Prevention (CDC) reported a cluster of six cases of transmission of human immunodeficiency virus (HIV) infection from a Florida dentist to his patients (Ciesielski et al. 1994; CDC 1993). These cases, in which the mode of transmission was never determined, had a direct effect on federal and state policy. In 1991, after a year-long national debate (Ciesielski et al. 1994), the CDC recommended that health care workers (HCWs) infected with HIV or HBV (HbeAg positive) should be reviewed by an expert panel and

L. O. Gostin (✉)
Georgetown University,
Center for Law and Public's Health,
600 New Jersey Avenue, N.W.,
Washington, DC 20001-2022, USA
e-mail: gostin@law.georgetown.edu

L. O. Gostin
Johns Hopkins University,
Baltimore, USA

should inform patients of their serologic status before engaging in exposure-prone procedures (CDC 1991). Later in 1991, Congress mandated states to adopt the CDC guidelines or their equivalent.[1]

Public health authorities, in the face of scientific uncertainty, took the path of caution (Gostin 1991a). However, considerable evidence has emerged since 1991 suggesting that Congress and the CDC should reform national policy. Data demonstrate that the risk of bloodborne pathogen transmission in the health care setting is exceedingly low. Current policy, moreover, does not improve patient safety. At the same time, implementation of CDC policy at the local level places significant human rights burdens on HCWs. Consequently, national policy should be changed to end professional practice restrictions and the requirement to disclose a HCW's HIV or HBV infection status to patients.

After describing current CDC guidelines, this chapter presents evidence from the fields of epidemiology and law to demonstrate why revision of national policy is desirable. While the focus is on HIV infection, much of the analysis is relevant to other bloodborne infections. The chapter concludes by proposing a new national policy. The new proposed policy emphasizes patient safety by ensuring that infection control procedures are systematically implemented in health care settings. The policy, therefore, focuses on safer systems of practice rather than on excluding and stigmatizing infected HCWs.

## Current National Policy for Protecting Patients from Bloodborne Pathogens

The CDC, in 1991, recommended that HCWs infected with HIV or HBV (HbeAg positive) should not perform exposure-prone procedures unless they have "sought counsel from an expert review panel and been advised under what circumstances, if any, they may continue to perform these procedures" (CDC 1991). Even if panels permit them to practice, HCWs must still inform patients of their serologic status. The CDC defined an exposure-prone procedure to include "digital palpitation of a needle tip in a body cavity or the simultaneous presence of the health care worker's fingers and a needle or other sharp instrument or object in a poorly visualized anatomic site." The CDC sought assistance in clarifying the definition of exposure-prone procedures, but professional medical and dental associations declined to specify such procedures (American College of Surgeons 1998).

In October 1991, Congress enacted a statute requiring each state, as a condition of receiving Public Health Service funds, to certify that CDC guidelines "or their equivalent" have been instituted.[2] During the following year, the CDC notified states that the agency would be flexible in accepting the certifications of equivalency. States could determine exposure-prone procedures "on a case-by-case basis, taking into consideration the specific procedure as well as the skill, technique, and possible impairment of the infected HCW" (Roper 1992). As a result, variability exists in state law and practice. In particular, many states do not require disclosure to patients even though this is currently recommended by the CDC (Tereskerz et al. 1999; McIntosh 1996).

In December 1995, the Presidential Advisory Council on HIV/AIDS asked President Clinton to "instruct the CDC to review its guidelines that arbitrarily restrict HIV-infected HCWs and lead to discrimination." Later, professional organizations recommended a change in policy so that HCWs are not required to be tested, hospitals are not required to notify patients, and infected-HCWs are not excluded from practice.[3] The CDC, although it has the legal power to do so, has not changed its policy about testing and exclusion of HIV-infected HCWs.

If the CDC were to change its guidelines, it would significantly affect national policy for two reasons. First, as explained above, current federal legislation requires states to adopt CDC guidelines or their equivalent. Thus, changes in CDC guidelines should result in state-wide reforms. Second, under state tort

[1] PL 102–141, Title VI, §663, 42 U.S.C. §300ee–2 (2001).

[2] PL 102–141, Title VI, §663, 42 U.S.C. §300ee–2 (2001).

[3] Committee on Pediatric AIDS and Committee on Infectious Diseases (1999) Issues related to Human Immunodeficiency Virus Transmission in Schools, Child Care, Medical Settings, the Home, and Community. *Pediatrics* 104, 318–324; AIDS/TB Committee of the Society for Healthcare Epidemiology of America (1997) Management of Healthcare Workers Infected with Hepatitis B Virus, Hepatitis C Virus, Human Immunodeficiency Virus, or Other Blood-borne Pathogens. *Infection Control and Hospital Epidemiology* 18, 349–363; American College of Surgeons (1998) Statement on the Surgeon and HIV Infection.

law, courts usually measure professional and hospital practices against a national standard of care. CDC guidelines do not necessarily set that standard, but they are highly influential in judicial cases (Noble et al. 1997).

It should be emphasized that the other branches of government may not necessarily agree with new federal agency guidelines. The issue of infected HCWs is still politically charged and Congress holds the ultimate power to set policy (Summers 2001). Congress, therefore, could enact new legislation reinstating an exclusionary policy with respect to infected HCWs. Further, the courts are not bound by CDC guidelines. Judges retain discretion in applying tort law and disability discrimination law. Consequently, the courts could continue to decide cases against the interests of infected HCWs. As a result, hospitals might still insist that infected HCWs refrain from practice or, at least, inform patients, due to the hospital's fear of liability.

## New Scientific Evidence

The published data suggest that the risk to patients of contracting HIV infection in a health care setting is exceedingly remote. While the data for HBV and HCV are not as clear, transmission to patients appears to be rare. The risks of bloodborne disease transmission, moreover, are significantly lower than other risks faced by patients such as the possibility of adverse outcomes from medical error (Kohn et al. 1999). Risks can be further minimized if HCWs take recommended precautions. Further, if all transmission from HCWs to patients were entirely prevented, the public health burden from the HIV epidemic would be reduced infinitesimally (Robinson and de Bliek 1996).

## Health Care Worker-to-Patient Transmission of HIV

At the time of the 1991 guidelines, little evidence existed to assess the risk of HIV transmission from HCWs to patients. Since that time, data from reported cases, retrospective investigations, and national HIV/AIDS surveillance show that the risk is exceedingly remote. Since the beginning of the HIV epidemic nearly two decades ago, more than 22,000 HCWs have been diagnosed with AIDS (CDC 2000). Yet as of 1999, the CDC was aware of only 56 cases where health care workers were infected with HIV following an occupational exposure (CDC 2000), and to date, fewer than ten episodes of HIV transmission from HCWs to patients have been documented. In addition to the six infected patients in the Florida dental cluster, a single case was reported in 1997 involving an orthopedic surgeon in France with advanced symptomatic, but undiagnosed, HIV disease (Lot et al. 1999 and Blanchard et al. 1998). A further possible case of nurse-to-patient transmission in France was reported in 2000 (Goujon et al. 2000).

Comprehensive retrospective investigations, particularly among physicians engaged in invasive procedures, have not identified additional cases (Robert et al. 1995; Rodgers et al. 1993). As of July 1999, CDC had analyzed HIV test results for more than 22,000 patients of 63 HIV-infected HCWs, and no documented case of transmission had occurred (CDC 1999). Similarly, in 1997, 1,180 surgical patients of an HIV-infected physician in obstetrics and gynecology were tested in the United Kingdom; none was found to be positive (Donnely et al. 1999). Finally, state health department follow-up of reported cases of HIV or AIDS have failed to confirm additional cases of HCW-to-patient transmission.

There are theoretical reasons, in addition to the epidemiological data, to believe that the risk of transmission is exceedingly remote. New therapies can reduce HIV viral load in plasma to very low levels, and assays to measure viral load are available (Saag et al. 1996). Consequently, if HIV-infected HCWs are in treatment it ought to be possible to monitor their health status and ensure low viral loads,[4] thus reducing risks to patients even further (Quinn et al. 2000; Law et al. 2001).

## Health Care Worker-to-Patient Transmission of Hepatitis B

The likelihood of transmission of HBV is significantly greater than HIV. Model-based calculations esti-

[4] Panel for Clinical Practices for the Treatment of HIV, *Guidelines for the Use of Antiretroviral Agents in HIV-Infected Adults and Adolescents,* April 23, 2001 (viewed at http://www.hivatis.org/guidelines/adult/Apr23_01/text/index.html on August 8, 2001).

mate that the risk of surgeon-to-patient transmission of HBV is 0.24% during a single procedure as compared to a 0.0024% risk of HIV transmission from surgeon to patient (Ross et al. 2000a). Despite the elevated risk, HCW-to-patient transmission of HBV has also been rare since the early 1990s. In 1992, a cluster of 19 cases of transmission occurred from an HbeAg positive cardiothoracic surgeon in California who did not double-glove even after infection was diagnosed (Harpaz et al. 1996). Since this cluster of cases, no episode of HCW-to-patient HBV transmission has been documented in the United States, although transmission has been documented in the United Kingdom[5] and Canada.[6] A cluster of HBV infections did occur in the United States between December 1995 and May 1996 among chronic hemodialysis patients, but the apparent mode of transmission was through the use of medical equipment shared among infected and uninfected patients (Hutin et al. 1999).

## Health Care Worker-to-Patient Transmission of Hepatitis C

The 1991 guidelines did not address Hepatitis C Virus (HCV) because it had only recently been discovered, and there were few epidemiologic and laboratory data to support guidelines. In 1998, the CDC found the risk of HCV transmission to be "very low" (CDC 1998). There is a documented cluster of cases of HCV transmission from a cardiothoracic surgeon in Spain to five patients between 1988 and 1993, but investigation of those cases did not identify factors that might have contributed to transmission (Esteban et al. 1996). In 1998, an anesthesiology assistant in Germany transmitted HCV virus to five patients (Ross et al. 2000b). The anesthesiology assistant was himself infected through occupational exposure to a patient with HCV. Investigation revealed that the HCW never wore gloves and, at the time he treated all six patients, the HCW had a weeping wound on his right hand. Reports of the incident noted that the infections most likely could have been prevented by the use of universal precautions. A Spanish anesthetist, who was addicted to morphine, reportedly infected over 200 patients (Bosch 1998). When giving patients post-operative painkillers, the anesthetist would often inject himself with part of the syringe contents and then inject the remaining painkiller into the patients using the same syringe. Apart from these exceptional cases, reported transmission of HCV from HCWs-to-patients has been rare (Duckworth et al. 1999; Anonymous 1995). Model-based calculations similarly suggest a low rate of HCV transmission of about 0.014% from surgical staff to patients (Ross et al. 2000a). This risk is approximately the same as a patient's risk of anesthesia-associated mortality.

Currently, no federal policy exists regarding management of HCWs with HCV. However, the American College of Surgeons states that: "There is no indication for surgeons to take special measures to protect their patients except during acute, symptomatic illness with hepatitis C."[7] The level of risk entailed in HCV transmission in the health care setting appears to be comparable to other bloodborne infections. Consequently, national policy should include strategies for the management of HCV as well as HIV and HBV.

## Prevention Techniques Minimize the Risk of Health Care Worker-to-Patient Transmission

There is substantial evidence that preventive measures greatly reduce the risk of HCW-to-patient transmission of bloodborne pathogens. The CDC has long recommended the use of universal precautions to reduce blood-to blood contact between HCWs and patients (CDC 1989). OSHA's blood-borne pathogen standard also requires such precautions.[8] There is evidence that some clusters of HCW-to-patient transmission of

[0] Ngui, Siew L., Watkins, Ruth P.F., Heptonstall, Julia, and Teo, Chong G. (2000) Selective Transmission of Hepatitis B Virus after Percutaneous Exposure. *Journal of Infectious Diseases* 181, 838–843; Ross, Stefan R., Vlazov, Sergei, and Roggendorf, Michael (1999) Provider-to-Patient Transmission of Hepatitis B Virus. *Lancet* 353, 324–325; The Incident Investigation Team and Others. (1997) Transmission of Hepatitis B to Patients from Four Infected Surgeons Without Hepatitis B Antigen. *New England Journal of Medicine* 336, 178–184.

[0] Hepatitis B Outbreak Investigation Team. (2000) An Outbreak of Hepatitis B Associated with Reusable Subdermal Electroencephalogram Electrodes. *Canadian Medical Association Journal* 162, 1127–1131.

[7] American College of Surgeons (1999) Statement on the Surgeon and Hepatitis. *Bulletin of the American College of Surgeons* 84, 21–24.

[8] 29 C.F.R. §1910.1030 (2001).

bloodborne pathogens could have been prevented entirely had the HCW taken these universal precautions.[9] Moreover, by adopting changes in practice habits, HCWs can further reduce the probability of percutaneous injuries during invasive procedures (Gerberding 1999). For example, double-gloving protects both the patient and the provider against blood-to-blood exposure more effectively than single-gloving.[10]

In addition, experts encourage surgeons and other HCW's to manage intraoperative injuries in the same way as other occupational injuries (Gerberding 1999). Surgeons should avoid recontact between a contaminated instrument and the patient. The CDC recommends post-exposure prophylaxis for HCWs occupationally exposed to HIV or HBV-infected blood to prevent these HCWs from developing HIV (CDC 2001). Patients exposed to an infected HCW's blood can receive post-exposure prophylaxis if exposure is promptly recognized and reported.[11]

Scientists have made great strides in developing safer medical technology over the last decade. In fact, the CDC has estimated that 177,000 injuries in hospital settings can be prevented each year through the use of needles with safety devices, needleless technologies, and safer work practices.[12] In response to the availability of safer needles, Congress passed the *Needlestick Safety and Prevention Act* in November 2000 amending OSHA's bloodborne pathogens standard to require health care employers to develop plans for the use of safe technology where possible.[13]

[9] Hepatitis B Outbreak Investigation Team, An Outbreak of Hepatitis B Associated with Reusable Subdermal Electroencephalogram Electrodes; Ross, Stefan R. et al. (2000b) Transmission of Hepatitis C Virus from a Patient to an Anesthesiology Assistant to Five Patients.

[10] American Academy of Orthopaedic Surgeons, *Advisory Statement: Preventing the Transmission of Bloodborne Pathogens* (viewed at www.aaos.org August 8, 2001); Mangram, Alicia et al. (1999) Guideline for Prevention of Surgical Site Infection, 1999. *Infection Control and Hospital Epidemiology* 20, 247–278.

[11] Gerberding, J. (1999) Provider-to-Patient HIV Transmission: How to keep it Exceedingly Rare (stating, "[u]nfortunately, for most patient infections ...recontact is either not recognized or not reported in time to initiate prophylactic treatment").

[12] Correspondence from Janet Heinrich, Director of Health Care-Public Health Issues, GAO to Representative Pete Stark entitled Occupational Safety: Selected Cost and Benefit Implications of Needlestick Prevention Devices for Hospitals, dated 11/17/2000 (viewed at http://www.cdc.gov/niosh/pdfs/GOA-01-60R.pdf on 7/14/2001)

[13] Pub. L. No. 106–430 (2000)

## Human Rights Burdens

Sanctions against HIV-infected HCWs would be ethically permissible if they were necessary to avert a serious risk to patients or if the limitations on human rights were trivial. At present, however, the risks to patients are negligible, especially when appropriate preventive measures are taken, and the burdens on HIV-infected HCWs disproportionately high. Qualified and experienced professionals face discrimination, invasion of privacy, and potential liability. An unintended consequence of CDC guidelines is that they have become a nationally recognized standard of care used by health care organizations and the courts to justify adverse treatment of infected HCWs (Lo and Steinbrook 1992).

### Discrimination

The Americans with Disabilities Act (ADA), and similar state statutes (Gostin et al. 1999), proscribe employment discrimination against "qualified" persons with a disability. The Supreme Court has held that all stages of HIV disease, including asymptomatic infection, are covered disabilities.[14] A person is qualified if she is capable of performing the essential performance functions of the job. Notably, "qualification" standards include a requirement that a person does not pose a "direct threat" to the health or safety of others.[15] The ADA, however, requires reasonable accommodations if they would enable persons with disabilities to perform their job safely (i.e., without posing a significant risk) and effectively.[16] Thus, if reasonable accommodations could help HCWs practice safely, health care organizations must provide those accommodations.[17]

The critical questions, therefore, are whether HIV-infected HCWs pose a significant risk to patients and, if so, whether there are reasonable accommodations to reduce that risk. The Supreme Court assesses "significant risk" by its nature (the mode of transmission), probability (the likelihood of transmission), severity (the magnitude of the harm should the infection be

[14] *Bragdon v. Abbott*, 524 U.S. 624 (1998).

[15] 42 U.S.C. §12113(b) (2001).

[16] 42 U.S.C. §12112(b)(5)(A) (2001).

[17] *Parks v. Female Health Care Assoc., Ltd.*, No. 96C 7133, 1997 WL 285870 (N.D. Ill. May 23, 1997).

transmitted), and duration (the length of time the person remains infectious).[18] The EEOC, moreover, states that "an employer ... is not permitted to deny an employment opportunity to a person with a disability merely because of a slightly increased risk."[19]

Despite this clear language, the courts have held that because HIV infection carries grave consequences, even a theoretical risk of transmission can be sufficient to justify discrimination (Rohlfsen 1999). The courts have had little difficulty finding that HIV-infected HCWs pose a significant risk[20], often resolving the issue through summary judgment without medical facts and expert testimony (Van Detta 1999). These courts rely on the severity of harm *should the risk materialize.* One court allowed a hospital to reassign a surgical assistant to the procurement department while recognizing the "small" risk: "The duration of infection is perpetual. And the virus inevitably leads to the fatal disease AIDS."[21]

This kind of reasoning perverts the significant risk standard because it means that individuals can be discriminated against in the absence of an appreciable public threat. A federal Court of Appeals, for example, upheld the segregation of HIV-infected inmates arguing that they pose a threat to the prison population.[22] Because significant risk is a product of four criteria (nature, probability, severity and duration), if any criterion demonstrates a very low chance of serious harm, then the risk should be "insignificant" (Rhodes, et al. 1995). Notably, courts use CDC guidelines to support their position.[23] The court in *Estate of Mauro v. Borgess Medical Center* found that a surgical technician posed a "direct threat to the health and safety of others" even though the technician had never placed his hands near the patient's wound and his duties consisted primarily of handing the surgeon's instruments.[24] The court concluded: "[w]e must defer to the medical judgement in the report of the Centers for Disease Control."[25]

Even if HIV-infected HCWs pose a significant risk, hospitals have a duty to provide reasonable accommodations such as infection control, training, and a leave of absence for treatment.[26] If HIV-infected HCWs were to receive this kind of support, the great majority would be able to function effectively and safely.

Despite the potential of the ADA to safeguard the rights of workers, the courts and administrative agencies, with few exceptions[27], have upheld discrimination against HIV-infected HCWs. The judiciary has permitted decisions to exclude HCWs from medical[28] and nursing[29] practice. In response to concern about the Florida dental case, one court upheld the exclusion of an HIV-infected student from a dental school.[30] Despite the legal standard that the employer bears the burden of proving that the practice poses a significant risk of harm, in reality, the courts have shifted the burden to HCWs to show they pose virtually no risk (Webber 1997). The courts have approved discriminatory action not only for exposure-prone procedures, but also for less invasive procedures.[31] Notably, some courts have upheld restrictions despite expert review panel advice that the HCW should continue to practice.[32] These are cases where

[18] *School Bd. of Nassau County. v. Arline*, 480 U.S. 273, 287 (1987).

[19] 29C.F.R. §1630pt. 1630, App. (2001).

[20] *Scoles v. Mercy Health Corp.*, 887F. Supp. 765 (E.D. Pa. 1994); Forrest, Adam G. (1999). Is there a Significant Risk or High Probability of HIV Transmission from an Infected HealthCare Worker to Others? The Sixth Circuit's Answer Lies in *Mauro v. Borgess Medical Center.Creighton Law Review* 32, 1763–1803.

[21] *Bradley v. Univ. of Texas M.D. Anderson Cancer Ctr.*, 3F.3d 922, 924 (5th Cir. 1993).

[22] *Onishea v. Hopper*, 171F.3d 1289 (11th Cir. 1999) (en banc), *cert. denied sub. nom, Davis. v. Hopper*, 528 U.S. 1114 (2000)

[23] *Estate of Mauro v. Borgess Med. Ctr.*, 137F.3d 398, 404 (6th Cir. 1998); *Doe v. Univ. ofMaryland Med. Sys. Corp.*, 50F.3d 1261,1266 (4th Cir. 1995). But see *Tolman v. Doe*, 988. F. Supp. 582 (E.D. Va.1997) (determining that HIV infected cardiologist followed the CDC'sguidelines thus cardiologist had a valid defamation claim against his partner in practice whoimplied to patients that cardiologist was unfit for practice)

[24] *Estate of Mauro v. Borgess Med. Ctr.*, 137F.3d 398 (6th Cir. 1998).

[25] *Estate of Mauro v. Borgess Med. Ctr.*, 137F.3d 398 (6th Cir. 1998).

[26] See *Parks v. Female Health Care Assoc.*, 1997 WL 285870.

[27] *Doe by Laveryv. Attorney General*, 44F.3d 715, *opinion superceded by* 62F.3d 1424 (9thCir. 1995), *judgement vacated by* 518 U.S. 1014; *Doe v. Westchester County Med. Ctr.*, StateDiv. of Human Rights, No. 91-504-2, N.Y.L.J., Dec. 26, 1990, p. 30.

[28] *Doe v. Univ. of Maryland Med. Sys. Corp.*, 50F.3d 1261, 1264 (4th Cir. 1995).

[29] *Leckelt v. Bd. of Comm'rs*, 909F.2d 820 (5th Cir. 1990).

[30] *Doe v. Washington Univ.*, 780F. Supp. 628 (E.D. Mo. 1991).

[31] *Estate of Mauro v. Borgess Med. Ctr.*, 137F.3d 398 (6th Cir. 1998); *Leckelt v. Bd. ofComm'rs*, 909F.2d 820 (5th Cir. 1990).

[32] *Doe v. Univ. of Maryland Med. Sys. Corp.*, 50F.3d 1261 (4th Cir. 1995); *Doe v. WashingtonUniv.*, 780F. Supp. 628 (E.D. Mo. 1991).

public health authorities have complied with the ADA's mandate for individualized determinations and the judiciary has nonetheless declined to protect HCWs' rights.

## Privacy

The CDC requirement to disclose a HCW's HIV-status to patients before performing exposure-prone procedures has become common practice. Patient notification is supported by cultural, ethical, and legal reasoning (Fost 2000). American cultural thought strongly supports a patient's "right to know." Patients want to be informed and to make decisions for themselves whether to incur risks. Similarly, infected physicians may feel they owe an ethical duty to patients and the wider public to disclose their serological status. Physicians may choose to "put patients first" by disclosing their serological status, even if the risk of transmission is very low. Finally, the legal doctrine of informed consent appears to support disclosure. In many states, the law requires physicians to disclose risks that "reasonable" patients would want to know; and many patients do want to know if their physician is infected with HIV (Rediger 2000; Tereskerz et al. 1999).

Despite these significant arguments, the law should not *require* HCWs to disclose their HIV-status to patients. A legal obligation to notify patients is an invasion of the HCW's privacy. It is important to recall that the HCW is also a patient who is being treated for a stigmatizing disease. Forced disclosure of this sensitive information may be socially embarrassing and harm the HCW's livelihood and professional reputation.[33] Moreover, the invasion of privacy is extensive because patients have no duty of confidentiality and may spread the information to other patients and the media (Gostin 1991b).

The doctrine of informed consent, moreover, should not require HIV-infected HCWs to disclose their HIV status to patients. First, informed consent requires disclosure of "material" risks, not remote risks. The risk of HIV transmission from HCW-to-patient is too low to meet the legal standard for disclosure. Moreover, if the risk were significant, the logical remedy would be to restrict the HCW's right to practice, not to notify the patient. Public health authorities would not permit a clinician to practice knowing he/she poses a meaningful risk even if patients were notified. Second, informed consent usually requires disclosure of risks entailed in the medical procedure, not those posed by the HCW herself. HCWs ordinarily are not required to inform patients about their personal health status or disability (whether temporary or permanent). For example, HCWs who have depression, have had insufficient sleep, or have had alcoholic beverages at a social occasion in the hours preceding a patient encounter are not ordinarily required to disclose these facts to patients. In each case, the HCW may pose a risk that is the same as, or greater than, the risk of HIV transmission. Yet, provided the HCW is considered competent and reasonably safe, she is entitled to practice without a duty to disclose.

State courts have affirmed hospital decisions to disclose the HCW's HIV status to patients. Relying on CDC guidelines, these courts require compulsory disclosure as part of the informed consent process.[34] Some courts even permit disclosure for the purposes of retrospective investigations.[35] In *Faya v. Almaraz*, for example, an HIV-infected oncological surgeon performed partial mastectomies on two patients. When the patients read that the physician had died of AIDS, they brought a law suit alleging emotional distress. The court allowed damages for the period between the time that the patients learned of the physician's HIV status and their conclusively testing negative for HIV.[36] Similar results occurred in other court decisions.[37] In these kinds of cases, hospitals and HCWs face liability even though patients suffer

[33] Daniels, Norman (1992) HIV-infected Professionals, Patient Rights, and the 'Switching'Dilemma. *Journal of the American Medical Association* 267, 1368–1371; See also American-College of Surgeons, Statement on the Surgeon and HIV Infection (stating that the CDC'spolicy towards HCWs with HIV is "intrusive in the extreme).

[34] *Estate of Behringer v. Princeton Med. Ctr.*, 592 A.2d 1251 (N.J. Super. Ct. Law Div. 1991).

[35] In re Milton S. Hershey Med. Ctr., 634 A.2d 159 (Pa. 1993).

[36] *Faya v. Almaraz*, 620 A.2d 327 (Md. 1993).

[37] *Williamson v. Waldman*, 696 A.2d 14 (N.J. 1997) (granting emotional distress damages tocleaning employee who feared contracting AIDS after she was pricked by a discarded lancetwhile cleaning a medical office); *Madrid v. Lincoln County Med. Ctr.*, 923 P.2d 1154 (N.M.1996) (granting emotional distress damages without evidence of actual exposure to workerwho feared exposure to HIV when body fluid samples she was transporting to lab leaked).

no tangible harm or infection (Fisher 1997). This litigation, moreover, is not restricted to HIV, but could apply equally to other infectious diseases such as HBV, HBC, or TB.

Fortunately, most state courts require plaintiffs to show actual exposure to HIV in order to recover emotional distress damages.[38] However, even if litigation is unsuccessful, it can influence hospitals to restrict HCW rights more than they think may be justified in the public interest. Hospitals, fearing potential liability, may assume it is less costly to mandate patient notification or restrict a HCW's practice than to face litigation. The problem is exacerbated by malpractice liability concerns if insurers urge "screening out" infected HCWs rather than incur liability risks.

## Compulsory Testing

The CDC does not recommend HIV testing in the absence of behavioral risk factors. Nor does the agency recommend mandatory testing. Nevertheless, hospitals occasionally require HCWs to be tested against their will and courts have approved policies of this kind. For example, a federal Court of Appeals upheld a hospital's decision to fire a licensed practical nurse who was suspected of being HIV-infected, but refused to be tested. The court reasoned that the hospital was prevented from "deciding what, if any, measures were necessary to protect the health of patients."[39] Courts have held that HIV testing can be "job related and consistent with business necessity."[40] In one case, a training school obtained a medical assistant's blood purportedly to test for rubella, but instead performed an HIV test.[41] The court found an invasion of privacy, but the case shows the lengths to which some facilities will go to identify HIV-infected HCWs. If the standard of care remains that HCWs must notify patients and possibly discontinue practice, then health care organizations and the courts may believe that compulsory testing is an appropriate response.

## HCWs' Rights and the Public's Health

HCWs living with HIV/AIDS face loss of their livelihood, professional status, and self-image. HCWs, have been terminated, forced to resign, re-assigned, denied rotations, or not permitted to continue their education (Schatz 1995). Many HCWs, because of the fear of discrimination, do not seek diagnosis and treatment because they have greater legal protection if they can honestly say that they did not know their serologic status. Some pay for treatment out of their own pockets to avoid filing claims with their health insurance carriers. Others travel outside their geographic areas to protect their anonymity or avoid treatment altogether.[42]

Current policy and practice not only adversely affect the professional and personal interests of HCWs, but also may not be in the public interest. By denying talented health care professionals the opportunity to treat patients, the current policy may limit patients' ability to obtain care.[43] Punitive policies may provide disincentives for HCWs to determine their HIV status or to disclose it to their employers or personal physicians. Consequently, the CDC policy's restrictive approach may reduce HCWs' opportunity for therapy, thereby increasing risks to patients.

## Proposals for Reform of National Policy

Current national policy offers no discernable risk reduction for patients – very few, if any, new bloodborne infections are prevented. At the same time, the policy imposes human rights burdens, undermines efforts to retain experienced professionals, and poses liability risks. Consequently, new national policy should focus on structural changes to make the health care workplace safer for both patients and HCWs rather than on identification and management of infected HCWs (Gerberding 1996). Certainly, patient safety remains the most important part of any

[38] *Majca v. Beekil*, 701N.E.2d 1084 (Ill. 1998); *K.A.C. v. Benson*, 527N.W.2d 553 (Minn.1995); *Brzoska v. Olsen*, 688 A.2d 1355 (Del. 1995); *Kerins v. Hartley*, 33 Cal. Rptr. 2d 172 (Cal. Ct. App. 1994).

[39] *Leckelt v. Bd. of Comm'rs*, 909F.2d 820 (5th Cir. 1990).

[40] *Watson v. City of Miami Beach*, 177F.3d 932 (11th Cir. 1999); *EEOC v. Prevo's FamilyMarket, Inc.*, 135F.3d 1089 (6th Cir. 1998).

[41] *Doe v. High-Tech Inst.*, 972 P.2d 1060 (Colo. Ct. App. 1998).

[42] Letter from the Gay and Lesbian Medical Association to the CDC, dated June 26, 1996.

[43] American College of Surgeons (1998) "Statement on the Surgeon and HIV Infection."

national policy, but it ought to be possible to assure patient safety, while not undermining the HCW's interests in autonomy, privacy, and livelihood. The following five recommendations should ensure that patients receive care in a safe environment, while treating HCWs with respect and dignity.

1. *Program to prevent bloodborne pathogen transmission*

Health care organizations should be responsible for planning, implementing, enforcing, and evaluating effective strategies for prevention of bloodborne pathogen transmission. Prevention programs should include policies and procedures for: (a) standard (universal) precautions (e.g., barrier equipment such as gloves, gowns and face protection) (Garner 1996; Beekman et al. 1994); (b) reprocessing patient-care equipment (e.g., cleaning, disinfecting, and sterilizing) and cleaning environmental surfaces; (c) infection control training (in professional schools and in the health care setting); (s) prevention and management of infectious conditions (e.g., HBV vaccination); (d) injury and exposure prevention during surgical, obstetric, and dental procedures-such as less invasive alternatives to conventional interventions (e.g., laparoscopy), practice changes (e.g., "no touch" techniques and double-gloving), and safer instruments (e.g., blunted suture needles and use of staples instead of sutures); and (e) surveillance for transmission of bloodborne pathogens (e.g., reporting and evaluating parenteral injuries).

2. *Responsibilities of infected HCWs*

HCWs, as professionals, have ethical responsibilities to promote their own health and well-being and to assure patient safety. HCWs should learn their serological status through testing with informed consent. Infected HCWs should seek medical care and treatment, including ongoing monitoring of viral load, as well as evaluations of physical and mental health status. HCWs are responsible for notifying patients and hospitals in all cases of significant exposure to the HCW's blood.

3. *Discontinue expert review panels and special restrictions for exposure-prone procedures*

Identifying infected physicians, requiring expert review panels, and adopting special restrictions for exposure-prone procedures have served to single-out and stigmatize HCWs. The term "exposure-prone procedure" has not been clearly defined, so the courts have erred on the side of restricting HCW practice. Expert review panels, moreover, are constituted differently in each state so there are multiple standards of care; even when panels permit practice, health care organizations sometimes disregard their advice. The requirement to disclose a HCW's serologic status to patients has rendered expert review panels virtually irrelevant since few patients are willing to be treated by an infected HCW. Review panels, therefore, should be replaced by expert consultants who would be available for advising about HCWs' health and patients' safety, but not empowered to restrict HCW practice.

4. *Discontinue mandatory disclosure of a HCW's infection status*

HCWs may feel morally obliged to voluntarily notify patients of their infection-status, but the law should not require disclosure of very low-level risks. HIV, in particular, is a highly personal, and sometimes stigmatic, health condition that usually has little relevance to patient safety. Because notification represents an invasion of privacy and may result in loss of livelihood, it should not be legally mandated.

5. *Impose practice restrictions to avert significant risks to patients*

Public health authorities owe a public duty to assure patient safety. Consequently, health care organizations and/or public health authorities should issue practice restrictions if a HCW:

(a) suffers from a physical or mental impairment that affects his professional judgment or practice;
(b) has exudative lesions or weeping dermatitis;
(c) has a history of poor infection control technique and practice; or
(d) has had an incident of transmission of a bloodborne pathogen. In these kinds of cases, the HCW cannot practice competently and safely. Consequently, health care organizations and public health authorities owe a primary duty to safeguard patient safety.

## Conclusion

The health care system must be made as safe as possible for both patients and their care providers.

The HIV epidemic has driven government and the public toward achieving near-zero risk. Such a standard is not achievable and, in the process, existing national policy has imposed human rights burdens, driven qualified HCWs from the profession, and posed unfair liability risks. A new national policy, focused on management of the workplace environment and injury prevention, would achieve high levels of patient safety without discrimination and invasion of privacy.

**Acknowledgments** This article is revised and updated from: Lawrence O. Gostin. (2000) A Proposed National Policy on Health Care Workers Living with HIV/AIDS and Other Bloodborne Pathogens. *Journal of the American Medical Association* 284, 1965–1970.

## References

AIDS/TB Committee of the Society for Healthcare Epidemiology of America. 1997. Management of healthcare workers infected with hepatitis B virus, hepatitis C virus, human immunodeficiency virus, or other bloodborne pathogens. *Infection Control and Hospital Epidemiology* 18: 349–363.

Alicia, Noble, Troyen A. Brennan, and Andrew L. Hyams. 1997. Snyder v. American association of blood banks: a re-examination of liability for medical practice guideline promulgators. *Journal of Evaluation in Clinical Practice* 4: 49–62.

American Academy of Orthopaedic Surgeons. 2001. *Advisory statement: preventing the transmission of bloodborne pathogens* (viewed at www.aaos.org August 8).

American College of Surgeons. 1998. Statement on the surgeon and HIV infection. *Bulletin of the American College of Surgeons* 83: 27–29.

American College of Surgeons. 1999. Statement on the surgeon and hepatitis. *Bulletin of the American College of Surgeons* 84: 21–24.

Anonymous. 1995. Hepatitis C virus transmission from health care worker to patient. *Communicable Disease Report Weekly* 5: 121.

Beekman, Susan E., et al. 1994. Temporal association between implementation of universal precautions and a sustained progressive decrease in percutaneous exposures to blood. *Clinical Infectious Diseases* 18: 562–569.

Blanchard, Alain, et al. 1998. Molecular evidence for nosocomial transmission of human immunodeficiency virus from a surgeon to one of his patients. *Journal of Virology* 72: 4537–4540.

Bosch, Xavier. 1998. Hepatitis C Outbreak Astounds Spain. *Lancet* 351: 1415.

*Bradley v. Univ. of Texas M.D. Anderson Cancer Ctr.* 1993. 3F.3d 922, 924 (5th Cir).

*Bragdon v. Abbott.* 1998. 524 U.S. 624.

Centers for Disease Control and Prevention. 1989. Guidelines for Prevention of Transmission of Human Immunodeficiency Virus and Hepatitis B Virus to Health-Care and Public-Safety Workers. *Morbidity and Mortality Weekly Report* 38(S–6), 1–36.

Centers for Disease Control and Prevention. 1991. Recommendations for Preventing Transmission of Human Immunodeficiency Virus and Hepatitis B Virus to Patients During Exposure-prone Invasive Procedures. *Morbidity and Mortality Weekly Report* 40, RR-8, 1–9.

Centers for Disease Control and Prevention. 1993. Update: investigations of persons treated by HIV-infected health-care workers. *Morbidity and Mortality Weekly Report* 42: 329–331.

Centers for Disease Control and Prevention. 1998. Recommendations for Prevention and Control of Hepatitis C Virus (HCV) Infection and HCV-related Chronic Disease. *Morbidity and Mortality Weekly Report* 47, RR-19, 1–39.

Centers for Disease Control and Prevention. 1999. *Fact sheet: HIV and its transmission* (Atlanta: Centers for Disease Control and Prevention) (viewed at http://www.cdc.gov/nchstp/hiv_aids/pubs/facts/transmission.htm on August 8, 2001).

Centers for Disease Control and Prevention. 2000. *Fact sheet: surveillance of health care workers with HIV/AIDS* (Atlanta: Centers for Disease Control and Prevention) (viewed at http://www.cdc.gov/hiv/pubs/facts/hcwsurv.htm on August 8, 2001).

Centers for Disease Control and Prevention. 2001. Updated U. S. Public Health Service Guidelines for the Management of Occupational Exposures to HBV, HCV and HIV and Recommendations for Postexposure Prophylaxis. *Morbidity and Mortality Weekly Report* 50, RR-11, 1–52.

Ciesielski, Carol, et al. 1994. The 1990 Florida dental investigation: the press and the science. *Annals of Internal Medicine* 121: 886–888.

Committee on Pediatric AIDS and Committee on Infectious Diseases. 1999. Issues related to human immunodeficiency virus transmission in schools, child care, medical settings, the home, and community. *Pediatrics* 104: 318–324.

Daniels, Norman. 1992. HIV-infected professionals, patient rights, and the 'switching' dilemma. *Journal of the American Medical Association* 267: 1368–1371.

Donnely, Michael, et al. 1999. Are HIV look backs worthwhile? Outcome of an exercise to notify patients treated by an HIV infected health care worker. *Communicable Disease and Public Health* 2: 126–129.

Duckworth, Georgia J., et al. 1999. Transmission of hepatitis C virus from a surgeon to a patient. *Communicable Disease and Public Health* 2: 188–192.

Esteban, Juan I., et al. 1996. Transmission of hepatitis C by a cardiac surgeon. *New England Journal of Medicine* 334: 555–560.

*Faya v. Almaraz*, 620 A.2d 327 (Md. 1993).

Fisher, Eric S. 1997. Aidsphobia: a national survey of emotional distress claims for the fear of contracting AIDS. *Tort and Insurance Law Journal* 33: 169–226.

Forrest, Adam G. 1999. Is there a significant risk or high probability of HIV transmission from an infected health care worker to others? The sixth circuit's answer lies in Mauro v. Borgess Medical Center. *Creighton Law Review* 32: 1763–1803.

Fost, Norman. 2000. Patient access to information on clinicians infected with bloodborne pathogens. *Journal of the American Medical Association* 284: 1975–1976.

Garner, Julia S. 1996. Hospital infections practices advisory committee. Guideline for isolation precautions in hospitals. *Infection Control and Hospital Epidemiology* 17: 53–80.

Gerberding, Julie L. 1996. The infected health care provider. *New England Journal of Medicine* 334: 594–595.

Gerberding, Julie. 1999. Provider-to-patient HIV transmission: how to keep it exceedingly rare. *Annals of Internal Medicine* 130: 64–65.

Gostin, Lawrence O. 1991a. The HIV-infected health care professional: public policy, discrimination and patient safety. *Archives of Internal Medicine* 151: 663–665.

Gostin, Lawrence O. 1991b. CDC guidelines on HIV or HBV-positive health care professionals performing exposure-prone invasive procedures. *Law, Medicine and Health Care* 19: 140–143.

Gostin, Lawrence O., C. Feldblum, and D.W. Webber. 1999. Disability discrimination in America: HIV/AIDS and other health conditions. *Journal of the American Medical Association* 281: 745–752.

Goujon, Christophe P., et al. 2000. Phylogenetic analyses indicate an atypical nurse-topatient transmission of human immunodeficiency virus type 1. *Journal of Virology* 74: 2525–2532.

Harpaz, Rafael, et al. 1996. Transmission of hepatitis B virus to multiple patients from a surgeon without evidence of inadequate infection control. *New England Journal of Medicine* 334: 549–554.

Hepatitis B Outbreak Investigation Team. 2000. An outbreak of hepatitis B associated with reusable subdermal electroencephalogram electrodes. *Canadian Medical Association Journal* 162: 1127–1131.

Hutin, Yvan J.F., et al. 1999. An outbreak of hospital-acquired hepatitis b virus infection among patients receiving chronic hemodialysis. *Infection Control and Hospital Epidemiology* 20: 731–735.

Kohn, Linda T., Janet M. Corrigan, and Molla S. Donaldson (eds.). 1999. *To err is human: building a safer health system.* Washington: National Academy.

Law, M.G., et al. 2001. Modeling the effect of combination antiretroviral treatments on HIV incidence. *AIDS* 15: 1287–1294.

Lo, Bernard, and Robert Steinbrook. 1992. Health care workers infected with the human immunodeficiency virus. *Journal of the American Medical Association* 267: 1100–1105.

Lot, Florence, et al. 1999. Probable transmission from an orthopedic surgeon to a patient in France. *Annals of Internal Medicine* 130: 1–6.

Mangram, Alicia, et al. 1999. Guideline for prevention of surgical site infection, 1999. *Infection Control and Hospital Epidemiology* 20: 247–278.

McIntosh, Phillip L. 1996. When the surgeon has HIV: what to tell patients about the risk of exposure and the risk of transmission. *University of Kansas Law Review* 44: 315–364.

Ngui, Siew L., Ruth P.F. Watkins, Julia Heptonstall, and Chong G. Teo. 2000. Selective transmission of hepatitis B virus after percutaneous exposure. *Journal of Infectious Diseases* 181: 838–843.

Panel for Clinical Practices for the Treatment of HIV. 2001. Guidelines for the Use of Antiretroviral Agents in HIV-Infected Adults and Adolescents, April 23 (viewed at http://www.hivatis.org/guidelines/adult/Apr23_01/text/index.html on August 8, 2001).

Parks v. Female Health Care Assoc., Ltd. 1997. No. 96C 7133, 1997 WL 285870 (N.D. Ill. May 23).

Quinn, Thomas C., et al. 2000. Viral load and heterosexual transmission of human immunodeficiency virus type 1. *New England Journal of Medicine* 342: 921–929.

Rediger, Byron B. 2000. Living in a world with HIV: balancing privacy, privilege, and the right to know between patients and health care professionals. *Hamline Journal of Public Law and Policy* 21: 443–487.

Rhodes, Robert S., Gordon L. Telford, Walter J. Hierholzer Jr., and Mark Barnes. 1995. Bloodborne pathogen transmission from health-care workers to patients. Legal issues and provider prospective. *Surgical Clinics of North America* 75: 1205–1217.

Robert, Laurie M., et al. 1995. Investigations of patients of health care workers infected with HIV. *Annals of Internal Medicine* 122: 653–657.

Robinson Jr., Edward N., and Ruth de Bliek. 1996. The college student, the dentist, and the North Carolina senator: risk analysis and risk management of HIV transmission from health care worker to patient. *Medical Decision Making* 16: 86–91.

Rodgers, Audrey S., et al. 1993. Investigation of potential HIV transmission to patient of an HIV-infected surgeon. *Journal of the American Medical Association* 269: 1795–1801.

Rohlfsen, Ryan J. 1999. HIV-infected surgical personnel under the ADA: do they pose a threat or are reasonable accommodations possible. *Journal of Contemporary Health Law and Policy* 16: 127–144.

Roper, William L. 1992. Letter to state health departments, dated June 16.

Ross, Stefan R., Sergei Vlazov, and Michael Roggendorf. 1999. Provider-to-patient transmission of hepatitis B virus. *Lancet* 353: 324–325.

Ross, Stefan R., Sergei Viazov, and Michael Roggendorf. 2000a. Risk of hepatitis C transmission from infected medical staff to patients: model-based calculations for surgical settings. *Archives of Internal Medicine* 160: 2312–2316.

Ross, Stefan R., et al. 2000b. Transmission of hepatitis C virus from a patient to an anesthesiology assistant to five patients. *New England Journal of Medicine* 343: 1851–1854.

Saag, Michael S., et al. 1996. HIV viral load markers in clinical practice. *Nature Medicine* 2: 625–629.

Schatz, Benjamin. 1995. Supporting and advocating for HIV-positive health care workers. *Bulletin of the New York Academy of Medicine* 72: 263–272.

Summers, Todd. 2001. Public policy for health care workers infected with human immunodeficiency virus. *Journal of the American Medical Association* 285: 882.

Tereskerz, Patti Miller, Richard D. Pearson, and Janine Jagger. 1999. Infected physicians and invasive procedures: national policy and legal reality. *Milbank Quarterly* 77: 511–529.

The Incident Investigation Team and Others. 1997. Transmission of hepatitis B to patients from four infected surgeons without hepatitis B antigen. *New England Journal of Medicine* 336: 178–184.

Van Detta, Jeffrey A. 1999. Typhoid Mary meets the ADA: a case study of the direct threat standard under the Americans with disabilities act. *Harvard Journal of Law and Public Policy* 22: 853–949.

Webber, David W. (ed.). 1997. *AIDS and the Law*. New York: Wiley.

Bioethical Inquiry (2009) 6:181–185
DOI 10.1007/s11673-009-9155-4

# Do Physicians' Legal Duties to Patients Conflict with Public Health Values? The Case of Antibiotic Overprescription

Carl H. Coleman

Received: 8 January 2009 / Accepted: 14 April 2009 / Published online: 5 May 2009


**Abstract** Among the many explanations for antibiotic overprescription, some doctors cite the risk of malpractice liability if they deny a patient's request for an antibiotic and the patient's condition worsens. In this paper, I examine the merits of this concern—i.e., whether physicians could, in fact, face malpractice liability for refusing to prescribe an antibiotic when, from a public health perspective, the use of the antibiotic would be considered inappropriate. I conclude that the potential for liability cannot be dismissed entirely, but the risk is remote—even in cases where there is a chance that the antibiotic might have benefited the patient.

**Keywords** Over-prescription · Malpractice · Anti-biotics

The overprescription of antibiotics is an important contributing factor in the development of antibiotic resistance, a serious public health problem that has recently become even more urgent with the emergence of multi-drug resistant tuberculosis. According to some studies, at least half of all antibiotic prescriptions are "unnecessary, poorly chosen, or incorrectly dosed" (Solomon et al. 2001). In addition to prescribing antibiotics for illnesses that are not caused by bacteria, physicians frequently prescribe antibiotics for conditions that, although bacterial in nature, are likely to clear up quickly even if no treatment is provided. Even when an antibiotic prescription is medically warranted, doctors may fuel resistance by writing prescriptions for broad-spectrum antibiotics capable of fighting multiple bacteria, instead of waiting for the results of a culture test that would enable them to prescribe a narrow-spectrum antibiotic targeted to the patient's particular infection.

Among the many explanations for antibiotic overprescription, some doctors cite the risk of malpractice liability if they deny a patient's request for an antibiotic and the patient's condition worsens (Selgelid 2007). In this paper, I examine the merits of this concern from the perspective of malpractice law in the United States. Specifically, I consider whether physicians could, in fact, face malpractice liability for refusing to prescribe an antibiotic when, from a public health perspective, the use of the antibiotic would be considered inappropriate. I conclude that the potential for liability cannot be dismissed entirely, but the risk is remote—even in cases where there is a chance that the antibiotic might have benefitted the patient. Nonetheless, if physicians believe they could be held liable, this perception is likely to affect their behavior, even if it is grossly disproportionate to the risk they actually face.

C. H. Coleman (✉)
Center for Health & Pharmaceutical Law & Policy,
Seton Hall University School of Law,
One Newark Center,
Newark, NJ 07102, USA
e-mail: colemaca@shu.edu

From a public health perspective, when physicians think about the legal implications of prescribing antibiotics, they should be motivated to act cautiously. To the extent that fears of liability are pushing physicians in the opposite direction, policy-makers should adopt counterbalancing legal mechanisms that would create incentives for physicians to prescribe antibiotics more judiciously. I close the paper by offering a few preliminary suggestions about how this might be done.

## The Problem

The overprescription of antibiotics can be defined as the prescription of antibiotics in excess of legitimate clinical need. The most obvious example of overprescription is the physiologically futile use of antibiotics, such as when a physician prescribes an antibiotic to treat a viral infection. In these situations, the antibiotic will simply not work. Overprescription can also occur when an antibiotic might provide some medical benefit, but the expected benefits are small and are outweighed by the potential promotion of resistance. An example of this second category would be an antibiotic prescription for an ear infection likely to clear up quickly without treatment.

Numerous causes of antibiotic overprescription have been identified in the literature (see Laxminarayan and Malani 2007). Patient-related factors include misunderstanding about how antibiotics work, the attitude that a visit to doctor is not productive unless it ends with a prescription (Howard 2007), an unwillingness to delay treatment until culture tests are available, and the fact that the primary risk of overprescription—the development of drug-resistant strains—is a societal problem that may never directly affect the individual receiving care. For physicians, overprescription often stems from a desire to placate worried patients (or, in the case of children, who make up a large percentage of ear infection patients, their parents). As a recent report on antibiotic overuse observed, "The average patient suffering from a cold or an ear infection wants immediate relief and sees a prescription for antibiotics as the ticket to recovery, and the physician may be only too happy to oblige if writing it benefits her practice" (Laxminarayan and Malani 2007, 3–4). The economics of antibiotic production and distribution do not help matters, as manufacturers' profits are based on the number of sales, not the medical legitimacy of the prescriptions, and the out-of-pocket costs to purchasers of antibiotics do not reflect the social cost of overuse.

## Antibiotic Prescriptions and Malpractice Liability: What are the Real Risks?

Assessing the risk of malpractice liability for refusing to write a physiologically futile antibiotic prescription is easy: there is no risk. First, the "standard of care" cannot plausibly be interpreted to require physicians to provide medically useless treatment simply because the patient asks for it. This is true whether the standard of care is defined in terms of what physicians customarily do (the traditional approach to malpractice liability) or as what a "reasonable physician" would do under the circumstances (a more modern approach used in some jurisdictions that allows juries to evaluate the expert witnesses' testimony and make their own assessment of what a competent physician would have done under the circumstances) (Peters 2000). Second, if the antibiotic would truly have been futile, a patient who is denied the antibiotic will not be able to satisfy the causation element of a malpractice claim—i.e., the requirement that the patient establish that it is "more likely than not" that her injuries were caused by the conduct about which she complains. No matter how sick the patient becomes after being denied an antibiotic, if the antibiotic had no chance of working, the refusal to provide it could not possibly have caused any harm.

Of course, physicians who express concern about malpractice liability for refusing patients' requests for antibiotic prescriptions are probably not thinking about cases of true physiological futility. Rather, they are concerned with situations in which the antibiotic might provide some benefit, albeit a small and uncertain one—such as with an ear infection that might clear up a bit earlier if an antibiotic is provided, or a case of diagnostic uncertainty in which the potential benefits of an antibiotic cannot be ruled out (Selgelid 2007, 222). In these situations, if the patient insists on an antibiotic prescription, does the physician who refuses to comply face a genuine liability risk?

In jurisdictions that follow the traditional approach to malpractice liability, this question would be analyzed by asking whether it is customary for physicians to prescribe antibiotics under the circumstances at issue. Given how many physicians are known to accede to patients' requests for antibiotics even when the potential medical benefits are minimal, it might appear that a custom-based analysis would be favorable to plaintiffs. However, despite the frequency of antibiotic overprescription, the practice has been widely criticized by the organized medical profession (e.g. Gonzales et al. 2001), whose views have a significant impact on the assessment of medical custom. Moreover, even if a plaintiff could establish that many physicians do prescribe antibiotics when the potential benefits are minimal, physicians could still avoid liability in a traditional malpractice jurisdiction by showing that a conservative approach to antibiotics is supported by a "respectable minority" of the profession.[1] This should be fairly easy to establish in light of professional statements endorsing conservative use.

The standard of care analysis becomes more complicated in jurisdictions that use the "reasonable physician" approach to malpractice liability, under which juries are given greater leeway to evaluate, rather than merely to identify, what physicians customarily do. At first glance, it might seem that an objective reasonableness standard would be even more favorable to physicians than one that simply defers to customary practice, given that, in the cases we are considering, the potential benefits of antibiotics are minimal and the public health risks are great. However, resistance does not result from a single antibiotic prescription; it takes many prescriptions over an extended period of time until an antibiotic no longer works. Because the incremental risks of a single antibiotic prescription are minimal, a jury might conclude that the reasonable physician would take the risk if there is even a small chance that the patient's condition would improve.

Further complicating the reasonableness analysis is the fact that the primary risks of antibiotic overprescriptions extend to the public at large, not to the individual seeking care. Because physicians are commonly regarded as fiduciaries of their patients (Rodwin 1995), courts may take the position that, in assessing the reasonableness of the physician's conduct, the only risks and benefits the jury should consider are those the individual patient would experience. If the public health risks of antibiotic resistance are taken out of the equation, a refusal to provide a potentially beneficial antibiotic prescription may well be viewed as "unreasonable" medical care.

Finally, in jurisdictions that rely on the reasonable physician approach to malpractice, the patient's subjective desire for an antibiotic may play a greater role in the analysis than in jurisdictions that define the standard of care solely in terms of physicians' customary practices. In general, reasonableness assessments depend on a weighing of the risks and benefits of actions, so the issue in a "reasonable physician" jurisdiction would be whether the potential benefits of an antibiotic prescription outweigh the associated risks. In the area of informed consent litigation, courts have emphasized that identifying and valuing the risks and benefits of medical treatment depends as much on individual values and preferences as on objective medical information (see Canterbury v. Spence). If the patient's subjective desire for an antibiotic is taken into consideration in identifying the potential benefits of an antibiotic, physicians might be expected to take greater risks for such patients to satisfy the standard of reasonable medical care.

This deference to patient-driven assessments of the risks and benefits of treatment finds some support in the handful of cases in which physicians have sought to withhold or withdraw life-sustaining treatment over the objections of a patient or surrogate. In many of these cases, courts have found that the patients are entitled to treatments they or their surrogates deem subjectively beneficial, even if those treatments seem unjustifiable from an objective point of view (Pope 2007). Read broadly, these cases could be construed as standing for the general proposition that, as long as a treatment has the potential to provide some benefit to the patient (i.e., as long as it is not physiologically futile), determining whether the benefits are "worth it" is for the individual patient to decide.

Despite these observations, it is doubtful that a physician who refuses to prescribe a minimally beneficial antibiotic faces more than a theoretical risk of malpractice liability.[2] First, even in jurisdictions that rely on the reasonable physician approach to

[1] As Barry Furrow explains, "If a defendant has established that distinctive practices are supported by a minority within the professional group, the judge may direct a verdict for the defendant rather than leaving the issue to the jury." Barry R. Furrow. 1997. Managed care organizations and patient injury: Rethinking liability. *Georgia Law Review* 31: 419-509, at 486 n.300.

[2] Indeed, "there are no documented cases in the medical literature of a physician being sued for failing to prescribe an antibiotic and a board member of a malpractice insurer reported that he was unaware of such cases" (Howard, 76).

malpractice, the views of professional organizations remain influential. With a clear professional consensus in favor of conservative use of antibiotics, plaintiffs are likely to have a hard time convincing a jury that a reasonable physician would choose to take a more aggressive approach.

Moreover, while individual autonomy is clearly an important legal value, the relative importance of autonomy vis-à-vis other values depends on the specific situation. Thus, the fact that patients have the right to refuse proposed interventions based on subjective or idiosyncratic value considerations suggests that individual autonomy is paramount when the patient's bodily integrity is at issue. However, in the antibiotic context the patient is not seeking information to help decide whether to accept a bodily invasion, but is instead seeking to compel a physician to provide treatment the physician believes is inappropriate. The fact that courts have emphasized the subjective nature of risk-benefit assessment in the context of informed consent litigation does not mean they would place an equivalent emphasis on individual autonomy when the patient is seeking to *compel* treatment, rather than to refuse it.

Admittedly, some of the end-of-life cases do appear to support a broader right to affirmatively insist on treatments, but in those cases the potential efficacy of the treatment was not seriously at issue. Rather, the physicians in these cases were claiming that, even though the treatments were likely to work—in the sense that they would keep the patients alive—the patients were so debilitated that keeping them alive would be pointless. Whether life is worth living seems quite clearly to be a philosophical, not a medical, determination. Thus, rather than reflecting a broad willingness to defer to patient preferences in all situations, the end-of-life cases can be read as standing for the more limited proposition that doctors have no right to tell patients that they would be better off dead.[3]

More broadly, despite the fact that physicians are normally required to act exclusively in their patients' interests, there is precedent for allowing physicians to take the interests of non-patients into account. For example, physicians are permitted, and in some cases required, to breach patient confidentiality when a patient poses a direct threat to others (see Tarasoff v. Regents of the University of California). While an antibiotic prescription does not pose an imminent threat to an identifiable individual—the standard courts have generally used for permitting or requiring physicians to breach confidentiality—the third-party disclosure cases demonstrate that courts will sometimes subordinate patients' wishes to broader societal concerns.

Similarly, the entire field of medical research can be seen as an exception to the general principle that physicians must always promote the individual's best interests, given that research subjects are frequently exposed to risks from which they will derive no direct benefits (Coleman 2005). To be sure, individuals who participate in medical research usually consent to enter into a relationship in which promoting their individual interests is not the primary objective. However, in the U.S. the law permits limited forms of nonconsensual research when the risks to individuals are minimal, provided the research cannot otherwise be conducted and an independent ethics committee approves it (Department of Health and Human Services 2005). As with the third-party disclosure cases, the permissibility of minimally risky, non-consensual medical research suggests that societal interests can sometimes trump the usual supremacy of individual choice.

Finally, even if a patient is able to convince a jury that the physician acted unreasonably by denying her request for an antibiotic, she must also establish that the denial of the prescription caused compensable damages. If the expected benefits of the antibiotic to the patient are minimal, any damages caused by refusing to prescribe the antibiotic are also likely to be minimal—unless the physician grossly miscalculated the patient's need for the antibiotic, in which case malpractice liability may well be appropriate. Unless the damages caused by the physician's conduct are substantial, it is unlikely that a malpractice lawsuit would even be brought.

## Changing the Incentives: Legal Measures to Promote Conservative Antibiotic Use

The foregoing discussion suggests that physicians who refuse to provide antibiotics to patients who

[3] As one commentator has observed, "It is as presumptuous and ethically inappropriate for doctors to suppose that their professional expertise qualifies them to know what kind of life is worth prolonging as it would be for meteorologists to suppose their professional expertise qualifies them to know what kind of destination is worth a long drive in the rain" (Ackerman 1991, 27–28 cited in Pope, 41).

demand them may face a theoretical risk of malpractice liability, but in the absence of other wrongdoing (such as negligent misdiagnosis) the real liability risk is probably remote. Yet, it is the perceived, not the actual, risk that is likely to drive behavior. In the area of pain management, for example, physicians commonly cite fear of criminal liability as a barrier to aggressively prescribing narcotics (Ziegler and Lorich 2003), despite the fact that criminal actions against physicians who prescribe narcotics appropriately are fairly rare events (Meier 2008).

Theoretically, one way to address this problem would be to educate physicians about the real risk of liability, in the hopes that better-informed physicians will be more likely to resist inappropriate patient requests. Yet, changing physicians' perceptions about the law is notoriously difficult, particularly when the legal issues are ambiguous and there is no case law directly on point. Moreover, because physicians' concerns about liability are just a small piece of the overprescription problem, it is not clear how much of an impact educating physicians about the law would actually have.

A better response would be to counterbalance the negative incentives stemming from fear of malpractice liability by creating additional legal incentives inspired by public health norms. For example, legislatures could draw on tools designed to discourage the overprescription of other potentially dangerous medications, such as requirements that antibiotic prescriptions be written on special forms, with copies of the prescriptions sent to state officials (Brushwood 2003).[4] They could require general practitioners to consult with specialists before prescribing broad-spectrum antibiotics, or prohibit the prescribing of antibiotics without an in-person consultation.

Measures like these would not necessarily eliminate physicians' fears of malpractice liability, but they would counterbalance those fears with incentives to prescribe antibiotics more cautiously. Rather than being a barrier to the pursuit of public health objectives, the law could become a tool for aligning physicians' incentives with important public health goals.

[4] These monitoring programs have been criticized for over-deterring the legitimate use of controlled substances. However, under-prescribing does not appear to be a significant problem in the area of antibiotics (as it is with controlled substances), so the risk of over-deterrence is a much less significant concern.

## References


Ackerman, F. 1991. The significance of a wish. *Hastings Ctr. Rep* 21: 27–30. doi:10.2307/3562998.

Brushwood, D.B. 2003. Maximizing the value of electronic prescription monitoring programs. *The Journal of Law, Medicine & Ethics* 31: 41–54. doi:10.1111/j.1748-720X.2003.tb00058.x.

Canterbury v. Spence, 150 U.S. App. D.C. 263, 464 F.2d 772 (D.C. Cir. 1972).

Coleman, C.H. 2005. Duties to subjects in clinical research. *Vanderbilt Law Review* 58: 387–449.

Department of Health and Human Services.2005. Part 46: Protection of Human Subjects. http://www.hhs.gov/ohrp/humansubjects/guidance/45cfr46.htm. Accessed 4 April 2009.

Furrow, B.R. 1997. Managed care organizations and patient injury: Rethinking liability. *Georgia Law Review (Athens, Ga.)* 31: 419–509.

Gonzales, R., et al. 2001. Principles of appropriate antibiotic use for treatment of acute respiratory tract infections in adults: Background, specific aims, and methods. *Annals of Internal Medicine* 134: 479–486.

Howard, D. 2007. Patient and physician demand for antibiotics. In *Extending the Cure: Policy responses to the growing threat of antibiotic resistance*, ed. Laxminarayan Ramanan, and Malani Anup. Washington: RFF Press.

Laxminarayan, R., and Malani, A. (Eds.). 2007. *Extending the Cure: Policy responses to the growing threat of antibiotic resistance.* Washington: RFF Press.

Meier, B. (2008). Study finds few pain doctors face criminal prosecutions. *The New York Times*, 20 September, A16.

Peters, P.G. 2000. The quiet demise of deference to custom: Malpractice law at the millennium. *Washington and Lee Law Review* 57: 163–205.

Pope, T.M. 2007. Medical futility statutes: No safe harbor to unilaterally refuse life-sustaining treatment. *Tennessee Law Review* 75: 1–80.

Rodwin, M.A. 1995. Strains in the fiduciary metaphor: Divided physician loyalties and obligations in a changing health care system. *American Journal of Law & Medicine* 21: 241–257.

Selgelid, M.J. 2007. Ethics and drug resistance. *Bioethics* 21 (4): 218–229. doi:10.1111/j.1467-8519.2006.00542.x.

Solomon, D.H., et al. 2001. Academic detailing to improve use of broad-spectrum antibiotics at an academic medical center. *Archives of Internal Medicine* 161: 1897–1902. doi:10.1001/archinte.161.15.1897.

Tarasoff v. Regents of the University of California, 17 Cal.3d 425, 551 P.2d 334 (1976).

Ziegler, S.J., and N.P. Lorich Jr. 2003. Pain relief, prescription drugs, and prosecution: A four-state survey of chief prosecutors. *The Journal of Law, Medicine & Ethics* 31: 75–100. doi:10.1111/j.1748-720X.2003.tb00060.x.

# Part III: Vaccination Policy

Poiesis Prax (2005) 3:229–241
DOI 10.1007/s10202-005-0002-3

FOCUS

# Risk Perceptions and Ethical Public Health Policy: MMR Vaccination in the UK

**Angus Dawson**

Published online: 14 October 2005


**Abstract** This paper is concerned with how public health policy makers should respond to the public's perception of risks. I suggest that we can think of this issue in terms of two different models of responding to the public's view of such perceived risks. The first model I will call the "public perception" view (PP view) and the second the "public good" view (PG view). The PP view suggests that the public's perception of any risks is so important that public health policies should be formulated in direct response to knowledge about them. I will consider two possible ethical arguments that might be offered in support of such a view: the first argument is an "autonomy" argument and the second a "consequences" argument. I suggest there are serious problems with both arguments. I then outline an alternative model of public health policy formation that I call the "public good" or PG model. This model focuses on drawing distinctions between the clinical and the public health context, and argues that most of public health policy is primarily concerned with the creation and maintenance of various public goods. This latter fact means that the PP model is inappropriate for public health policy formation.

A. Dawson (✉)
Centre for Professional Ethics, Keele Hall,
Keele University,
Staffordshire ST5 5BG, UK
e-mail: a.j.dawson@keele.ac.uk

**Zusammenfassung** Dieser Beitrag beschäftigt sich damit, wie Entscheidungsträger in der Gesundheitspolitik der Wahrnehmung von Risiken in der Öffentlichkeit begegnen sollten. Mein Vorschlag ist hier, diese Frage im Rahmen zweier verschiedener Modelle der Reaktion auf die öffentliche Sichtweise solcher wahrgenommender Risiken zu betrachten. Das erste Modell bezeichne ich als die Perspektive der öffentlichen Wahrnehmung ("PP (Public Perception)-Modell"), das zweite als die Perspektive des öffentlichen Nutzens ("PG (Public Good)-Modell"). Nach dem PP-Modell sind allgemeine Risikowahrnehmungen von solcher Wichtigkeit, dass Gesundheitspolitiken als direkte Reaktion auf das Wissen über solche Wahrnehmungen zu formulieren wären. Ich betrachte zwei mögliche ethische Argumente, die zur Stützung dieses Standpunkts angeführt werden könnten, das erste ein "Autonomieargument", das zweite ein "Folgenargument". Ich zeige auf, dass beide Argumente mit ernsten Schwierigkeiten behaftet sind. Dann skizziere ich ein Alternativmodell zur Gestaltung öffentlicher Ge-sundheitspolitik, das so genannte PG-Modell, in dem der öffentliche Nutzen im Vordergrund steht. Dieses Modell konzentriert sich auf die Unterschiede zwischen Fragen des klinischen Gesundheitswesens einerseits und solchen der öffentlichen oder Volksgesundheit. Das Argument lautet dann, dass es in der Politik zur öffentlichen Gesundheit weitgehend und in erster Linie um die Schaffung und Erhaltung verschiedener öffentlicher Güter geht, was allerdings bedeutet, dass das PP-Modell für die

Politikformulierung zur öffentlichen Gesundheit ungeeignet ist.

**Résumé** Le présent article s'interroge sur la manière dont les décideurs dans le domaine de la politique de santé publique devraient répondre à la perception des risques par l'opinion publique. Je suggère que nous réfléchissions sur ce thème dans le cadre de deux modèles différents de réaction à la vision de l'opinion publique des risques ainsi perc¸us. J'appelle le premier modèle le point de vue de la perception publique (point de vue PP (Public Perception)), et le deuxième le point de vue de l'intérêt public (point de vue PG (Public Good)). Le modèle PP suggère que la perception publique des risques revêt une telle importance que les politiques de santé publique devraient être formulées en réponse directe à ce qu'on en sait. Prenons deux arguments éthiques possibles pour étayer ce point de vue : le premier argument est un argument<d'autonomie>et le second un argument<de conséquences >. Je montre que ces deux arguments posent de sérieuses difficultés. J'esquisse ensuite un modèle alternatif pour l'élaboration de politiques de santé publique, le modèle PG ou<d'intérêt public >. Ce modèle se concentre sur les différences entre l'aspect hospitalier de la santé et son aspect public, et argue que la politique de santé publique porte essentiellement sur la création et la préservation de biens publics. Ceci signifie que le modèle PP ne convient pas à l'élaboration d'une politique de santé publique.

## Introduction

A paper written by Andrew Wakefield and others was published in The Lancet in 1998 suggesting grounds for a possible association between the measles, mumps and rubella (MMR) combined vaccine and bowel problems and autism.[1] The paper was based on a study of only 12 children and explicitly stated that the authors had no evidence strong enough to establish a causal link between the vaccine and the health problems. However, they suggested the need for further investigation of their findings. The hypothesis was widely reported in the media, not always accurately. The main author of the paper has been widely interviewing in the media, when he often proposes a stronger version of the hypothesis than that contained in the published paper. Uptake rates for MMR have dropped significantly in the UK since the publication of this paper, presumably as a direct result of the public's perception of MMR based upon the media reporting of the paper's content.[2] A significant minority of the population are either not getting their child vaccinated with MMR or are seeking vaccination through single vaccines which they suppose are safer.[3] Despite these events a dispassionate consideration of the available empirical evidence about the safety of MMR is likely to conclude that the combined vaccine is the best option available to parents and the supposed side-effects are either rare or nonexistent.[4]

This paper is concerned with the following question: how should those given the task of formulating public health policy in relation to vaccination respond to such a situation? Should they insist upon a policy based upon the best possible empirical evidence or should they respond to public concerns about the alleged risks of harm by basing their policy on what many parents want (as they have been urged by some commentators)?[5] What will count as an ethical public health policy in such a situation? In this paper I will use the recent

[1] Wakefield et al. (1998). See also Wakefield and Montgomery (2000).

[2] The most recent statistics available for the whole of the UK on MMR uptake are those published in: NHS Immunisation Statistics (2003–2004). Across the UK only 83% of children received a second MMR vaccination by the time of their fifth birthday. Parallel rates for other vaccines are much higher (e.g., diphtheria, tetanus and petussis (DTP) vaccination covered 94% of people by year 2. MMR vaccination rates are on the way back up from their lowest point, but it should be noted that there are still pockets of resistance to MMR and coverage in some areas is only around 50%. Indeed, it is likely that there will remain a cohort of children (some now at school) susceptible to measles (and mumps and rubella), and this increases the risk of an epidemic in the future as herd protection does not exist. For specific discussion of the media's role in this public health crisis see Hargreaves et al. (2003).

[3] Although, ironically, there is less evidence about effectiveness and safety for such single vaccines than there is for MMR.

[4] See, for example, Elliman and Bedford (2001), Patja et al. (2000), Peltola and Heinonen (1986), Madsen et al. (2002) and Smeeth et al. (2004).

[5] See Heller (2001) for an indirect call for separate vaccines and Jarmulowicz (2002) for an explicit request for government support for single vaccines.

discussions about MMR in the UK as an example to illustrate this issue, but the argument should be relevant to vaccination policies in general and other aspects of public health policy.[6]

In the course of this paper I consider two arguments for taking the public's perceptions of such risks seriously. However, I argue that they do not prove to be decisive in suggesting the need to adopt a policy based upon such perceptions. Whilst such factors are relevant and certainly need to be taken into account, they should not simply be used to determine policy in this area. It is proposed that we should adopt a different model of public health policy formation within which the important factor is what will bring the greatest benefit to the public's health. I argue that a vitally important aspect of this is to concentrate upon the production and maintenance of public goods such as herd protection.[7] I suggest that we can think of this issue in terms of the adoption of two different models of responding to the public's perception of risk. The first model I will call the "public perception" view (PP view) and the second the "public good" view (PG view). In brief, the PP view suggests that the public's perception of any risks is so important that public health policies should be formulated in direct response to knowledge about the public's perceptions of the relevant risks. I will consider two possible ethical arguments that might be offered in support of such a view: the first argument is an "autonomy" argument and the second a "consequences" argument. I suggest there are serious problems with both arguments if used to support the PP view. I then outline an alternative model of public health policy formation that I will call the "public good" or PG view. This model focuses on drawing distinctions between the clinical and the public health context, and argues that much public health policy is primarily concerned with the creation and maintenance of various public goods. This latter fact means that the PP view is inappropriate for public health policy formation. I now turn to consider the first argument that might be used in support of the PP view.

[6] Of course, the current reaction to MMR is only one of a long line of situations where such issues need to be considered. Other examples include the argument about the pertussis element in DTP in the 1970s; and smallpox vaccination in the US in the last few years.

[7] I talk of herd protection rather than herd immunity deliberately. See Paul (2004).

## The "Autonomy" Argument for the PP View

The "autonomy" argument is based upon the claim that when the public propose a change in policy the relevant authorities should respond to that request because that is what the public want. This view takes the role of public perceptions very seriously indeed and suggests that we can treat public health considerations as if they were in this respect just like individual clinical encounters. In both situations the central factor in decision making is what the autonomous patients request or wish for. The argument might go that given the respect deserving of such autonomous choices within a broadly liberal and democratic culture, we should use our knowledge about patient wishes to formulate the relevant public health policy. This appeal to autonomy will, of course, in turn have to be justified; but it is a truism that various different moral theoretical positions might support the idea that autonomy is an important moral consideration or value. However, it looks as though the appeal to autonomy in this argument must be to some sort of absolute principle of autonomy, where it is suggested that autonomy takes priority over all other moral concerns. It will be for the supporter of such a view to justify this rather implausible claim.[8]

Putting this justificatory issue to one side, there are clear objections to such a view if applied in the public health context. One obvious difference between the clinical situation and the public health situation is that it is unlikely that in the latter case there will be a single view in a population in relation to such public health measures that can then be used as the basis of such an autonomy-based policy. However, I suggest we put this type of practical objection to one side as well. I am more interested in this paper in the possibility of more fundamental objections to the argument than this. I will consider two such possible "fundamental" objections here. The first is that there is an important difference between public health and clinical situations because of the difference in aims behind the interventions. The second is that what people want should not be the decisive issue in the formulation of public health policy.

[8] I will assume for the purposes of this paper that this can be done, but see Garrard and Dawson (2005) for some discussion on the status of autonomy in a set of moral principles.

The first objection to the autonomy argument is based upon a real difference between clinical and public health situations, in that the potential harms and benefits of any public health policy arguably extend beyond the sum of the harms and benefits for each participating individual.[9] If this is true then it can be argued that it is not clear why we should base policy making about public health matters upon the autonomous expressions of individuals in the sense proposed in the "autonomy" argument (even if we can make sense of what "population autonomy" might be). The idea is that such a judgment cannot be determined purely on the basis of adopting what individuals might want such a policy to be. On this critical view, considerations about the public's health should be the driving force in the formulation of public health policies as we cannot make any sense of how individuals can directly contribute as individuals to such policy formation.

The second objection is to the way that the autonomy argument relies upon giving weight to the idea of wants. We can ask why we should choose to base a policy upon such a notion? It is clearly possible to want something inappropriate for your own health. It might be decided in the clinical case to respect your autonomy even to the point of allowing you to potentially harm yourself (perhaps after being fully informed about such likely consequences). However, in the public health realm it is not clear that we should adopt the same approach. Once again, this is because in the public health arena, at least in relation to vaccination for contagious diseases, individuals are not just deciding about something with consequences for their own health when they decide to forego a vaccination as their decision may have consequences for others. Your decision not to vaccinate your child for measles might mean that my child, too young to receive her scheduled vaccinations, is infected by yours. Your choice has resulted in harm to another. In terms of standard liberal theory you are required to take harm-toothers concerns seriously in your deliberations.[10] Just as individual choice has potential implications for others, so do the choices of policy makers in devising their policy. By definition, then, in shaping public health policy in relation to such vaccinations, policy makers are deciding a policy that has implications for all. This means that if there are fewer individuals vaccinated, chances are that it will not just be the individual(s) that requested that particular approach that are thereby put at risk. As I have just suggested it might well be "innocent" others unable to take any steps to protect themselves who are at greatest risk.[11]

Consider the example that I mentioned before. In the UK there have been many requests for separate single vaccines rather than the use of the combined MMR vaccine. The Department of Health has, so far, rejected these requests. Should public health policy respond to such requests for single vaccines (or offer a choice between MMR or single vaccines)? It might be argued by appeal to the autonomy argument that it should as this will respond to parental autonomous requests and this is a good thing. However, the counterargument is that adopting such a policy will impact upon all citizens, and that the public's health will be worse off as a result. This is because a policy of encouraging single vaccines through state support is likely to result in lower coverage for at least some diseases as each child will need to have so many more injections on a number of different occasions. For example, MMR vaccination requires two sets of injections in pre-school children, whereas separate vaccines would require six sets of injections. This will increase the risk of harm to each individual child from these diseases as it will take much longer for immunity to be established, but it will also almost certainly result in poorer levels of immunity in the population as a whole as it is more likely that scheduled vaccinations will be missed, so increasing the risk of epidemics.[12] This increased risk of harm will be a particular danger to those who are not vaccinated either because they are too young (e.g., neonates) or because they are allergic to one or more component of a vaccine.

[9] See Verweij and Dawson (2005) for an exploration of such a claim.

[10] See Dawson (2005b) for some discussion of harm to others considerations in relation to vaccinations.

[11] Of course decision making in relation to third parties (such as parents for their children) is a complex issue. See Dawson (2005a) for some discussion of these issues.

[12] The claim that single vaccines will result in poorer coverage can be supported by looking at the situation in Japan, where single vaccines were introduced in 1993 after worries about MMR. Vaccine coverage rates for measles, mumps and rubella are much lower, and disease rates much higher, than in countries using MMR. See the Japanese Infections Disease Surveillance Center website at: idsc.nih.go.jp for details.

For the sake of completeness I will consider two further possible arguments in favour of PP here, though in less detail, one based upon the importance of public trust in public health policies and another based on an appeal to parental perceptions of harm. Public trust in public health interventions is vital, as otherwise participation will fall, and the aims of any such programme will not be achieved.[13] In addition, once trust is lost it is an extremely difficult business to rebuild it. It takes time and effort. In the MMR case, it might be that ignoring the minority of the public requesting single vaccines means that such trust in the MMR vaccination programme or vaccination programmes as a whole may be reduced or lost. However, from a policy maker's perspective this is a difficult issue as trust will also be lost if the vaccines used either cause harm through sideeffects, fail to protect the individuals vaccinated due to vaccine failure, or if they fail to prevent outbreaks. If evidence exists that a combined vaccine such as MMR is safe and there is no such comparative evidence in relation to the corresponding single vaccines, it might be that public trust in the long-term is better protected by continuing to advocate the use of MMR even if some public trust is lost in the short-term.

Another possible argument in favour of PP is that all parents are seeking to do by not accepting MMR vaccination is, to protect their children from what they perceive as a significant risk of harm. Of course the formation of public health policies, just like any other medical practices, should involve a consideration of the risks of harm involved in any proposed intervention. But this does not mean that we should seek to avoid every single proposed risk (e.g., from possible side-effects), and if we did so, life would be impossible. Everything (including doing nothing) carries some degree of risk of harm. In addition, in this particular case, any advocate of such a view is almost certainly ignoring the (greater) risk of harm arising from non-vaccination. Public policy should indeed respond to evidence about any risks, but once again this is likely to be a difficult exercise, to be made in the light of all relevant evidence. Any such assessment of the risks of harm must consider a number of factors, such as not only the fact that possible risks might follow from that measure, but also that there are risks involved in not continuing with an existing policy or that risks will arise from changing an existing measure.

Of course, one potentially serious problem is that very often the relevant empirical evidence for assessing the various risks is either not available or is less than perfect in some way.[14] In addition, there has been a great deal of empirical work looking at the way that people understand and react to different risks.[15] What these factors together suggest is that when considerations involving risks are discussed, special care should be taken to ensure that the relevant risks are not either inappropriately magnified or reduced. There have been some efforts to take this issue to heart, such as the UK Department of Health's advice on communicating risks to patients.[16] However, despite these efforts it might still be possible to argue that this provides another reason for decision making to be made by well-informed policy makers on the basis of the best possible medical evidence rather than on the basis of a response to the attitudes of the public. This is because if it is true that there are systematic biases in the way that people make decisions (such as tending to overestimate immediate risks and underestimate long-term risks), and the empirical evidence looks quite robust in relation to such "framing effects", this provides a good reason to be cautious about basing policy on PP.[17] Of course, "experts" will not always be right either, as most would instantly concede, but they are less likely to make these systematic errors in judging the relevant evidence.

## The "Consequences" Argument for the PP Model

The "consequences" argument is very different to the "autonomy" argument. This argument does not rely upon the fact that (some of) the public have particular attitudes about certain risks as such, but rather the focus is upon what the consequences or results of

[13] See Verweij and Dawson (2004).

[14] Although it is not clear this is the case in relation to MMR where all credible evidence is overwhelmingly in favour of the vaccination.

[15] See Tversky and Kahneman (1981) and Tversky and Kahneman (1984).

[16] See Department of Health (1998) for discussion of some of these issues.

[17] See Dawson (2004) for discussion of these problems in relation to the understanding of the concept of "randomisation" in clinical trials.

such beliefs might be. It relies upon the idea that where policy does not change in response to public attitudes in relation to the relevant risks this may itself have consequences for the public's health. Therefore, the focus here is upon the whole population in question, and what is best for that population's health, rather than focusing on the attitudes of individual members of that population and their individual attitudes to the vaccination in question. For example, it might be argued that the policy of only promoting MMR, and not making single vaccines available, may over time actually reduce the effectiveness of the whole vaccination programme as individuals opt out of all vaccinations (even those that they would otherwise have agreed to).[18] This in turn might impact adversely upon immunity rates within the population and so increase the overall risk of harm to the public's health.

I would argue that this argument is a stronger one than the autonomy argument and that it in fact gains in power as more people decline vaccination for their children. Indeed, there must come a point where vaccination rates become so low that the advocacy of a policy defending a particular vaccine (such as MMR) becomes untenable. In such a situation, the full power of the consequences argument kicks in and policy makers would need to think carefully about the best way to protect the public's health. This might mean that in some cases defeat would have to be reluctantly conceded by policy makers, not on the basis of the empirical evidence, which may still support the vaccine in question, but in response to the practical realities about the need to maintain the maximum level of vaccination across the population and thereby protect the public's health. Indeed, it might be argued that to do otherwise would be unethical, on the grounds that practical considerations should trump ideological commitments in such situations. Of course any policy maker is unlikely to publicly endorse such a view, but in reality, they might have to respond to such a situation. In the MMR case, this point would be reached if the current policy of only providing MMR itself threatens to bring about greater public health harms than the provision of single vaccines. However, it has been well argued by the UK government that the problem is that we have little evidence as to potential benefits and harms from single vaccines (whereas we have significant evidence for the effectiveness and safety of MMR).

Note that it is unlikely that any advocate of the PP model will appeal to the consequences argument, but it is something for the policy makers to take into account. It will not be used by the supporter of the PP model because until the tipping point described above is reached, any argument appealing to consequences is probably going to be based upon the best available evidence of effectiveness (even in situations where a minority are allocating a disproportionate weight to a particular perceived risk). So, for example, in the MMR case a consequences argument in the current situation will be likely to support the status quo in favour of MMR. The power of the argument comes about because anyone truly committed to seeking to protect the public's health will have to accept that at some point the existing policy may have to be abandoned as this could prove to be the best way of protecting the public's health.

## The "Public Good" Model of Public Health Policy Formation

In response to a model of public health decision making that is actively shaped by patients' perceptions of assumed risks, I would like to propose an alternative. This I will call the "Public Good" or PG model. The main idea behind this approach is that whilst those with the job of formulating public health policy should take into account the public's perceptions of the relevant risks (as suggested in the "autonomy" argument) as well as the consequences of not doing so (as suggested in the "consequences" argument), they should not just note the public's view and then infer from these facts their decision about the relevant policy. Such elements must inform the policy making, but other factors remain important as well. A vital consideration is what sort of policies will actually benefit the public's overall health. This factor might mean that the other two elements are not decisive when it comes to policy formation.

In fact, in beginning to construct an alternative, we can offer a diagnosis of the problem that lies behind the PP model. One of the issues is that it is in danger

[18] Interestingly, it looks as though this has not taken place. The NHS Immunisation Statistics (2003–2004), suggests that coverage rates for other childhood vaccinations remain high.

of ignoring the differences between clinical medicine and public health. These differences are often lost in the application of principles constructed in the sphere of medical ethics to the field of public health. It is clear that the issues relating to the health of populations are different from those of the doctor–patient relationship. Whilst appeals to autonomy might be central to determining the right thing to do in relation to deciding an appropriate clinical treatment, it is not clear that the same is true in relation to public health decision making.[19] For example, it can be argued that when risks of harm are considered within a public health context, it is vital to give special consideration to what the wider impact of a particular measure might be upon the population as a whole. This is because the focus of attention within public health is not just upon individual patients alone but also upon the health of the public as a collective group. It can be argued that this means that consideration of such issues must go beyond the sum of interests of each of the individual patients. The easiest way to see the importance of this point is to see the centrality of public goods to most public health activity. What do I mean by public goods?

Vaccination for a contagious disease can be seen as an act that not only has potential benefits for the individual themselves but as also making a contribution towards a collective benefit as everyone profits where herd protection exists in the population, including those who are not vaccinated (for whatever reason) and those who do not show sufficient immune response despite vaccination (for example, because they were ill at the time of vaccination and their immune system was already stimulated by other infectious agents). One way to think of these two positive outcomes is as being both a private (or individual) and a public (or collective) good. A private good is a good that benefits only the individual concerned and a public good benefits all of the members of a group or population. It is because of such a shared population benefit from the existence of herd protection that we might think of the existence of such a state as being a public good. We can think of public goods in general, following Klosko, as being characterised by two main properties: non-excludability and dependence upon cooperation by a large number of people.[20] "Non-excludable goods" are those where no one can be excluded from the benefits of the existence of the relevant good, even when they have not contributed towards bringing it about.[21] This is the case where herd protection exists: the non-vaccinated benefit from the high immunity in the population. In addition, herd protection can only be generated through collaborative endeavour as it cannot be created, obtained or controlled by any individual acting alone. In addition to these two aspects of public goods suggested by Klosko, I would add another proposed by Rawls.[22] He suggests that public goods must also be indivisible: that is, they cannot be broken down or divided into individual or private goods to be distributed amongst the members of a group or population. This is true of herd protection in the sense that the equal collective benefit can only come about as a result of collective action. Herd protection where it exists can therefore be seen to be a public good as it is indivisible, non-excludable and dependent upon the cooperative actions of a group.[23]

Many interventions in public health aim to create or maintain public goods as defined above. Herd protection in a population, where it exists, serves as an excellent example of such a public good. Herd protection is a public good because it creates a benefit that goes beyond that of the vaccinated individuals qua individuals. The whole population derives a substantial benefit from the existence of herd protection in addition to any individual benefit to the vaccinated individuals. Such benefits are felt directly by those that are unvaccinated, such as children too

[19] Of course even in the clinical context we might doubt that autonomy is always going to be the supreme consideration. It is highly likely that in at least some situations other moral considerations should take priority.

[20] Klosko (1987).

[21] An excludable good would be one created jointly where the benefits are only enjoyed by the participants themselves. Examples of excludable goods might include a library created by subscription open to private members or a private health insurance scheme. In such cases, contributing members control as to who benefits from their actions. By contrast, all of the relevant population benefit from the existence and maintenance of a public good whatever their views about whether or not they will personally benefit or whether or not it should be maintained.

[22] Rawls (1971).

[23] A more substantive list of features of public goods is given by many authors such as Cullity (1995). However, the characterisation given here is sufficient for the needs of the argument in this paper.

young to be vaccinated, but also indirectly by society as a whole. By indirect benefits here I mean that a society is better off if it knows that the threat of a potentially devastating disease is reduced. Such a benefit does not come about through the direct protection of the vaccination itself, but the knowledge that normal life is less likely to be affected by the consequences of any epidemic.[24]

It should be noted that one possible objection to the PG model of policy formation is that it might be held by the advocates of the PP position to be paternalistic. Paternalism is best defined as acting so as to promote the overall best interests of another individual. If I intervene to prevent you from smoking by removing your cigarettes then I am being paternalistic. We might then go on to argue about whether my action was justified or not. This might depend upon a range of factors such as whether you are competent or not, whether you are aware of the risks you run to your health, perhaps even whether you have asked me to do this in the past whenever I see you smoking. However, doubts might be expressed about whether the PG model of public policy formation is a form of paternalism because the focus of action is not merely upon the good of the relevant individuals in society, but it also takes account of the good of society as a whole resulting from the existence and maintenance of the relevant public good. The intention to create or maintain public goods is very different to a decision relating to an individual's health. It might well be that the existence of such a public good as herd protection is in any individual's best interest in that particular society where it exists, but this does not mean that action in relation to creating and maintaining public goods is paternalistic in any straightforward sense.

It should also be noted that the PG view provides a different perspective upon public health from that of the consequences argument, despite sharing some similarities. The consequences argument is a purely consequentialist argument concerned with all of the relevant outcomes of an act. Such an approach may be used to justify many public health actions.[25] However, the PG view provides a different type of justification: one focused on the creation and maintenance of public goods (as defined above). Whilst the PG view can be supported by consequentialists (and often will be as public goods are likely to contribute to human welfare) it may also be supported by more deontologically inclined individuals (because public goods are also likely to contribute towards non-maleficence and beneficence). Arguments about public goods are therefore distinct from arguments about consequences.

If we return to the MMR issue, the PG view will produce an outcome as follows. Worries about the supposed risks of MMR and the possible subsequent actions by parents (e.g., non-vaccination) mean that policy in this area must take account of these concerns, but these must be weighed against the important benefits to the public health following from the maintenance of the existing MMR programme (e.g., fewer injections; greater immunity in the relevant population, etc.) and the judgment on the basis of the existing good quality medical evidence about what the best possible policy to protect the public's health will actually be. This view suggests that the relevant "experts" will have an essential role in deciding the relevant policy. Whilst such experts are, of course, open to bias and manipulation they are also trained to make judgments about the relevant material medical evidence and not base their policies on partial media reporting or selective reading of the relevant literature. Any such judgments and policies are then, of course, open to public scrutiny and debate.

## Conclusions

In conclusion, I have argued that ethical public health policies need to be formulated in the light of evidence about public attitudes, but this does not mean that those same attitudes should directly determine public health policies.[26] Far more important to the formulation of ethical public health policy is the creation and maintenance of public goods such as herd protection. Such a basis to policy requires action at the level of government and should be informed by the best possible evidence about the

[24] See Verweij and Dawson (2004), op cit.

[25] See Bayer and Fairchild (2004) for discussion of this type of justification for public health actions.

[26] Of course, the discussion in this paper is only about one particular vaccine. The arguments are likely to differ, at least to some extent, when considering other public health interventions.

risks and benefits of the relevant vaccines. Such policy should only consider taking public perceptions of risk as the basis of policy when what I have called the consequences argument becomes so strong that the credibility of vaccination in general is threatened. Otherwise the right thing to do is to keep an eye on public perceptions, take them into account, but work with the PG model of policy formation. The supreme moral obligation of government in relation to public health is to create and maintain relevant public goods such as herd protection.[27]

**Acknowledgements** Thanks to audiences at the 6th World Congress of the International Association of Bioethics (Brasilia, October 2002); the 121st Annual Conference of the American Public Health Association (Philadelphia, November 2002); and the Health Protection Agency conference (September 2004) for comments on earlier versions of this paper.

## References

Bayer, R., and A. Fairchild. 2004. The genesis of public health ethics. *Bioethics* 18(6): 473–492.

Cullity, G. 1995. Moral free riding. *Philosophy & Public Affairs* 24(1): 3–34.

Dawson, A. 2004. What should we do about it? implications of the empirical evidence in relation to comprehension and acceptability of randomisation. In *Engaging the world: the use of empirical research in bioethics and the regulation of biotechnology*, ed. S. Holm and M. Jonas. Netherlands: IOS.

Dawson, A. 2005a. The determination of "Best Interests" in relation to childhood vaccinations. *Bioethics* 19(2): 188–205.

Dawson, A. 2005b. Herd protection as a public good: vaccination and our obligations to others. In *Ethics, prevention and public health*, ed. A. Dawson and M. Verweij. Oxford: Oxford University Press.

Department of Health. 1998. *Communicating about risks to public health*. London: Department of Health.

Elliman, D., and H. Bedford. 2001. MMR vaccine: the continuing saga. *BMJ* 322: 183–184.

Garrard E, Dawson A (2005) What is the role of the REC? Paternalism, inducements and harm in research ethics. J Med Ethics (in press)

Hargreaves, I., J. Lewis, and T. Speers. 2003. *Towards a better map: science, the public and the media*. Swindon: ESRC.

Heller, T. 2001. Ethical debate: vaccination against mumps, measles, & rubella: is there a case for deepening the debate? *BMJ* 323: 838–840.

Jarmulowicz, M. 2002. Single measles vaccine should be allowed. *BMJ* 324: 733.

Klosko, G. 1987. Presumptive benefit, fairness and political obligation. *Philosophy & Public Affairs* 16(3): 241–259.

Madsen, K., et al. 2002. A population-based study of measles, mumps and rubella vaccination and autism. *NEJM* 347 (19): 1477–1482.

NHS (2003–2004) NHS immunisation statistics, England. Bulletin 2004/16, London

Patja, A., et al. 2000. Serious adverse events after measles–mumps–rubella vaccination during a fourteen-year prospective follow-up. *The Pediatric Infectious Disease Journal* 19(12): 1127–1134.

Paul, Y. 2004. Letter: herd immunity and herd protection. *Vaccine* 22: 301–302.

Peltola, H., and O. Heinonen. 1986. Frequency of true adverse reactions in measles–mumps–rubella vaccine. A double-blind placebo-controlled trial in twins. *Lancet* 1: 939–942.

Rawls, J. 1971. *A theory of justice*. Oxford: Oxford University Press.

Smeeth, L., et al. 2004. MMR vaccination and pervasive developmental disorders: a case-control study. *Lancet* 364: 963–969.

Tversky, A., and D. Kahneman. 1981. The framing of decisions and the psychology of choice. *Science* 211: 453–458.

Tversky, A., and D. Kahneman. 1984. Choices, values and frames. *The American Psychologist* 39: 341–350.

Verweij, M., and A. Dawson. 2004. Ethical principles for collective immunisation programmes. *Vaccine* 22: 3122–3126.

Verweij, M., and A. Dawson. 2005. What is meant by "public" in public health? In *Ethics, prevention and public health*, ed. A. Dawson and M. Verweij. Oxford: Oxford University Press.

Wakefield, A., and S. Montgomery. 2000. Measles, mumps and rubella vaccine: through a glass, darkly. Adverse drug react. *Toxicological Reviews* 19(4): 265–283.

Wakefield, A., et al. 1998. Ileal–lymphoid–nodular hyperplasia, non-specific colitis and pervasive developmental disorder in children. *Lancet* 351: 637–641.

[27] In the light of this argument, the Department of Health in the UK is to be congratulated for not conceding defeat on the issue of MMR despite the intense pressure it was no doubt under to do so.

Bioethical Inquiry (2009) 6:219–228
DOI 10.1007/s11673-009-9153-6

# A New Vaccine for Tuberculosis: The Challenges of Development and Deployment

**Helen A. Fletcher · Tony Hawkridge · Helen McShane**

Received: 3 March 2009 / Accepted: 24 March 2009 / Published online: 5 May 2009


**Abstract** Tuberculosis (TB) is one of the world's leading causes of death due to infection and efforts to control TB would be substantially aided by the availability of an improved TB vaccine. There are currently nine new TB vaccines in clinical development, and the first efficacy trials are due to commence in 2009. There are many complex ethical issues which arise at all stages of TB vaccine development, from the need to conduct trials in developing countries to informed consent and the process of ethical review. While it is important that these issues are discussed, it may also be timely to consider the challenges which may arise if a vaccine in clinical development proves to be highly effective. We examine a number of scenarios where decisions on the deployment of a new TB vaccine may impact on the rights and liberty of the individual.

**Keywords** BCG vaccine · Tuberculosis vaccines · Biological markers · Tuberculosis

**Competing Interest Statement** Helen McShane is an inventor on a composition of matter patent and a shareholder in a Joint Venture, Oxford-Emergent Tuberculosis Consortium, formed to develop MVA85A. The views expressed in this article are those of the author(s) and do not necessarily represent those of the Oxford-Emergent Tuberculosis Consortium Ltd

H. A. Fletcher (✉) · H. McShane
The Jenner Institute, Nuffield Department of Clinical Medicine, The University of Oxford,
Oxford, UK
e-mail: helen.fletcher@ndm.ox.ac.uk

T. Hawkridge
Aeras Global TB Vaccine Foundation, Africa Office,
Cape Town, South Africa

## Introduction

The World Health Organization (WHO) declared tuberculosis (TB) a global health emergency in 1993 with good reason; sixteen years later the scale of the problem remains an urgent global challenge. With more than 9 million new cases and almost two million deaths each year, TB is one of the world's leading infectious causes of illness and death (WHO 2007). Effective methods of diagnosing and treating TB already exist and yet, due to (population increases and) increases in HIV-associated TB in Africa and the emergence of multidrug-resistant strains of *Mycobacterium tuberculosis* (*M. tb*), the global incidence of TB is increasing (Corbett et al. 2003). Despite its global impact there has been a lack of discussion of the ethical issues related to TB (Selgelid et al. 2008a, 2008b). These issues include individual obligations to avoid infecting others, coercive social distancing measures to prevent the spread of infection, breaching confidentiality through notification of contacts of TB patients and health workers' duty to treat contagious patients (Selgelid et al. 2008b). There are both moral and self-interested reasons for wealthy nations to do more to help reduce the burden of TB in developing countries; and ethicists should evaluate whether it would be more effective to focus spending on research and development, or on improving healthcare infrastructure. Ethical policy for infectious disease control should aim to strike a balance between protecting rights/liberties of infected individuals and promoting the greater good of society in the way of public health (Selgelid 2005). Many of the ethical issues related to infectious disease, such as coercive social distancing and breaching of confidentiality through notification of contacts, could be avoided if diseases were eradicated or infection prevented. The most effective and cost-effective tool for disease prevention is vaccination. The only existing licensed vaccine against TB is a substrain of *M. bovis*, Bacille Calmette Guérin, or BCG. This vaccine, developed around the turn of the last century and first administered in 1921, is given to a large proportion of newborn infants throughout the world in the hope that it will protect them against TB. However, the protection BCG confers against TB is both incomplete and variable (Colditz et al. 1994).

We submit that a new TB vaccine, or vaccine regimen, which would ideally be effective in all populations and all age groups, against all stages of TB infection and disease (for example latent, pulmonary and extra-pulmonary TB) is the only affordable and realistic long-term solution to the global TB epidemic.

There are many important ethical issues to be considered in the development of a new vaccine for an epidemic disease such as TB. As with all medical research on humans, TB vaccine trials must be conducted according to the principals of the Declaration of Helsinki, most recently updated in 2008 (WMA 2008), and the Belmont Report (U. S. Department of Health, Education and Welfare 1979). The latter establishes the principles of 1) Respect for persons 2) Beneficence and 3) Justice. Most previously published work on TB vaccines has focused primarily on the issue of informed consent (Ibanga et al. 2006; Minnies et al. 2008; Snider 2000). Selgelid et al. have previously described the ethical issues associated with TB disease (Selgelid et al. 2008a, 2008b). Using these documents as guides, we consider the ethical challenges which face TB vaccine development and deployment; and we highlight some of the ethical issues that warrant further consideration.

## Challenges to Decision Making in Vaccine Development

One of the first efficacy trials of a new generation vaccine designed to boost an antigen specific T cell response was the STEP trial, which assessed the efficacy of an adenovirus type 5 (Ad5)-based vaccine designed to prevent HIV infection. In the STEP trial, vaccination of men with pre-existing Ad5 immunity unexpectedly resulted in a higher incidence of HIV-1 infection, when compared to placebo-vaccinated men (Buchbinder et al. 2008). This led to an extensive and detailed review of the preclinical efficacy and preclinical and clinical immunogenicity data obtained with the Ad5-based vaccine, to determine if the outcome of the STEP trial could have been predicted (McElrath et al. 2008). The vaccine was protective in most animal models and immunogenic in both animals and humans. This highlights two critical problems with the development of vaccines for cell mediated immunity: 1) a lack of validated preclinical models which predict the efficacy of a vaccine in humans; and 2) an incomplete understanding of the components of a protective immune response. It is important that we learn from the experiences of the STEP trial in order that we protect patient-subjects, use what limited resources we have in the most effective manner and develop and deploy a more effective TB vaccine.

### Progression from Pre-clinical to Clinical Testing

One ethical issue raised by progression from preclinical to clinical vaccine testing is distributive justice. There are limited resources for conducting TB vaccine trials, so some fair means of allocating scarce resources must be determined. In addition to safety, the two primary methods used for selecting a TB vaccine candidate are discussed below.

#### *Efficacy Testing in Animal Models*

The first experiments which demonstrated that a subunit TB vaccine could protect mice against challenge with virulent *M. tb* were published in 1996 (Huygen et al. 1996; Tascon et al. 1996). There was optimism at the time that an improved TB vaccine would soon be available for human use. Since that time, there have been hundreds of reports of experimental vaccines demonstrating protection against challenge with *M. tb* in mice; yet, to date, only nine of these vaccines have progressed to clinical trials. The most commonly used murine model can be highly variable and the same vaccine candidate can demonstrate 100% protective efficacy to no protective efficacy depending on factors such as the species of animal used, the route of vaccination, the interval between vaccination and challenge, the route and dose of challenge and the interval between challenge and termination (Orme 2005). The limitations of the murine model are well illustrated by the consistent protective effect of BCG vaccination in mice. If BCG were as consistently good in humans, the need for a new TB vaccine would be much less urgent.

Limitations of the murine model have led to the experimental use of other animal species including guinea pigs, rabbits, non-human primates and cattle. All preclinical animal experiments are expensive, and time consuming (usually running for more than 6 months); and they require highly specialized Category 3 biocontainment facilities, which are not widely available.

Do we understand enough about the strengths and limitations of our models to use animal data as a basis for the selection of vaccine candidates? Is it ethical to accept or reject a candidate on the basis of preclinical animal efficacy data? It is unlikely that any candidate vaccines would progress through preclinical testing to early stage clinical testing without any evidence of efficacy. Collaborative efforts such as those funded by the NIH and European Commission Framework 6 TBVAC cluster have tested many TB vaccine candidates in multiple animal species (Baldwin et al. 1998; Williams et al. 2005). In the TBVAC project funding was provided for head-to-head testing of several new TB vaccine candidates from various sponsors. Such comparative experiments will remain necessary if we are to maximize the possibility of selecting the safest and most protective vaccine candidates for further development.

## Measurement of Immunogenicity

There is no proven immunological correlate of protection with which one can select vaccines to progress from early, small scale Phase I/IIa clinical trials to late, larger scale Phase IIb/III efficacy trials.

The identification of an immunological correlate of protection or "biomarker" would greatly facilitate the development of a vaccine for TB, as such a biomarker could be used to identify protective vaccines early in clinical development. Currently, interferon-gamma (IFN-γ) is used as a biomarker for TB vaccine selection, despite the fact that IFN-γ alone is insufficient for the prevention of TB disease.

Is it reasonable to select vaccine candidates on the basis of an ability to induce antigen-specific IFN-γ, when we know that this immunological measurement alone is not sufficient for protection? Although we do not yet have a better biomarker than IFN-γ, efforts should be made to harmonise the immunological assays in use for the measurement of IFN-γ in clinical trials which are currently being conducted in various countries worldwide (Hanekom et al. 2008). Finally, it is also important that we store samples from larger efficacy trials to enable the identification of biomarkers that could be used to select promising vaccines and aid in the just distribution of the limited resources available for TB vaccine development.

## Progression from Phase I Safety Trials to Phase III Efficacy Trials

Ethical principles considered here include beneficence and distributive justice.

### *Non-inferiority, Clinical Superiority and Placebos*

A double blind, randomized, placebo controlled trial is considered the optimum design for a phase III efficacy trial. For a disease where no current vaccine is available (such as for HIV or malaria) the ethics of trial design is focused on appropriate sample size and selection of placebo. The rabies vaccine is considered a good placebo for malaria as this will offer some benefit to those participants not receiving the malaria vaccine. For a new TB vaccine the scenario is different due to the currently available TB vaccine, BCG. BCG is one of the most widely administered vaccines in the world and despite varying efficacy does provide some protection against childhood forms of TB. To date it has been the view of researchers, ethics committees and regulatory agencies that in a country where TB is endemic it would be unethical to withhold the BCG vaccine in a randomized control trial of a new TB vaccine. This view has driven the development of vaccines designed to work in combination with BCG and slowed the development of vaccines designed to replace BCG. For a vaccine designed to enhance previous BCG vaccination, a randomized placebo controlled trial of the boosting vaccine is possible without withdrawing BCG vaccination. To facilitate the development of vaccines designed to replace BCG the European Commission TBVAC consortium with co-sponsorship of the Aeras Global TB Vaccine Foundation and the WHO have formed a consensus document of the proposed entry criteria for replacement vaccines (Kamath et al. 2005). The availability of the BCG vaccine also raises the question of whether a new TB vaccine should demonstrate non-inferiority or clinical superiority to BCG. A non-inferiority trial aims to demonstrate that the new vaccine is not worse than the comparator by more than a pre-specified, small amount. There has been much debate about the ethics of performing non-inferiority trials relating to the principle of beneficence where it is the duty of healthcare workers to provide a benefit to the patient. While some argue that the introduction of a non-inferior drug would increase availability and affordability (Soliman 2008) the alternative view is that non-inferiority trials are unethical since a product tested in this way is not (afterwards) proven to offer benefit when compared to the existing treatment and may indeed be less safe and less effective than the existing treatment (Garattini and Bertele 2007). The first clinical efficacy trials of two new TB vaccines are due to commence in 2009 and both these trials are designed to show clinical superiority when compared to BCG.

### *Lack of Global Capacity for Vaccine Efficacy Evaluation*

A major challenge facing TB vaccine developers is the limited availability of suitable field sites where TB vaccine efficacy trials can be conducted, together with a relative lack of funding for such sites. TB trials are likely to be very costly, because of their size and because of the length of follow-up required, which is directly linked to the lack of an acceptable validated immunological surrogate endpoint. Clinical efficacy endpoints take time to develop, so follow up in a TB efficacy trial is unlikely to be less than a year and probably two or more years. The result is that a restricted number of vaccine candidates can progress to Phase IIb and III efficacy trials, and efforts are being made to address this bottleneck by Aeras and by the European and Developing Countries Clinical Trials Partnership (EDCTP). Until more trial sites become available ethicists should examine how clinical trial sites are used to ensure that the principles of distributive justice are adhered to as vaccine candidates are selected for efficacy testing.

A new, more protective TB vaccine could potentially be used anywhere where BCG is currently used, including in many lower burden countries and even in areas where BCG is not currently used. The available literature on BCG shows that its efficacy in preventing TB disease varies widely with factors such as geographical latitude; for example BCG has been demonstrated to be efficacious in Britain and North America, but not so in India and Africa (Colditz et al. 1994).

Given this variability, it is possible that a new TB vaccine which is of benefit in one population may not be of benefit in different regions of the world. How many countries or regions of the world should be included in efficacy evaluations and how do you determine if such multiple evaluations are an effective use of scarce resources? Given the high burden of TB disease in sub-Saharan Africa, we feel that any new TB vaccine must first be evaluated there. It would be desirable also to show efficacy within the Indian subcontinent and in South-East Asia, in part because of the appreciable burden of disease in these two areas (both in terms of TB incidence rates, but more especially in terms of absolute numbers of cases of TB). A non-inferiority trial may be an ethical trial design when comparing the efficacy of a new TB vaccine between different countries.

### *Exclusion of HIV Infected Individuals from Trials*

All early trials of new TB vaccines have thus far excluded HIV infected individuals. This group is considered to be at higher risk for adverse events than the HIV negative population and vaccines are only evaluated in HIV positives once safety has been demonstrated in HIV negative people. Whilst this cautious approach is logical, there is a need to evaluate new TB vaccines in the HIV-infected, since they are arguably the population most in need of a new TB vaccine, with annual TB incidence rates of between 5–10% (and potentially higher) depending on the degree of immune suppression and access to antiretroviral therapy. This higher incidence of TB means that efficacy can be evaluated using smaller numbers of participants, once safety (in others) has been confirmed. TB efficacy trials for HIV positive populations are currently in the planning stages and study participants will receive the usual standard of care provided by their National Control Programme. For this reason the first trials will be conducted in countries that have a National Control Programme which includes the availability of anti-retroviral drugs. To ensure safety we will work in close contact with the healthcare workers who usually provide care and HIV viral loads and CD4 counts of study participants will be closely monitored.

*Involvement of Pharmaceutical Companies*

Ideally, we need the involvement of pharmaceutical companies in the development of drugs and vaccines for poverty related diseases, in order to work with the Global Alliance for Vaccines and Immunization (GAVI), UNICEF and the Global Fund to ensure these products reach the markets for which they are intended in a timely fashion. Historically, these companies have been reluctant to invest time and resources into developing such products, possibly because—at least in part—of perceptions that any financial return on such an investment would be improbable. More recently, several innovative schemes and mechanisms have been established, in order to encourage pharmaceutical involvement in this field. Firstly, under the European Medicines Agency (EMEA) and the U.S. Food and Drug Administration (FDA) is the Orphan Drug Scheme (http://www.emea.europa.eu/htms/human/orphans/intro.htm and http://www.fda.gov/orphan/). If a market is considered small enough (e.g. for a rare disease) or if the financial return on a product is likely to be very low (e.g. for prophylactic vaccination against a poverty related disease), then the developers can apply to the regulatory authorities (the FDA and/or the EMEA) to have their product designated an Orphan Drug. Such a designation provides benefit to the developer, including free regulatory advice estimated by the EMEA to be worth €6,000,000. Another benefit of being accorded Orphan Drug status is the award of 7-year and 10-year market exclusivity by the FDA and EMEA respectively. There is an ethical concern that such exclusivity could lead to excessive pricing of drugs for rare diseases (Samson 2008). As 95% of the market for a poverty related disease, such as TB, will be developing-country based the pricing of the vaccine will be restricted, and therefore even 10-years market exclusivity in Europe is not expected to provide a sufficient return on investment. The exclusivity period may also be broken if the holder of the original orphan vaccine gives consent; is unable to supply sufficient quantities; or if the second vaccine is proved clinically superior.

Secondly, under the GAVI Alliance, the Advance Purchase/Market Commitment Scheme (http://www.vaccineamc.org/) involves promises by governments and agencies to procure stated quantities of new drugs and vaccines (meeting pre-specified criteria) at a predetermined price. Such commitments provide pharmaceutical companies with reassurance concerning a financial return on their investment and thus provide an incentive to conduct more research and development of drugs and vaccines for neglected diseases.

Thirdly, the FDA recently launched the Priority Review Voucher Scheme (http://www.fda.gov/cber/gdlns/tropicaldisease.htm). In return for filing an application on a product designed for a listed disease of poverty, a company receives a voucher which allows for "priority regulatory review" of one other product that the company is developing. These vouchers may be traded and sold—and they have high expected value when used to expedite approval of potential new "blockbuster" drugs.

Such schemes make it more likely that pharmaceutical companies will invest in the development of a vaccine for a disease such as TB. Whilst they offer reasonable incentives for pharmaceutical companies, mechanisms should be established to ensure that, once licensed, such a vaccine is made available at or below (subsidized) cost-price to the governments of high TB burden countries, where it is most needed.

A related question is whether the incentives provided by the Orphan Drug Scheme are sufficient, and whether there is scope for this to increase. Just as many governments offer motorists tax breaks for using environmentally friendly cars, they might offer pharmaceutical companies tax breaks for investing in diseases such as TB, HIV and malaria. We posit that such additional incentives would increase the number of pharmaceutical companies which invest in vaccines for diseases of poverty, as well as the fraction of their budgets which they are prepared to commit to this end.

### Registration Issues

#### *Regulatory Authority Capacity Issues*

Generally, the regulatory authorities which are the best resourced—and consequently the most capable—of efficiently conducting competent and rigorous reviews of clinical development plans, clinical trial protocols and applications for licensure, are located in countries or regions of the world which do not have a high burden of TB. Examples are the FDA in the United States, the European EMEA, and the regulatory authorities of Japan and Australia. The converse is unfortunately also largely true: many high TB burden countries have poorly resourced, inexperienced regulatory authorities which do not have such capacity. In the worst case, a high burden country may have no regulatory authority and very little ethical review capacity. This potentially creates an opening for unethical, insufficiently regulated trials to be conducted by unscrupulous researchers. In the middle ground are high burden countries with some resources and some structures which can render a competent review; but, because of their resource constraints, review in such countries can take a disproportionately long time. Limited capacity and resources results in delays, not only for protocol approval but also for registration of new, effective products. In high burden countries, this is far from an ideal situation.

The WHO has established a task force with the specific aim of improving regulatory capacity in developing countries (Brennan et al. 2007). Experienced regulators from both the FDA and EMEA are working together with developing world regulators in order to build capacity, exchange experiences and provide support. Ideally, a new TB vaccine will undergo parallel registration with either the EMEA or the FDA, and simultaneously within the developing world, for example, with the South African Medicines Control Council (MCC).

One further regulatory issue relates to how wide such registration can and should be. If the efficacy of a new TB vaccine is satisfactorily demonstrated in one population in one country (e.g. in South African infants), could the vaccine, on the basis of the same results, also be registered for use in other age groups within the same country and/or for use in the same age group in other countries? Careful regulatory advice regarding bridging studies will be required.

## Deployment

### Post Registration Issues

When a TB vaccine is granted registration we will have an ethical obligation to ensure that it is made available to those most at risk. Given that approximately one third of the world's population is infected with TB and that tens of millions of infants born every year are at risk of acquiring infection, supplying enough vaccine will be a challenge and raises issues of international distributive justice.

Many public funding agencies and universities incorporate humanitarian access rights into their stated missions, statutes or charters. For example, the stated mission of the Aeras Global TB Vaccine Foundation (www.aeras.org) is to develop effective TB vaccine regimens that will prevent TB in all age groups and will be affordable, available and adopted worldwide. To ensure future access, Aeras

> obtains rights and/or licenses to distribute vaccines in resource-poor countries … partners with vaccine developers that agree to adequate supply and affordable production and distribution costs … shares financial risk to spur investment by outside vaccine developers … [and] develops manufacturing capacity to accelerate production and distribution at the lowest possible cost.

Many other charities and funding organizations have similar aims. The mission of The Wellcome Trust (www.welcome.ac.uk) is "to foster and promote research with the aim of improving human and animal health". The European & Developing Countries Clinical Trials Partnership (EDCTP, www.edctp.org) was created in 2003 as a European response to the global health crisis caused by the three main poverty-related diseases of HIV/AIDS, malaria and tuberculosis. The mission of EDCTP is to accelerate the development of new or improved drugs, vaccines and microbicides against HIV/AIDS, malaria and tuberculosis, with a focus on phase II and III clinical trials in sub-Saharan Africa. To achieve this, EDCTP supports multicentre projects which combine clinical trials, capacity building and networking. The aim of integrating these three activities is to ensure that the developed capacity is utilised to successfully conduct the clinical trials in a sustainable way. All EDCTP-funded projects are undertaken in partnership with sub-Saharan African countries, to ensure synergy and optimal use of resources and to create a win-win situation for all parties involved.

## Use of an Un-registered Vaccine

### *Should We be Using these Vaccines as Immunotherapeutics in Drug Resistant TB?*

At the World Lung Health meeting in Paris in October 2008, early results of the "DarDar trial", a Phase III efficacy trial of a novel TB vaccine, *M. vaccae,* in HIV infected adults in Tanzania, were presented (Alcorn 2008). The trial showed a significant reduction (37%) in the rate of culture positive TB disease in those who received the vaccine compared to those who received placebo. These results show that a TB vaccine can not only prevent disease but may be useful in the treatment of existing TB disease.

The last few years have seen the identification of extensively drug resistant strains of *M. tb* (XDR TB) and a greater understanding of the extent of multi drug resistant (MDR) strains of *M. tb* throughout the world (CDC 2006; Gandhi et al. 2006). Treatment of MDRTB and particularly XDR TB is much more expensive, more toxic and less successful than treatment of drug sensitive strains of *M. tb*

Once we have an indication that a particular new TB vaccine may be effective in preventing TB disease, should such vaccines be made available, prior to full registration and licensure for therapeutic use in patients suffering from XDR or MDR TB?

The FDA does have a mechanism for distribution of a medicinal product after efficacy has been demonstrated but before marketing has been authorized called "Treatment Investigational New Drugs" or "Treatment IND" (entered into the Federal Register, May 22, 1987). However, very few applications have been granted and safety and efficacy data on test subjects must still be collected.

It is important to consider the impact this could have on the registration process if there were an adverse event (AE). The risk of an AE if a new vaccine were to be administered to a patient with TB disease, particularly a drug-resistant strain of *M. tb*, is potentially high. It may be difficult to ascertain the causality of such an AE, and either (a) the AE may be reported as being related to vaccination, which may delay or even prevent registration of the vaccine for prophylactic use or (b) the AE may be reported as not being related to vaccination, but the timing may mean it is impossible to prove this conclusively. Development of a vaccine which may have been of enormous use as a prophylactic vaccine in one population could therefore be stopped because of the occurrence of an AE in very high risk group.

## Further Challenges Which may Arise if a Vaccine Works

What follows are some "thought experiments" using a number of different scenarios and illustrating some of the ethical issues relating to vaccine deployment, particularly in the early stages after licensing.

### *Justice and the Distribution of a TB Vaccine*

It is unlikely that any new vaccine will be immediately available in sufficient quantity to meet the urgent and enormous global need. In addition to vaccine availability, logistical requirements such as a public health infrastructure for vaccine deployment and cold chain storage will need to be met. This will be the case particularly if an effective vaccine is to be administered to adolescents and young adults. At present there are no routine vaccination programmes outside of infancy in most developing countries, yet adolescents and young adults form an important target population for a new TB vaccine. It is possible, therefore, that some form of prioritization will have to be instituted, at least with regard to the initial rollout of the new vaccine.

Factors which would need to be considered when prioritizing countries (or groups within countries) include the incidence (and incidence rate) of TB infection and disease; the prevalence (and prevalence rates) of HIV infection and AIDS; the ability of an immunization program to effectively deliver the new vaccine (including the ability to maintain the cold chain if required, reach all communities, maintain records and conduct post-licensing surveillance for adverse events following immunization); the presence of competing priorities on their health agenda (for example a health ministry may not wish to divert scarce resources from a campaign which aims to get insecticide treated bed-nets to families with young children if that is the national priority at the time); the presence or absence of political support at various levels for such a campaign (e.g. the regional offices of UNICEF and the WHO, the national health department); and the availability of other means of preventing progression from TB infection to TB disease (e.g. chemoprophylaxis). Some might argue that it would be illogical and even unethical to deploy a new vaccine unless a reasonably well-functioning TB control program is already in place; a surveillance programme, for example, would be necessary to demonstrate an effect of the vaccine on rates of TB infection and disease. However, countries or cities without such programmes will be among the places most in need of a new, effective vaccine, as decades of ineffective and suboptimal case detection and treatment programs have had little or no effect on the burden of disease there.

If efficacy trials of a vaccine demonstrate higher efficacy in some subgroups than others (e.g. one gender, a particular age group, or those with HIV infection), then it might be logical to target these groups first, if vaccine supplies are limited and if this approach is practical. Another approach would be to target the most vulnerable (e.g. those living in extreme poverty, children and the elderly) on the basis that they are less able to effectively compete for humanitarian aid and are most likely to benefit from vaccination.

### *Duty to Treat TB Patients and Vaccination of Healthcare Workers*

We use the term "healthcare workers" here in the broadest sense and intend it to include physicians, nurses, radiographers, physiotherapists, social workers, Directly Observed Treatment, Short-course (DOTS) supporters and supervisors, support staff such as hospital cleaners: everyone with whom TB patients may come into significant contact. Healthcare workers are a special case for a number of reasons. Firstly they are at higher risk of exposure and consequently infection, because of their work. Secondly, their continued health and well being and ability to work is necessary for the welfare of those already suffering from TB and requiring or receiving TB treatment. Thirdly, should they develop TB, they may well present a risk of infection to other patients and colleagues. Lastly, healthcare workers in some settings have been shown to have a higher prevalence of HIV infection (Connelly et al. 2007; Shisana et al. 2004), placing them more at risk of developing TB should they become infected with the bacillus.

In view of the above, it may be appropriate to consider healthcare workers as a priority group when allocation decisions regarding a new TB vaccine are made. In a developing country setting, where the prevalence of TB disease is high, this would most realistically be achieved by vaccinating all healthcare workers.

### *Third-party Notification*

Close contacts of TB patients, particularly of patients with smear positive disease, are at increased risk of infection and 50% of those who progress on to develop disease do so within the first 1–2 years (Morrison et al. 2008). An effective new vaccine may well reduce either the establishment of infection in those exposed, or the development of disease in those infected. Prophylactic vaccination of such contacts may therefore be an effective public health measure.

It is likely that any new TB vaccine would be as effective against drug resistant strains of *M. tb* as it would against drug sensitive strains. In addition, drug resistant strains of *M. tb* are not currently considered intrinsically any more infectious than fully sensitive *M. tbs* isolates, although patients may remain sputum smear and/or culture positive for longer (National Institute for Health and Clinical Excellence 2006). Contacts of MDR/XDR TB patients should therefore be at least as entitled to prophylactic vaccination as contacts of drug sensitive TB patients. However, the fact that therapeutic options for the treatment of drug resistant strains of *M. tb* are more limited, less effective, more prolonged, more toxic, more expensive and less readily available in many high burden countries may mean that public health is best served by such contacts being given priority over contacts of patients with drug sensitive strains of *M. tb*. MDR/XDR TB patients may voluntarily inform their close contacts of their exposure to the disease; but they sometimes choose not to do so. In the latter case an ethical dilemma arises, because a breach of patient confidentiality may be necessary to protect the exposed individual's right to life.

*Mandatory Treatment*

If there was an outbreak of XDR-TB, as for example in the Tugela Ferry outbreak (Gandhi et al. 2006), and an effective vaccine existed, a reasonable public health measure might be to "ring vaccinate" everyone in the immediate geographical area. The effectiveness of such a strategy would depend on the level of herd immunity achieved. Thus it might be necessary for a national authority to insist on vaccination, and to thereby override the rights of individuals. Such a measure may be seen as the most efficient and cost effective way to control such an outbreak.

Factors to be considered before such a decision could be made would include the magnitude of the risk (the closeness and duration of the contact, the risk of infection given contact, estimates as to the transmissibility of the strain, the risk and likely timing of disease given infection, the prognosis and treatment options and effectiveness should disease develop and the risk of adverse reactions to the vaccination) and the likely magnitude of the benefit (the demonstrated vaccine efficacy against ordinary and MDR/XDR TB).

## Conclusions

There are many complex ethical issues which arise at all stages of TB vaccine development. Many of these are common to those previously described in the context of TB disease and further ethical discussion about how to strike a balance between rights/liberties of infected individuals and the greater good of society would be useful for considering the ethical issues arising from TB vaccine development. Vaccination has enabled the eradication of smallpox and virtual eradication of polio from the world. Development of a TB vaccine could be considered a moral obligation as reducing the morbidity and mortality of TB disease through the development and deployment of an effective vaccine would reduce the occurrence of conflict between the rights and liberties of the infected individual versus those of society.



## References

Alcorn, K. 2008. TB vaccine reduces new cases by almost 40% in people with HIV. Aidsmap News. 20 October. http://www.aidsmap.com/en/news/0C1FB0AF-9BC6-4A7A-8D47-7D8ABBD3C8E9.asp. Accessed 4 April 2009.

Baldwin, S.L., C. D'Souza, A.D. Roberts, B.P. Kelly, A.A. Frank, M.A. Lui, J.B. Ulmer, K. Huygen, D.M. McMurray, and I.M. Orme. 1998. Evaluation of new vaccines in the mouse and guinea pig model of tuberculosis. *Infection and Immunity* 66(6): 2951–2959.

Brennan, M.J., U. Fruth, J. Milstien, R. Tiernan, S. de Andrade Nishioka, and L. Chocarro. 2007. Development of new tuberculosis vaccines: A global perspective on regulatory issues. *PLoS Medicine* 4(8): e252. doi:10.1371/journal.pmed.0040252.

Buchbinder, S.P., D.V. Mehrotra, A. Duerr, D.W. Fitzgerald, R. Mogg, D. Li, P.B. Gilbert, J.R. Lama, M. Marmor, C. Del Rio, M.J. McElrath, D.R. Casimiro, K.M. Gottesdiener, J.A. Chodakewitz, L. Corey, and M.N. Robertson. 2008. Efficacy assessment of a cell-mediated immunity HIV-1 vaccine (the Step Study): A double-blind, randomised, placebo-controlled, test-of-concept trial. *Lancet* 372(9653): 1881–1893. doi:10.1016/S0140-6736(08)61591-3.

Centers for Disease Control, Prevention (CDC). 2006. Emergence of Mycobacterium tuberculosis with extensive resistance to second-line drugs–worldwide, 2000–2004. *MMWR. Morbidity and Mortality Weekly Report* 55(11): 301–305.

Colditz, G.A., T.F. Brewer, C.S. Berkey, M.E. Wilson, E. Burdick, H.V. Fineberg, and F. Mosteller. 1994. Efficacy of BCG vaccine in the prevention of tuberculosis. Meta-analysis of the published literature. *Journal of the American Medical Association* 271(9): 698–702. doi:10.1001/jama.271.9.698.

Connelly, D., Y. Veriava, S. Roberts, J. Tsotetsi, A. Jordan, E. DeSilva, S. Rosen, and M.B. DeSilva. 2007. Prevalence of HIV infection and median CD4 counts among health care workers in South Africa. *South African Medical Journal* 97(2): 115–120.

Corbett, E.L., C.J. Watt, N. Walker, D. Maher, B.G. Williams, M.C. Raviglione, and C. Dye. 2003. The growing burden of tuberculosis: Global trends and interactions with the HIV epidemic. *Archives of Internal Medicine* 163(9): 1009–1021. doi:10.1001/archinte.163.9.1009.

Gandhi, N.R., A. Moll, A.W. Sturm, R. Pawinski, T. Govender, U. Lalloo, K. Zeller, J. Andrews, and G. Friedland. 2006. Extensively drug-resistant tuberculosis as a cause of death in patients co-infected with tuberculosis and HIV in a rural area of South Africa. *Lancet* 368(9547): 1575–1580. doi:10.1016/S0140-6736(06)69573-1.

Garattini, S., and V. Bertele. 2007. How can we regulate medicines better? *BMJ (Clinical Research Ed.)* 335(7624): 803–805. doi:10.1136/bmj.39281.615706.94.

Hanekom, W.A., H.M. Dockrell, T.H. Ottenhoff, T.M. Doherty, H. Fletcher, H. McShane, F.F. Weichold, D.F. Hoft, S.K. Parida, and U.J. Fruth. 2008. Immunological outcomes of new tuberculosis vaccine trials: WHO panel recommendations. *PLoS Medicine* 5(7): e145. doi:10.1371/journal.pmed.0050145.

Huygen, K., J. Content, O. Denis, D.L. Montgomery, A.M. Yawman, R.R. Deck, C.M. DeWitt, I.M. Orme, S. Baldwin, C. D'Souza, A. Drowart, E. Lozes, P. Vandenbussche, J.P. Van Vooren, M.A. Liu, and J.B. Ulmer. 1996. Immunogenicity and protective efficacy of a tuberculosis DNA vaccine. *Nature Medicine* 2(8): 893–898. doi:10.1038/nm0896-893.

Ibanga, H.B., R.H. Brookes, P.C. Hill, P.K. Owiafe, H.A. Fletcher, C. Lienhardt, A.V. Hill, R.A. Adegbola, and H. McShane. 2006. Early clinical trials with a new tuberculosis vaccine, MVA85A, in tuberculosis-endemic countries: Issues in study design. *The Lancet Infectious Diseases* 6(8): 522–528. doi:10.1016/S1473-3099(06)70552-7.

Kamath, A.T., U. Fruth, M.J. Brennan, R. Dobbelaer, P. Hubrechts, M.M. Ho, R.E. Mayner, J. Thole, K.B. Walker, M. Liu, and P.H. Lambert. 2005. New live mycobacterial vaccines: The Geneva consensus on essential steps towards clinical development. *Vaccine* 23(29): 3753–3761. doi:10.1016/j.vaccine.2005.03.001.

McElrath, M.J., S.C. De Rosa, Z. Moodie, S. Dubey, L. Kierstead, H. Janes, O.D. Defawe, D.K. Carter, J. Hural, R. Akondy, S.P. Buchbinder, M.N. Robertson, D.V. Mehrotra, S.G. Self, L. Corey, J.W. Shiver, and D.R. Casimiro. 2008. HIV-1 vaccine-induced immunity in the test-of-concept Step Study: A case-cohort analysis. *Lancet* 372(9653): 1894–1905. doi:10.1016/S0140-6736(08)61592-5.

Minnies, D., T. Hawkridge, W. Hanekom, R. Ehrlich, L. London, and G. Hussey. 2008. Evaluation of the quality of informed consent in a vaccine field trial in a developing country setting. *BMC Medical Ethics* 9: 15. doi:10.1186/1472-6939-9-15.

Morrison, J., M. Pai, and P.C. Hopewell. 2008. Tuberculosis and latent tuberculosis infection in close contacts of people with pulmonary tuberculosis in low-income and middle-income countries: A systematic review and meta-analysis. *The Lancet Infectious Diseases* 8(6): 359–368. doi:10.1016/S1473-3099(08)70071-9.

National Institute for Health and Clinical Excellence (NICE). 2006. Tuberculosis: Clinical diagnosis and management of tuberculosis, and measures for its prevention and control. http://www.nice.org.uk/nicemedia/pdf/CG033niceguideline.pdf. Accessed 4 April 2009.

Orme, I.M. 2005. The use of animal models to guide rational vaccine design. *Microbes and Infection* 7(5–6): 905–910. doi:10.1016/j.micinf.2005.03.008.

Samson, K. 2008. Orphan economics: The downside of supplyside pharmacology. *Annals of Neurology* 64(3): A13–A16. doi:10.1002/ana.21432.

Selgelid, M.J. 2005. Ethics and infectious disease. *Bioethics* 19 (3): 272–289. doi:10.1111/j.1467-8519.2005.00441.x.

Selgelid, M.J., P.M. Kelly, and A. Sleigh. 2008a. Ethical challenges in TB control in the era of XDR-TB. *The International Journal of Tuberculosis and Lung Disease* 12(3): 231–235.

Selgelid, M.J., P.M. Kelly, and A. Sleigh. 2008b. In *International Public Health Policy and Ethics*, ed. M. Boylan. Dordrecht: Springer.

Shisana, O., E.J. Hall, R. Maluleke, J. Chauveau, and C. Schwabe. 2004. HIV/AIDS prevalence among South African health workers. *South African Medical Journal* 94(10): 846–850.

Snider Jr., D.E. 2000. Ethical issues in tuberculosis vaccine trials. *Clinical Infectious Diseases* 30(Suppl 3): S271–S275. doi:10.1086/313872.

Soliman, E.Z. 2008. The ethics of non-inferiority trials. *Lancet* 371(9616): 895. doi:10.1016/S0140-6736(08)60406-7. author reply 896-7.

Tascon, R.E., M.J. Colston, S. Ragno, E. Stavropoulos, D. Gregory, and D.B. Lowrie. 1996. Vaccination against tuberculosis by DNA injection. *Nature Medicine* 2(8): 888–892. doi:10.1038/nm0896-888.

U.S. Department of Health, Education and Welfare. (1979). The Belmont report: Ethical principles and guidelines for the protection of human subjects of research. *Federal Register, 44*(76): 23191–23197. http://ohsr.od.nih.gov/guidelines/belmont.html. Accessed 4 April 2009.

Williams, A., G.J. Hatch, S.O. Clark, K.E. Gooch, K.A. Hatch, G.A. Hall, K. Huygen, T.H. Ottenhoff, K.L. Franken, P. Andersen, T.M. Doherty, S.H. Kaufmann, L. Grode, P. Seiler, C. Martin, B. Gicquel, S.T. Cole, P. Brodin, A.S. Pym, W. Dalemans, J. Cohen, Y. Lobet, N. Goonetilleke, H. McShane, A. Hill, T. Parish, D. Smith, N.G. Stoker, D. B. Lowrie, G. Kallenius, S. Svenson, A. Pawlowski, K. Blake, and P.D. Marsh. 2005. Evaluation of vaccines in the EU TB Vaccine Cluster using a guinea pig aerosol infection model of tuberculosis. *Tuberculosis (Edinburgh, Scotland)* 85(1-2): 29–38. doi:10.1016/j.tube.2004.09.009.

World Health Organization. 2007. *Global tuberculosis control: surveillance, planning, financing. WHO Report*. Geneva: World Health Organisation.

World Medical Association. 2008. Declaration of Helsinki. http://www.wma.net/e/policy/b3.htm. Accessed 4 April 2009.

# Part IV: Coercion and Compensation

Bioethical Inquiry (2009) 6:197–205
DOI 10.1007/s11673-009-9160-7

# Should Persons Detained During Public Health Crises Receive Compensation?

**Søren Holm**

Received: 15 October 2008 / Accepted: 6 May 2009 / Published online: 26 May 2009


**Abstract** One of the ways in which public health officials control outbreaks of epidemic disease is by attempting to control the situations in which the infectious agent can spread. This may include isolation of infected persons, quarantine of persons who may be infected and detention of persons who are present in or have entered premises where infected persons are being treated. Most who have analysed such measures think that the restrictions in liberty they entail and the detriments in welfare they impose can be justified and this paper proceeds from the assumption that detention measures are justifiable in some circumstances. Such measures are often implemented without any compensation being given to the persons who are detained. This raises the question: What do we owe to those whose liberty is justifiably restricted (e.g. through isolation, quarantine or detention) as a public health measure during a public health emergency? More specifically, do we owe them compensation for any losses they experience? The paper falls in four main sections. The first section provides examples of the current regulatory state of affairs from the US, Canada and WHO. The second section lays out the liberal, welfarist and pragmatic arguments for providing compensation. The third section discusses the arguments against compensation and the fourth and final section provides the conclusion. It is argued that the arguments for providing compensation clearly outweigh the counterarguments and that the default public policy therefore should be that compensation is provided.

**Keywords** Compensation · Isolation · Justice · Public health · Quarantine

A preliminary version of this paper entitled "Justifiable detention and the question of compensation" was first presented at the *Limiting Liberty in Contexts of Contagion* workshop held at Oxford University, July 2007.

S. Holm (✉)
Cardiff Law School,
Museum Avenue,
Cardiff CF10 3XJ, UK
e-mail: holms@cardiff.ac.uk

S. Holm
Section for Medical Ethics, University of Oslo,
Fredrik Holsts Hus, Blindern, Postboks 1130, 0318 Oslo,
Norway

## Introduction

One of the ways in which public health officials control outbreaks of epidemic disease is by attempting to control the situations in which the infectious agent can spread from one person to another in order to minimise the number of people exposed to the infectious agent. This may include isolation of infected persons, quarantine of persons who may be infected, the detention of persons who are present in or have entered premises where infected persons are being treated, general closures of venues in which large number of people congregate and mix like schools, cinemas, churches, restaurants and shops or encouraging voluntary social distancing. In the following I will, unless differentiation is needed, use the term "detention in the public health context" or similar to cover isolation, quarantine and detention.

Most who have analysed such measures from an ethical point of view think that the restrictions in liberty they entail and the detriments in welfare they impose can be justified either 1) on purely consequentialist grounds because there are many situations where the benefits derived from curtailing the spread of infectious disease outweigh the costs (broadly conceived) created by the liberty infringing measures or 2) from considerations of the public interest outweighing the liberty claims of those who pose a potential threat (Upshur 2002; Cetron and Landwirth 2005; Coker et al. 2007). In this paper the analysis will proceed on the assumption that detention measures are justifiable in some circumstances and that public health officials can make reasonably reliable judgements about when detention is justifiable.

Currently such measures are often implemented without any compensation being given to the persons who are quarantined or have their liberty severely restricted in other ways. The question that the present paper seeks to answer is:

> What do we owe to those whose liberty is justifiably restricted (e.g. through isolation, quarantine or detention) as a public health measure during a public health emergency?

More specifically, do we owe them compensation for any losses they experience?

Throughout the analysis will focus on persons whose liberty is significantly curtailed or who experience serious losses. The paper will not discuss whether we owe something in cases involving minimal inconvenience (for example, having your temperature measured in the airport), or in cases where there is only a minor infringement of liberty but no other harm or loss. But in some situations there are significant economic and non-economic losses. The following is not an exhaustive list but persons who are detained may lose their income during the detention period, they may be fired from their work or their own business may fold, they may be separated from their family for a significant period or they may in the case of quarantine with others be put at increased risk of contracting the disease.

The paper falls in four main sections. The first section provides some illuminating examples of the current regulatory state of affairs from the US, Canada and WHO. The second section lays out the liberal, welfarist and pragmatic arguments for providing compensation. The third section discusses the arguments against compensation and the fourth and final section provides the conclusion. Not all of the arguments discussed here are new or original but at least some are (Rothstein and Talbott 2007; Ly et al. 2007).

When thinking through these arguments it is important to remember that detention in the public health context may not only occur in relation to large scale global epidemics like flu or SARS, but may also be the response to quite localised outbreaks of disease or even single potentially contagious individuals where there is no risk of spread outside a small area. The issues discussed therefore do not only arise in times of great crisis and even full compensation does not always require great expense. In industrialised countries detention is, for instance, sometimes used in cases of extensively drug-resistant tuberculosis but the number of cases in any particular jurisdiction is very small. If the arguments for compensation hold in the case of large scale public health emergencies, they are even more likely to hold in individual cases.

## The Current Regulatory State of Affairs–Some Illuminating Examples

It is impossible to give a complete global overview of the public health detention powers and compensation arrangements worldwide and it is also unnecessary for the purposes of the present paper. It is, however, useful to give a few pertinent examples.

The US regulatory situation is complex because public health only becomes a Federal responsibility if the problem at hand involves international or interstate transport or commerce. Each state has its own legislation and these vary considerably (Rothstein and Talbott 2007). Here we will therefore use the provisions of "The Model State Emergency Health Powers Act, MSEHPA. 2008a, b" drafted by The Center for Law and The Public's Health for the Centers for Disease Control and Prevention in 2001 as an example of the general approach. By July 2006 parts of this Model Act had been incorporated into the legislation in 38 states in the USA (The Model State Emergency Health Powers Act (MSEHPA) 2008a, b).

The relevant sections in the Model Act are Sections 601–608 dealing with the protection of persons and Section 805 providing for compensation. Sections 601–608 provides wide ranging powers for compulsory testing, treatment, vaccination, isolation and quarantine. In Section 604, subsections b.6– 8 the conditions of isolation and quarantine are specified:

6. The needs of persons isolated and quarantined shall be addressed in a systematic and competent fashion, including, but not limited to, providing adequate food, clothing, shelter, means of communication with those in isolation or quarantine and outside these settings, medication and competent medical care.
7. Premises used for isolation and quarantine shall be maintained in a safe and hygienic manner and be designed to minimize the likelihood of further transmission of infection or other harms to persons isolated and quarantined.
8. To the extent possible, cultural and religious beliefs should be considered in addressing the needs of individuals, and establishing and maintaining isolation and quarantine premises (MSEHPA).

Section 805 on compensation is only concerned with "Compensation for property" (805.a) and specifies that "The amount of compensation shall be calculated in the same manner as compensation due for taking of property pursuant to non-emergency eminent domain procedures…" (805.c).

There is thus no compensation provided for individuals in the Model Act and although Rothstein and Talbott make the observation that this may be slowly changing the stance in the Model act is compatible with the current approach in US state laws (Rothstein and Talbott 2007).

In Canada the issue of public health regulation was brought to the fore during the 2003 Toronto SARS outbreak. The existing public health legislation in Ontario, the province in which Toronto is located, gave public health officials wide ranging powers to detain people and a large number of people were detained. Subsequently, it became obvious that there was no protection against economic losses for those who had been detained. This lead to the "SARS Assistance and Recovery Strategy Act 2003". The most important sections of this act are section 6 which defines absence from work due to a number of SARS related public health interventions as legally protected "leave of absence without pay" and section 8 which creates a legal right to reinstatement in the previously held position (SARS Assistance and Recovery Strategy Act 2003).

The Government of Ontario also established a specific economic assistance program to help those who had lost wages during the SARS outbreak. This was capped at CAD 500 per day or CAD 6000 in total per person (Canadian Press 2003).

These measures strictly speaking only apply to Ontario and only to the specific 2003 SARS outbreak, but it is difficult to see how any Canadian province could refuse to institute broadly similar measures if a comparable situation arose in the future. The compensation provided cannot under any description be deemed as excessive and the total payout created no fiscal problems for Ontario. In the future non-comparable situations may arise that would give policy makers pause before instituting compensation (for example, if SARS-like outbreaks become common), but this does nothing to show that there would not be a large political (and moral) problem in denying compensation in *comparable* cases.

International regulation is almost completely silent on the issue of compensation but the WHO International Health Regulations 2005 contains sections on isolation and quarantine of travellers and it does briefly mention how travellers ought to be treated when subject to public health procedures:

> **Article 32 Treatment of travellers**
> In implementing health measures under these Regulations, States Parties shall treat travellers with respect for their dignity, human rights and fundamental freedoms and minimize any discomfort or distress associated with such measures, including by:

(a) treating all travellers with courtesy and respect;
(b) taking into consideration the gender, sociocultural, ethnic or religious concerns of travellers; and
(c) providing or arranging for adequate food and water, appropriate accommodation and clothing, protection for baggage and other possessions, appropriate medical treatment, means of necessary communication if possible in a language that they can understand and other appropriate

assistance for travellers who are quarantined, isolated or subject to medical examinations or other procedures for public health purposes.

This short set of examples reveal two interesting facts: 1) that although there is concern for the conditions under which people are detained there are in general no provisions for compensation and 2) there are at least some circumstances where property owners will be compensated for their losses when property is compulsorily taken during a public health emergency.

## Why Should People Be Compensated?

It is in one way slightly strange to ask why persons should be compensated when their liberty is significantly infringed and they suffer harm or loss as a result of that infringement.

When the state takes or expropriates specific items of property for important or even not so important social purposes it usually provides compensation to the property owners, even if the property is taken in an emergency situation.

But it is equally plausible that the state should compensate when it takes away my ability to work or run my business, or when it significantly affects my welfare in a negative way.

There thus seems to be a good *prima facie* claim for compensation in a liberal state. Explicating the exact nature of the claim is complicated by the fact that not all liberty restrictions cause harm or loss to the person whose liberty is restricted. There is thus a question concerning whether a person should be compensated for a harmless liberty restriction imposed by the state. This is a question of great theoretical interest but one that can be bracketed here since most cases of public health detention involves harmful liberty restriction. This is the case even if a person's earning power is not diminished, but her welfare is as a result of the detention. Think for instance of a pensioner detained outside of her home in conditions just fulfilling the requirements of Article 32 of the WHO International Health Regulations 2005 (see above). She would have been harmed even if her income was not affected.

There is also a potentially troublesome threshold issue at play that was already alluded to in the introduction. At least some of the moral arguments for compensation are valid for a loss of any size and will therefore justify claims for compensation for even minimal losses and / or liberty infringements. But this seems intuitively and pragmatically problematic, partly because we all have to accept some uncompensated losses as part of normal life in modern, complex societies. Intuitively the claim for compensation has to reach a certain threshold before a policy maker has to take it seriously. Exploring exactly where this threshold should be is beyond the scope of this paper and it may well differ from society to society. It is, however, important to note that at the public policy level we have reasons to institute such a threshold that are not merely based on intuition and that are legitimately different from the argument an individual could make in relation to a compensation claim from another individual. The transaction costs in handling minimal claims through a publicly legitimate process may swamp the actual amount of compensation due and public support for a compensation scheme may depend on the scheme only giving compensation where compensation is clearly perceived to be due.

*Prima facie* claims are by their very nature defeasible and we therefore need to consider whether there are any obvious countervailing considerations to the claim for compensation. First we need to consider whether the persons are themselves responsible for their loss because they have full or partial causal and/ or moral responsibility. In almost all cases this will not be the case. Although the risk of being infected depends on a person's action and although it is a fact that many would not be put at risk of infection unless they had performed certain actions (e.g. gone to work, taken public transport, sent their child to school etc.) it is implausible to claim that they were the causes of their own risk of infection in any morally interesting sense. Everything that happens to a person is to some degree an effect of their own prior actions. But causal contribution does not imply causal responsibility; and causal responsibility does not imply moral responsibility or blameworthiness (for further elaboration of this point see Holm 2008). It is, for instance, pretty obvious that a person who was on a bus with an infectious person and who is therefore quarantined has not nullified a claim to compensation. We also need to note that there are cases where people are undoubtedly causally responsible, but where this does not defeat their claim. Health care professionals who go to work knowing that they will treat infected people and will be quarantined have not defeated their claim to compensation simply because they went voluntarily and in full knowledge of the consequences.

A second possible argument against compensation is that the vital interests of the community outweigh the claim, for instance because the costs of compensation will be very large and will undermine the continuation of the community. This will be discussed in more detail below in relation to arguments from analogy against compensation.

### The Welfarist Answer

If detention in the public health context succeeds in limiting the spread of the disease it constitutes a potential Pareto optimal social change compared to the situation where the disease outbreak is allowed to run its course unchecked. Analysis of the Toronto SARS outbreak does for instance seem to indicate that despite the very large costs of quarantine the economic benefits outweigh the costs (Gupta et al. 2005). A potential Pareto optimal social change is by definition a change where some lose and some win but where there is a net social welfare gain such that the winners could compensate the losers for their loss. A potential Pareto optimal social change can therefore, again by definition, be converted into an actual Pareto optimal change, i.e. a change where some gain welfare but no one loses welfare, if the winners compensate the losers for their loss.

Let us assume 1) that the number of detained persons is small compared to the general population and 2) that the principle of diminishing marginal utility of resources holds (at least approximately). Then it follows straightforwardly that the social state after compensation has been provided will have higher aggregate welfare than the state before compensation. The former losers will gain more welfare from the redistribution inherent in compensation than the former winners will lose, and the net loss to each former winner will be small.

There is thus a strong welfarist argument for providing compensation. This argument is even stronger if we accept a form of prioritarianism because this will direct us to give special weight to welfare improvements for those who are worst off in welfare terms (Rabinowicz 2001).

There may be situations where the public health intervention is not potentially Pareto optimal, i.e. where the intervention has caused a net, aggregate welfare loss. In such cases the non-prioritarian welfarist may have no compelling reason to redistribute.

### Pragmatic and Justice Considerations

There are also pragmatic considerations and issues of justice that support compensation for detention in the public health context. Some people who are detained fear for their livelihood (DiGiovanni et al. 2004; Blendon et al. 2006), and it is likely that the existence of a compensation system will improve adherence to the quarantine rules and will in general add to the perceived legitimacy and tolerability of detention.

It is furthermore likely that the burdens of detention will, at least sometimes, fall very unequally on different sectors of society. This may happen either because the rules are not applied completely impartially or because of the demographics of the disease outbreak (Jacobs 2007). If the burdens are very unequally distributed there is a justice argument for rectifying the resulting inequalities after the fact.

### Compensation and Restitution

This paper assumes that the detention is justifiable and that the issue that arises is therefore an issue of compensation. If, however, the public health detention is unjustifiable the claim will not be a claim for compensation but a claim for restitution. An unjustifiable detention is not only a harm but also a wrong and the person who has been wronged will have a strong claim to restitution against the wrongdoer.

## Arguments Against Compensation

If the arguments for compensation are so compelling why is compensation not the default regulatory option?

There is probably a historical reason in that the framing of public health regulations come from a time where governments were much more authoritarian and interventionist than they are now and where the freedom of citizens not as valued as it is now. There is little political incentive to change that stance. Public health detention without compensation is in many and probably most situations cheaper than detention with compensation and given that the public health powers are very rarely invoked there has been no mass mobilisation against them. This might however change if during some future crisis a large number of citizens in North America or Europe are detained as indicated by the government response to the Toronto SARS outbreak.

But there are also some philosophical arguments against compensation that we need to attend to.

## No Compensation for Doing Your Duty

Could it not be argued that people should not be compensated for doing their duty? Doing your duty is reward in itself. And there is plausibly a duty not to infect others with dangerous diseases (Harris and Holm 1995). There are at least three possible answers to this line of argument and these are not mutually exclusive. The first is that there are many situations where we praise people for doing their duty, but such praise becomes unintelligible in moral terms if doing your duty is sufficient reward in itself.

The second is that even if we accept a strong duty not to infect others, and some have questioned the strength of this duty (Verweij 2005), there is no direct deduction from this to a duty to be detained to reduce the risk of infection to others. You may, for instance not have a duty to accept detention if you can discharge your duty not to put others at risk effectively in a way that is less costly to you or leaves your liberty more intact.

The third answer is that individual duties do not occur in a moral vacuum. The duties of an individual living in society are always part of an intricate web of mutual obligations between individuals and between individuals and society. This aspect of morality can usefully be discussed under the rubric of "moral reciprocity" without thereby implying that reciprocity underlies all or even most of morality (Becker 1986). I should do my duty, but I have a legitimate expectation that this will be reciprocated by others, including my society doing their duty towards me (Harris and Holm 1993). What does reciprocity entail in the current context? There is probably no very specific answer to this, but it is implausible that society for instance fully discharges its duties by fulfilling the requirements of Article 32 of the WHO International Health Regulations quoted above by providing *inter alia* "adequate food and water".

## Arguments from Analogy

Another class of arguments against providing compensation are arguments from analogy showing that there are other similar situations where we detain persons justifiably and do not pay them compensation for the detention. There are a large number of possible analogies and although the five that will be discussed here may not fully exhaust the total field of analogies they are fairly representative. The five analogies are:

- Imprisonment for criminal activity
- Justifiable arrest eventually not leading to a prosecution
- Compulsory detention of the mentally ill in cases where they are a danger to others
- Preventive detention of enemy citizens in time of war
- Compulsory military (and other) service in time of war

In all of these cases the liberty of the persons are infringed by the state for a worthwhile social purpose and the persons suffer harm or loss, but are not compensated. Should we be convinced by these analogies that compensation should not be offered for detention in the public health context or are there significant disanalogies? In attempting to answer this question we have to remember that argument from analogy is notoriously tricky, especially in bioethics because the rhetorical force of analogies plays a significant role in bioethical argument, and that any analogy may be partially apt even if it is not perfect (Hofmann et al. 2007).

Let us first analyse the two "criminal analogies". With regard to these there are a number of significant disanalogies. The first and most obvious in relation to imprisonment is that one of the main purposes of imprisonment is precisely to curtail liberty and impose a loss on the persons who are imprisoned. Prison is supposed to be a punishment for past wrongdoing. We may discuss whether prisons ought to be penal institutions if our criminal justice systems were based on the best possible philosophical account of the function of justice (Braithwaite and Pettit 1992), but this does not entail that we can dispute that their current function is penal and that it would therefore be paradoxical and incoherent for society to compensate the intended losses they impose. Detention in the public health context is clearly not intended to be a punishment so the issue of compensation still arises.

If we had a criminal justice system that was purely based on deterrence, and this is clearly not our current system, then it would not be strictly incoherent for society to compensate those who were punished. As long as it was compatible with deterrence we could provide compensation for the liberty restrictions and losses imposed on those who where punished. This kind of reasoning might apply in the context of non-compliant patients with extensively drug-resistant tuberculosis (I owe this point to one of the anonymous reviewers).

Another disanalogy between the criminal and the public health context is that there is no actual or suspected wrongdoing involved in the public health context. There is very rarely any wrongdoing in the past, very few people set out to infect others deliberately; and there is little risk of wrongdoing in the future. Many people would be likely to adhere to quarantine voluntarily in their own home if they were made aware of the potential risk they posed to others and supported while maintaining social distancing. The last point is for instance evidenced by the classical Eyam village example (Wallis 2006).

A specific disanalogy also exists between quarantine and arrest since there is often a greater disproportion between those quarantined and those who are actual carriers than between the arrested and the convicted. And, given that quarantine often does not involve isolation it sometimes increases the risk of infection for those who were not infected when they were quarantined.

On further analysis the "criminal analogies" therefore provides very little support for denying compensation to those detained in the public health context.

There are also significant disanalogies between compulsory detention in the mental health and the public health context. In the mental health context there is an explicit assumption of irrationality and unreliability. We typically detain people who are dangerous to others and where this danger can clearly be linked to their mental illness. These assumptions are important because they can explain why the danger posed by the people we detain cannot be controlled by more standard means (because they are unreliable) and why there is an element of potentially acceptable paternalism (because they are irrational and do not really want to harm others). But the people detained for public health reasons during an infectious disease outbreak are rarely any more irrational or unreliable than other members of society and the harm they pose can therefore presumably be controlled in the same way as we control other people who pose potential harms to others, for example, by threat of punishment if they actually harm someone.

The "time of war" analogies are of limited use but need to be discussed, partly for completeness, partly because war-like metaphors abound in public discussions of communicable diseases (Sontag 1979; 1989). As noted above there are many public health emergencies where detention will be implemented that are localised and therefore not comparable to a time of war which is a much more generalised emergency situation. The time of war analogies are therefore only applicable to a limited range of detention situations even if we decide that they are valid analogies. But there are considerable problems with their validity. If we first consider compulsory military service it is often the case that we provide some compensation to those who are drafted for service, although we may call it "pay", and that we also sometimes provide specific services to them or their dependents after their service has ended in recognition of their special contributions to society (the services provided by the US Department of Veterans Affairs is a prime example). This analogy may therefore just as well be taken to support compensation for detention in the public health context.

The same cannot be said for the preventive detention of enemy citizens but it has other problems that weaken its force. There are many reasons for detaining enemy citizens (revenge, punishment of the enemy, use as bargaining chips, protection of them against vigilantes etc.) but let us accept 1) that there is a preventive element and that enemy citizens living amongst us are potentially dangerous because they may be spies, saboteurs or try to influence public opinion; 2) that general preventive detention is therefore justified, and 3) that we have traditionally not compensated them for the losses they experienced because of their detention. Does it follow from this that we should not compensate persons who are detained in the public health context? Not in any straightforward way. The danger that enemy citizens potentially pose is a danger that springs from their deliberate actions aimed at harming our society, but this is very different from the danger a potentially infected person poses. There is rarely an intention to harm and there are probably not very many Typhoid Marys around who deliberately put others at risk.

## Practicalities and the Argument from Limited Resources

A final set of counterarguments against compensation are related to considerations of practicalities and the drawing of boundaries in grey areas and to a worry about the resources necessary to provide the compensation.

We may worry about how we should set the level of compensation fairly. Should the person with a large salary get more per day than the person who is out of work? Should we take into account the conditions under which the person is detained? Should health care professionals who voluntarily take on infection risks get preferential compensation? All of these questions are relevant and have to be resolved when we design public policy, but the fact that they may not all have obvious principled answers and that any decision may be arbitrary does not show that compensation should not be provided. The compensation scheme that Ontario introduced in 2003 (see above) can be criticised in many ways, but it is better than nothing!

A related worry is that even though a government might accept the duty to compensate in the abstract constraints on available resources would mean that it could not discharge the duty. Or to put it more simply we ought to compensate but cannot do it because this is too expensive and would impinge on other vital interests of the community.

This argument comes in two versions, one focusing on the plight of poor countries and one focusing on a devastating epidemic with global spread.

Let us look at the second version first. This is a relevant objection and there may well be situations in which a given country would have to renege on a promise to compensate. If we had a global flu pandemic it might well be the case that it would have such a profound impact on the world economy that compensation to those who had been detained during the pandemic would have to be suspended or not paid at all. But this does nothing to show that people detained in the public health context should not be compensated in situations where compensation can be provided without imposing significant economic burdens on society. We may accept that ought implies can, and that cannot therefore implies ought not and thus extinguishes the obligation, but from this it only follows that the obligation is nullified when we really cannot honour it. In reality policy makers are likely to draw the line of the "cannot" in a different way than it would be drawn in moral theory, but this does nothing to show that society does not have a strong obligation to compensate in those cases where it is clearly possible.

With regard to the first version of the argument it is important to note that the cost of compensating one individual broadly tracks the economic resources and development of a particular country. Compensating for 10 days of average lost earnings does for instance not have the same price in Mali as it does in the UK. And we might also note, although a full exploration is far beyond the scope of this paper, that in the case of infectious diseases with potential transnational impact the agent(s) responsible for compensation may not be confined to the individual nation state. If country A implements effective infection control measures as soon as an outbreak is detected and thereby prevents or curtails the spread of the disease to countries B, C, D… these other countries have benefited greatly and may therefore have a plausible obligation to contribute to whatever costs country A has had to bear including the costs of compensation to those detained in country A. It is important to note that this obligation would not be derived from any claim that country B, C or D should have a cosmopolitan concern for the citizens of country A, but simply from the claim that these countries have benefited greatly from the actions of country A. And that they would, if asked *ex ante* have wanted country A to perform these actions. They may even have entered a mutual commitment to pursue disease control actions, for instance by signing up to the WHO International Health Regulations, and may therefore in a certain sense have relied on country A discharging its obligations under the mutual agreement.

## Conclusion

This paper has argued that providing compensation for losses incurred by persons who are justifiably isolated, quarantined or otherwise detained in a public context is supported by strong ethical arguments drawing on mutually supporting strands from liberal, welfarist, reciprocity and justice considerations. It has furthermore argued that the available ethical counterarguments against compensation in the individual case are weak, inapplicable on reflection or otherwise problematic and that the same is true of counterarguments against implementing compensation as a public policy.

The default public policy therefore ought to be that we will compensate those persons whom we detain during a public health crisis.

The presumption of compensation is defeasible but only in situations where in the aftermath of the public health crisis it is economically close to impossible to provide compensation.

There are significant practical problems in deciding on the level of compensation but these are both in principle and in practice no more difficult than deciding on levels of compensation for other compulsory or semi-compulsory services, such as jury service, citizens have to perform.

**Acknowledgements** The author is supported by the ESRC Centre for the Economic and Social Aspects of Genomics and the Cardiff Institute of Society, Health and Ethics.

I thank the participants at the *Limiting Liberty in Contexts of Contagion* workshop held at Oxford University, July 2007 for their helpful comments on a preliminary version of this paper. I also thank three anonymous referees for very helpful comments.

**Competing interests** None declared

## References

Becker, L.C. 1986. *Reciprocity*. London: Routledge & Kegan Paul.

Blendon, R.J., C.M. DesRoches, M.S. Cetron, J.M. Benson, T. Meinhardt, and W. Pollard. 2006. Attitudes toward the use of quarantine in a public health emergency in four countries. *Health Affairs* 25: w15–w25. doi:10.1377/hlthaff.25.w15. http://content.healthaffairs.org/cgi/content/abstract/25/2/w15 (accessed October 15, 2008).

Braithwaite, J. and P. Pettit. 1992. *Not just deserts–A republican theory of criminal justice*. Oxford: Oxford University Press.

Canadian Press. 2003. Ontario unveils SARS compensation package. http://www.ctv.ca/servlet/ArticleNews/story/CTVNews/20030613/sars_compensation_030613?s_name=&no_ads= (accessed October 15, 2008).

Cetron, M. and J. Landwirth. 2005. Public health and ethical considerations in planning for quarantine. *The Yale Journal of Biology and Medicine* 78: 325–330.

Coker, R., M. Thomas, K. Lock, and R. Martin. 2007. Detention and the evolving threat of tuberculosis: Evidence, ethics and law. *The Journal of Law, Medicine & Ethics* 35: 609–615.

DiGiovanni, C., J. Conley, D. Chiu, and J. Zaborski. 2004. Factors influencing compliance with quarantine in Toronto during the 2003 SARS outbreak. *Biosecurity and Bioterrorism* 2(4): 265–272. doi:10.1089/bsp.2004.2.265. http://www.liebertonline.com/doi/abs/10.1089%2Fbsp.2004.2.265 (accessed October 15, 2008).

Gupta, A.G., C.A. Mover, and D.T. Stern. 2005. The economic impact of quarantine: SARS in Toronto as a case study. *Journal of Infection* 50: 386–393. doi:10.1016/j.jinf.2004.08.006.

Harris, J. and S. Holm. 1993. If only AIDS was different!. *Hastings Center Report* 23: 6–11. doi:10.2307/3562917.

Harris, J. and S. Holm. 1995. Is there a moral obligation not to infect others? *BMJ (Clinical Research Ed.)* 311: 1215–1217.

Hofmann, B., J.H. Solbakk, and S. Holm. 2007. Analogical reasoning in handling emerging technologies: The case of umbilical cord blood biobanking. *The American Journal of Bioethics* 6: 49–57. doi:10.1080/15265160600938724.

Holm, S. 2008. Parental responsibility and obesity in children. *Public Health Ethics* 1: 21–29. doi:10.1093/phe/phn007.

Jacobs, L.A. 2007. Rights and quarantine during the SARS global health crisis: Differentiated legal consciousness in Hong Kong, Shanghai, and Toronto. *Law & Society Review* 41: 511–551. doi:10.1111/j.1540-5893.2007.00313.x.

Ly, T., M.J. Selgelid, and I. Kerridge. 2007. Pandemic and public health controls: Toward an equitable compensation system. *Journal of Law and Medicine* 15: 318–324.

The Model State Emergency Health Powers Act (MSEHPA). 2008a. *General page* http://www.publichealthlaw.net/ModelLaws/MSEHPA.php (accessed October 15).

The Model State Emergency Health Powers Act (MSEHPA). 2008b. *Text of Act* http://www.publichealthlaw.net/MSEHPA/MSEHPA2.pdf (accessed October 15).

Rabinowicz, W. 2001. Prioritarianism and uncertainty: On the interpersonal addition theorem and the priority view. http://mora.rente.nhh.no/projects/EqualityExchange/ressurser/articles/rabinowicz2.pdf (accessed October 15, 2008).

Rothstein, M.A. and M.K. Talbott. 2007. Job security and income replacement for individuals in quarantine: The need for legislation. *Health Care Law and Policy* 10: 239–257.

SARS Assistance and Recovery Strategy Act. 2003. http://www.e-laws.gov.on.ca/html/statutes/english/elaws_statutes_03s01_e.htm (accessed October 15, 2008).

Sontag, S. 1979. *Illness as metaphor*. New York: Farrar, Straus & Giroux.

Sontag, S. 1989. *Aids and its metaphors*. New York: Farrar, Straus & Giroux.

Upshur, R. 2002. Principles for the justification of public health intervention. *Canadian Journal of Public Health. Revue Canadienne de Sante Publique* 93: 101–103.

Verweij, M. 2005. Obligatory precautions against infection. 2005. *Bioethics* 19: 323–335.

Wallis, P. 2006. A dreadful heritage: Interpreting epidemic disease at Eyam, 1666–2000. *History Workshop Journal* 33: 31–56.

WHO. 2005. *WHO International Health Regulations 2005*. Geneva: WHO.

Bioethical Inquiry (2009) 6:207–217
DOI 10.1007/s11673-009-9149-2

# Your Liberty or Your Life: Reciprocity in the Use of Restrictive Measures in Contexts of Contagion

**A. M. Viens · Cécile M. Bensimon · Ross E. G. Upshur**

Received: 28 November 2008 / Accepted: 21 March 2009 / Published online: 15 May 2009


**Abstract** In this paper, we explore the role of reciprocity in the employment of restrictive measures in contexts of contagion. Reciprocity should be understood as a substantive value that governs the use, level and extent of restrictive measures. We also argue that independent of the role reciprocity plays in the legitimisation the use of restrictive measures, reciprocity can also motivate support and compliance with legitimate restrictive measures. The importance of reciprocity has implications for how restrictive measures should be undertaken when preparing and evaluating public health responses to contagion.

A. M. Viens (✉)
School of Law, Queen Mary, University of London,
67-69 Lincoln's Inn Fields,
London WC2A 3JB, UK
e-mail: a.viens@qmul.ac.uk

A. M. Viens · C. M. Bensimon · R. E. G. Upshur
Joint Centre for Bioethics, University of Toronto,
Toronto, Canada

R. E. G. Upshur
Department of Family and Community Medicine,
University of Toronto,
Toronto, Canada

R. E. G. Upshur
Dalla Lana School of Public Health, University of Toronto,
Toronto, Canada

**Keywords** Reciprocity · Restrictive measures · Infectious disease · Ethics · Quarantine · Isolation · Liberty

> Our business, daily and hourly, leads us to the depletion of men's pockets and the restriction of their liberty. We cannot expect the thanks of those who feel themselves aggrieved.
>
> *Dr Charles Chapin* (1894:12)

Recent history has indicated that restrictive measures are still an important intervention in modern public health. In the SARS outbreak of 2003, mass quarantine was employed in an effort to control the outbreak in Singapore, Hong Kong and Toronto. The emergence of extensively drug-resistant tuberculosis (XDR-TB) has also raised the issue of the use of isolative measures as a means of reducing spread to communities. The case of Andrew Speaker, an American lawyer who travelled extensively while harbouring a drug-resistant strain of tuberculosis, triggered the first use of American federal quarantine law in 40 years. More significantly, the increased prevalence of XDR-TB globally, and in South Africa particularly, has raised questions about the use of isolation for extended periods of time (perhaps even for life) in the context of a potentially untreatable disease posing a significant threat to the public (Singh et al. 2007).

Nevertheless, even if more nuanced accounts of public health action demonstrate that the use of restrictive measures is not simply a choice between one's liberty and one's life or health (Ignatieff 2005; Childress and Bernheim 2003; Ackerman 2006; Dyzenhaus 2006; also cf. Bensimon 2008; Viens, in preparation), we are still left with the need to provide—both in terms of theoretical grounding and practical guidance—some account of what justification and legitimacy conditions need to be met in order for the use of restrictive measures to be ethically permissible. In this paper, we explore the role of reciprocity in the employment of restrictive measures in contexts of contagion. The significance of reciprocity as a moral concept of relevance in public health is starting to gain more recognition, but its moral importance has yet to be fully articulated. We argue that reciprocity plays a vital role in establishing when public health action is legitimate when aiming to prevent, contain or eliminate the effects of infectious diseases. As such, reciprocity should be understood as a substantive value that governs the use, level and extent of restrictive measures. We also argue that independent of the role reciprocity plays in the potential to legitimise the use of restrictive measures, reciprocity can also help to motivate support and compliance with legitimate restrictive measures. The recognition of the centrality that reciprocity can and should play in public health action will have important implications for how restrictive measures should be undertaken when preparing and evaluating public health responses to contagion.

## Justifying the Use of Restrictive Measures

Protecting the public from communicable diseases is widely viewed as a fundamental obligation of the modern state (or the public health system as one of the organs of the state). As a corollary, it is widely established, at least in liberal democracies, that restrictive measures imposed by public health officials should only be used to protect important individual and societal interests. The threshold for invoking restrictive measures, however, is less categorical. When is the use of any restrictive measure justified to advance public health goals?

Traditionally, the control of communicable disease outbreaks has involved various kinds of restrictive public health measures with different levels of severity and varying implications for limits on liberty. For this reason, justifications for public health action involving restrictive measures have been grounded in different considerations on different occasions; that is, depending on the nature of the contagion and measures in play. Social distancing and voluntary isolation, for example, raise different issues and are presumably less problematic than forcible confinement or detention, which arguably require a greater burden of justification than less liberty-limiting measures. Although we believe that all restrictive measures require justification, our analysis will focus mainly on quarantine and isolation[1] because the exercise of such powers raises the most fundamental issues about the use of restrictive measures: in the case of quarantine, it usually imposes autonomy-limiting measures to *healthy* persons who may or may not pose a danger to others (and most often do not develop disease as noted in SARS); and decisions about quarantine and isolation may be shrouded in uncertainty, especially given the dearth of evidence of their effectiveness.

A closer examination of public health action, however, reveals a lack of explicit robust justification for the use of restrictive measures—because the dominant utilitarian approach of epidemiology and the rights-based approach of law do not pay adequate attention to *moral considerations*—such as reciprocity—relevant to the overall permissibility of such interventions. The morally problematic nature of restrictive measures is not adequately addressed. Even with increasing discourse on the recent emergence and re-emergence of communicable diseases, which has seen a significant shift towards public health requirements, the need for a satisfying account of necessary and sufficient grounds for the ethically permissible use of restrictive measures during public health emergencies remains unmet. Moreover, the too-narrow focus on scientific and legal grounds for restrictive measures has the downstream

[0] The distinction between quarantine and isolation is important to observe: *Quarantine* refers to the compulsory physical separation, including restriction of movement, of populations or groups of healthy people who have been potentially exposed to a contagious disease, or to efforts to segregate these persons within specified geographic areas. That is, these individuals do not manifest any signs and symptoms of disease, but are at risk of developing active disease and contributing to further spread due to exposure to a case. *Isolation* refers to the separation and confinement of individuals with signs, symptoms, or laboratory evidence of infection to prevent them from transmitting disease to others.

effect of shaping the conditions of legitimacy for their use through the very same scientific and legal lens that lacks adequate justificatory power.

In order to demonstrate the moral acceptability of restrictive measures, we must consider the conditions for *moral* legitimacy, which first requires that we can *morally justify* the use of restrictive measures. Before making the case for why moral legitimacy is a necessary part of an account of the morality of using restrictive measures, let us turn to a brief discussion of the problematic nature of scientific and legal justifications for restrictive measures.

In practical terms, public health has few modern referents or precedents on which to base decisions for the use of quarantine or isolation. The example of the recent SARS outbreak is a case in point. Even by the time that SARS was determined to be infectious, inadequate evidence and incomplete knowledge about the disease made decisions about the effectiveness of the use of restrictive measures difficult to reach with any degree of certainty. Yet, amid broader discussions about the justificatory basis of public health action involving restrictive measures in the context of any other communicable disease, many practitioners and scholars alike continue to call for greater evidence-based decision-making, going as far as proposing, as Coker et al. (2007, 612) have done, "to introduce into the language of ethics and rights the notion of evidence-based assessment of risk". It is argued that we only need scientific data to determine the validity of the use of restrictive measures in the control of communicable diseases. Even where there *is* reliable data to support interventions, scientific accounts remain problematic—and perhaps insufficient—because, given the nature of evidence in health care, (varying levels of) uncertainty is inevitable (Bensimon and Upshur 2007).

Similarly, as it stands, there are few legal precedents in communicable disease control that reflect modern developments in constitutional and human rights jurisprudence to adequately guide public health authorities to enforce restrictive measures—the most notable being *Jew Ho v. Williamson* and *Jacobson v. Massachusetts* in the US. In spite of this, the reliance on legal justifications for public health action involving restrictive measures—as an alternative to scientific justifications—is predominant. For example, in a recent article by Boggio et al. (2008), it was argued that international law provides legal justification for enforcing compulsory measures against tuberculosis patients who refuse diagnostic procedures, or who refuse to be monitored and treated once the disease is confirmed. That restrictive public health interventions have successfully prevailed against legal challenges does not, however, make them necessarily justifiable. In other words, a public health action is not justifiable *just because* it is carried out under the rubric of the law. Arguing that the use of restrictive measures is justified on legal grounds by virtue of the existence of laws supporting their use is sufficient because the justifiability existing law is not a given (cf. Enhorn v. Sweden).

Scientific and legal considerations are neither necessary nor sufficient to provide a moral justification of the use of restrictive measures. If they were necessary, no restrictive measures could be used in the absence of evidence or laws, as occurred in the case during SARS. If they were sufficient, public health would not have to consider the impact on individual rights. To impose restrictive measures without the guaranteed prospect of direct benefit, or assumed harm reduction for that matter, we must have a compelling moral justification.

## Moral Legitimacy of the Use of Restrictive Measures

When analysing the morality of public health action, we must differentiate between two separate notions: moral justification and moral legitimacy. The moral permissibility of using restrictive measures will depend upon whether such measures are both morally justified *and* morally legitimate.

The moral justification of an act depends on showing why the act under consideration would be morally right in the circumstances. In this case, the question of the moral justification of public health action concerns whether the state should be allowed to use restrictive measures on individuals or groups within its jurisdiction to achieve its public health goals. If the use of restrictive measures is morally justifiable, then it is open to the state to use such interventions in order to advance its public health goals. However, if the use of restrictive measures is morally unjustifiable, such measures are not a morally acceptable option. Within the literature, there are different moral justifications that have been advanced for using restrictive measures to prevent or mitigate contagion, including self-defense (Wilkinson 2007), and harm to others (Coker 2000; Gostin 2003; Parmet 2008, amongst others).

The moral legitimacy of an act depends on whether a justified act under consideration is performed in a morally acceptable manner. In this case, the question of the moral legitimacy of public health action concerns particular conditions that need to be met by the state using restrictive measures in the pursuit of public health goals. To put the point another way, the moral legitimacy of restrictive measures depends on the way in which the state goes about implementing justified options open to them. The way in which we are using the term *moral legitimacy* here is not to be confused with the notion of morally legitimate state authority, sometimes called *political legitimacy* or *political obligation* (cf. Edmundson 1998; Simmons 1999). Nor are we using legitimacy as Charles Taylor (1994, 58) does:

> to designate the beliefs and attitudes that members have toward the society they make up. The society has legitimacy when members so understand and value it that they are willing to assume the disciplines and burdens which membership entails. Legitimacy declines when this willingness flags or fails (also cf. Taylor 1985).

We are not concerned here with the matter of whether the state has an exclusive right to impose and coercively enforce binding duties on its citizens with its dictates. For the purpose of this paper, we assume that the state has the political legitimacy to undertake actions to protect the public's health. We shall only be concerned with which restrictive public health measures are morally justified and the conditions that need to be satisfied for such measures to be morally legitimate. This notion of the morally legitimacy of public health action is not arbitrary or unfounded. For instance, Gostin (2003) and Trotter (2007) employ a similar notion of legitimacy.

The question of moral justification is conceptually distinct and prior to the question of moral legitimacy. It is distinct because the question of moral justification is concerned with the act of quarantine or isolation *per se* (i.e., whether or not such measures are themselves morally right or wrong), while the question of moral legitimacy is concerned with how such restrictive measures are implemented (that is, whether or not the acts are performed in a way that is morally right or wrong). In contrasting these notions, we can say that the justification question concerns *what* actions the state can permissibly undertake in order to protect public health from the threat of contagion, while the legitimacy question concerns *how* these actions ought to be undertaken. Justification is conceptually prior in virtue of the fact that the legitimacy of public health action depends on satisfying particular conditions of implementing a public health measure that is already morally justified. On this view, public health action can be morally legitimate if and only if it is morally justified. As a consequence, although there can be morally justifiable public health action that is morally illegitimate, there cannot be morally legitimate public health action that is morally unjustifiable.

It is important to understand how these notions relate to each other. Morally illegitimate public health action can, in some circumstances, render the action morally unjustifiable. In the case of restrictive measures, the morally illegitimate implementation of such measures can have a corresponding effect on its moral justification; such that the state could conceivably lose such measures as a viable moral option open to advance its public health goals. The illegitimate implementation of restrictive measures can affect its justification in two ways.

On the one hand, the illegitimacy of public health actions can render such acts unjustifiable for empirical reasons. For instance, presume a particular public health action involving restrictive measures is morally justifiable on the grounds that it prevents harm and that one condition of the legitimacy of such measures is that it is effective. If the use of quarantine were employed in an arbitrary or inconsistent manner, which had the consequence of rendering the measures ineffective in preventing transmission of the contagion, then the illegitimate use of quarantine would prevent such interventions from preventing harm to the population and, thus, would render the moral justification for employing quarantine in the first place invalid.

On the other hand, the illegitimacy of public health action can render such acts unjustifiable for normative reasons. For instance, the use of restrictive measures might be employed in a discriminatory manner or in a way that violates another one of the state's obligations. The use of restrictive measures on Chinese immigrants in San

Francisco in response to the bubonic plague and the influenza pandemic in the late 19th and early 20th centuries would be an example of this (*Wong Wai v. Williamson*; *Jew Ho v. Williamson*; Shah 2001). In such cases, even if restrictive measures are implemented in a way that makes them measurably successful overall in containing the contagion, the fact that such an implementation failed to protect vulnerable populations or resulted in some proportion of the population suffering intolerably can render such measures morally unjustifiable. Returning again to the previous example, in which the moral justification for the use of restrictive measures is harm prevention, the morally illegitimate employment of quarantine—which denies a segment of the population the ability to benefit from the good of public health, for instance, as a result of discrimination—results in such measures failing to prevent harm to those individuals and fails to meet the justificatory burden for employing such measures.

Even though the term "legitimacy" is often used synonymously with "justification" (or even "acceptability" or "permissibility") in public health, we think there is an important philosophical distinction to preserve here and that it also provides further reason to investigate the putative conditions of the legitimacy of public health action. It is clear that any robust account of the use of restrictive measures in public health will have to provide a defence of the legitimacy conditions of these measures, how far their scope extends, and which of these conditions will be necessary, sufficient or (in some combination) jointly necessary and sufficient. Elucidating and analysing the different conditions of the legitimacy of public health action is not only important in itself—we need to ensure such conditions have an adequate theoretical grounding and are able to be articulated with sufficient clarity so as to provide practical guidance to public health officials—but also in terms of how these conditions relate to the moral justification of public health action.

While such an investigation and defense is beyond the remit of this paper, it is reasonable to believe that there are likely a number of conditions for the legitimacy of public health action. These conditions will be scientific, empirical, political/legal or ethical. Some of these conditions will be necessary, while others will be sufficient. For instance, conditions such as effectiveness (Kass 2001;Childress et al. 2001; Childress and Bernheim 2003; Gostin 2003; Verma et al. 2004), necessity (Childress et al. 2001; Childress and Bernheim 2003; Gostin 2003), proportionality (Childress et al. 2001; Childress and Bernheim 2003; Gostin 2003; Singer et al. 2003; Wilkinson 2007), and least infringement (Childress et al. Childress et al., 2001; Childress and Bernheim 2003; Wilkinson 2007) are often cited as putative conditions of moral legitimacy in normative frameworks and policy documents for public health action. Other conditions also cited include fairness (Kass 2001; Childress and Bernheim 2003), impartiality (Childress and Bernheim 2003), and public justification (Childress and Bernheim 2003; Trotter 2007).

## Reciprocity as a Legitimacy Condition for the Use of Restrictive Measures

Surprisingly, reciprocity is rarely cited as a condition of the legitimacy for public health action, especially in relation to the use of restrictive measures (Upshur 2002; Singer et al. 2003; Joint Centre for Bioethics 2005; Baylis et al. 2008; Selgelid 2008). Moreover, while reciprocity is also starting to be mentioned in some policy documents, for example in the UK (Nuffield Council on Bioethics 2007; Department of Health, United Kingdom 2007), it is not receiving the attention it warrants.

Reciprocity is generally understood to be based on the notion of mutual regard and fair play. Reciprocity demands an appropriate balancing of the benefits and burdens of the social cooperation necessary to obtain the good of public health. While the relevance of reciprocity is gaining further awareness within the literature, there is much philosophical work to be done on how we should understand the concept and scope of reciprocity in public health ethics and law. Our contribution to this volume is part of a larger project (Viens and Upshur, in preparation), and here we can only provide a partial account of reciprocity in public health ethics. In this paper, we shall not defend a substantive theory of reciprocity, but instead restrict our argument to the general notion of what is required by reciprocity within the context of public health action involving restrictive measures.

Reciprocity requires that one return the good one has received, or responds to harms performed, in a fitting manner. In the context of public health action a number of goods may be relevant, but we will focus on the good of public health. Reciprocity requires that we compensate those disproportionately burdened by complying with restrictive measures and make restitution to those individuals wronged by being subjected to unfair or intolerable treatment. Reciprocity not only requires that individuals should not be overly burdened by measures to protect public health, but also that individuals are supported in a way that allows them to fulfil their obligations. Reciprocity should be considered a condition of legitimate public health action in communicable disease control because it grants individual and societal interests equal and supporting weight as goods, and provides a common ground for the discharge of moral obligations and acceptance of moral responsibility associated with protecting public health.[2]

In the context of public health action involving restrictive measures, reciprocity will be an important ethical consideration for both how individuals ought to act in the context of a restrictive measures and the state's reasons for employing such measures.

For individuals, reciprocation requires that agents contribute in a way that promotes or returns the goods they have received (in this case, public health), or to prevent inflicting harms on others which affect participating in that good. This reciprocation contribution may take on many forms. One is the obligation not to infect others (cf. Harris and Holm 1993, 1995; Verweij 2005). Individuals have reciprocal obligations to not knowingly put others at risk of being infected by a communicable disease when avoidable. Another is the obligation to show deference to instructions from public health authorities and for individuals to, for example, sequester themselves in their homes and not attend public gatherings. Another is the obligation of individuals, such as physicians, to act as first responders, providing service to protect or restore public health.

For the state, reciprocation requires that it employ public health measures in such a way that those individuals who experience a burden as a result of such measures in order to obtain the good of public health should be supported in a number of ways by the state. Individuals, for instance, who experience a loss of freedom or autonomy as a result of restrictive measures must be adequately supported when experiencing such losses. This may take the form of a system of compensation for missed work, providing access to food and other necessities for those quarantined and isolated, assistance for first responders to balance their personal and professional obligations, amongst a number of other considerations. Reciprocation obligations also require the state to ensure there are several legal protections (both substantive and procedural) in place for those who are subjected to restrictive measures, such as the right to council, the right to a hearing, a right to appeal quarantine and detention decisions, and relief from punishment for non-compliance or violation of restrictive measures on judicial review. The state is additionally obligated to communicate all relevant information regarding the necessity of the restriction, including the expected duration of restriction and the precise time of reassessment of restrictions. Such orders should never be open-ended.

In employing restrictive measures in an effort to protect public health, in order to be morally legitimate the state must ensure that its public health action reflects that individuals are owed a fitting and appropriate return for what they have given up in order to secure the benefit of public health—just as the state is owed a fitting and appropriate return by individuals for their efforts to secure the public's health. Moreover, in understanding reciprocity as a requirement on both individual and state action, different circumstances may warrant that appropriate corrective measures can be undertaken in response to failures to reciprocate. For instance, in cases of individual failures of reciprocation, the state may be

[0] While it is claimed that reciprocity is one of the conditions of legitimacy of public health action, we shall remain neutral on the question of what processes or features confer legitimacy on public health action. Accepting our argument about reciprocity as a condition moral legitimacy leaves it open that moral legitimacy may be conferred on public health measures by democratic processes, legal authority, reasonable endorsement/rejection, etcetera. For instance, Trotter (2007, 30–7) maintains that we need to distinguish between two senses of legitimacy. On the one hand, there is *good reasons legitimacy*, which is "satisfied by well-formed arguments that show how a proposed intervention makes ethical, political and scientific sense" (Trotter 2007, 30). On the other hand, there is *public justification legitimacy*, which "results from a process in which proposed interventions and their rationale are properly discussed, articulated, marketed, explained, or otherwise brought to life before the general public" (ibid). Our focus shall be firmly with the former, though we do not discount the importance of the latter. Indeed, part of the robustness of our account of reciprocity is that it can accommodate both senses of legitimacy.

able to hold people responsible, blameworthy or liable, to restrict or coerce people into reciprocating, or denying compensation for those who fail to reciprocate. In cases of failures of reciprocation on the part of the state, individuals may be able to seek restitution for wrongdoing, or possibly engage in justified civil disobedience.

Of course, in addition to clarifying our obligations and responsibilities, we also need to pay attention to the circumstances that allow us to fulfill our reciprocation obligations. In particular, the reciprocation obligations of individuals and the state will hold in situations where communities are structured such that barriers to discharging those obligations are removed or mitigated. We can only reasonably expect reciprocation obligations to be discharged in circumstances where doing so does not leave individuals or institutions overburdened or unreasonably disadvantaged (cf. Powers and Faden 2006).

## Reciprocity as a Basis for Motivating Support and Compliance with Restrictive Measures

Our primary concern has been to argue for the importance of reciprocity as a condition of moral legitimacy for public health action involving restrictive measures. However, there is also an important motivational component that must be kept in mind when seeking support and compliance with the use of restrictive measures. Since the success of public health interventions can often depend on the public's support and compliance with the measures undertaken, the state also needs to be concerned with employing public health measures in a way that generally leads citizens to support policies and accept the decisions required to secure the public's health.

Clearly, the capacity to motivate individuals is not itself a condition of the moral legitimacy of public health action. It is hoped that individuals, in seeing that justified public health actions involving restrictive measures are legitimately implemented, will be motivated to support and comply with such measures; however, this need not be the case. There can be morally legitimate uses of restrictive measures that fail to gain support and compliance, and there can be morally illegitimate uses of restrictive measures that can, and have, gained support and compliance. Nevertheless, it may be the case that particular conditions of the moral legitimacy of restrictive measures may have a more efficacious effect on motivating individuals. While predicting how individuals will be motivated to act in the face of the threat of contagion is difficult, there is evidence to suggest that reciprocity may play an important role in motivating support and compliance with public health measures, especially those involving restrictive measures.

Within the literature, it has been demonstrated that reciprocity has a powerful and complex influence on how individuals behave. That being said, it is worth noting that different literatures—evolutionary biology, psychology, sociology and economics—do not always employ the same notion of reciprocity. However, the aspects of reciprocal behaviour they focus on can still have relevance for the issue of motivating support and compliance with restrictive measures.

Reciprocity is an influential social mechanism for voluntary cooperation between individuals and within society. Benefits provided to individuals—sometimes even unsolicited or unwanted benefits—are often reciprocated, and reciprocity can have both conscious and unconscious effects on how individuals go about discharging their obligations (Gouldner 1960; Pfaff et al. 2008). In the context of complying with restrictive measures, reciprocity would seem to have an important connection to both self-focused motivations (for example harm reduction, fear of negative evaluation) and other-focused motivations (such as empathy and shame) for compliance, or negative emotions for non-compliance (O'Keefe and Figgé 1997, 1999; Millar 2002; Viens 2008).

There are two broad ways in which we could understand reciprocity as a basis for supporting and complying with restrictive measures (Tyler 2006). On an instrumentalist view of motivation, individuals will be motivated to support and comply with public health measures if there is some direct benefit associated with compliance or sanction for non-compliance with the measures. On such a view, reciprocity could play a role in motivating compliance by, for example, compensating those individuals burdened by not being able to go to work or fining/detaining those individuals who fail to observe isolation orders and violate their reciprocal obligation not to infect others. While there are conceptual problems with equating reciprocity as being merely a tit-for-tat notion, it is evident how a tit-for-tat model would fit within an instrumentalist view of motivating compliance with public health measures.

On a normative view of motivation, individuals will be motivated to support and comply with public health measures if they regard such measures as morally appropriate, as opposed to contributing simply to their self-interest. On this view, reciprocity could play a role in motivating compliance because, for instance, the employment of restrictive measures is implemented in a way that is viewed as fair. In the 2003 SARS outbreak in Toronto, studies reported that individuals cited "civic duty" as their primary motivation for supporting and complying with requests by public health officials for work and home quarantine. While citing this obligation as the primary motivation would support a normative view, it is not clear that such a motivation had anything to do with the moral legitimacy of quarantine itself. However, it is quite plausible to think that illegitimate employment of restrictive measures, like work and home quarantines, will either vitiate that civic obligation or have another obligation (say to one's family) override their civic obligation.

We do not believe either view is exclusively correct. Individuals can be motivated by both instrumental and intrinsic considerations—often a combination of both.[3] However, it is relevant that reciprocity can address both the self-regarding and other-regarding basis of motivation.

Moreover, there is reason to believe that there is a mutually supportive connection between reciprocity and trust, which will be extremely important for support and compliance with restrictive measures (see, for instance, Meeker 1984; Berg et al. 1995; Ostrom and Walker 2005). In the context of a public health emergency, such as an influenza pandemic, individuals will almost certainly experience burdens and disadvantages associated with public health efforts seeking to mitigate the threat of contagion, and if those experiences become overly burdensome or unreasonably disadvantageous it will most likely lead to a reduction in trust in the state and its public health officials, and it could have a corresponding negative effect on the support and compliance individuals will have for the restrictive measures. To be sure, more research is needed on the relationship between reciprocity and considerations such as trust, allegiance, and deference, to help better understand the complexities of interpersonal and group behaviour in the context of contagion requiring restrictive measures.

In a recent survey more than 75% of Americans said they would co-operate with restrictive public health measures during an influenza pandemic, such as refraining from using public transit and practicing social distancing, by not going to school, malls, and places of worship (Blendon et al. 2006a; also cf. Blendon et al. 2006b). Quite surprisingly, 94% of respondents said they would sequester themselves at home for seven to ten days if they were infected with influenza. According to a substantial proportion of respondents, while their primary motivation for complying with restrictive measures are not instrumental in nature, there is a pervasive concern that complying with restrictive measures will lead them to experience various problems, including an inability to obtain health services and medications for themselves and care for elderly or disabled family members. Thus, it may be the case that reciprocity will be important not only for providing the initial motivation to support and comply with restrictive measures (before its negative effects are felt), but also for sustaining compliance when the force of the normative considerations that initially lead to an attitude of support begins to lose some of its motivational force.

A study of the SARS outbreak in Toronto revealed that the views on compliance and the means to achieve it varied greatly (Bensimon 2008). There were many contradictions, often by the same participant, clearly illustrating that many were conflicted about how to ensure compliance. In contrast, there was no debate regarding what most thought would greatly facilitate voluntary compliance: that of the

[0] As Koller (2007, 203) has so aptly put the point: "The motivating force of moral norms, however, has its limits too. In general, its strength depends on the extent of reciprocity of human interaction. Therefore, a public morality needs a social world in which individuals feel bound together by ties of social solidarity, a shared interest in mastering their problems of existence cooperatively, based upon an effective social practice. Without such an idea, we shall hardly succeed in establishing a widely acknowledged political and legal order, since the voice of morality will not be strong enough to gain attention against the parties' selfish interest in their struggle for power and benefit. It is, therefore, an important task to create and preserve a climate of social solidarity in order to bring forth the moral virtues without which a well-functional legal order cannot exist."

provision of services and adequate care. Indeed, just as participants vigorously supported quarantine in virtue of the common good, virtually all participants felt that providing support to those in quarantine was an obligation owed to them. It was thought to be a *sine qua non* condition for the implementation of quarantine.

Reciprocity should also be a key consideration in workplace. In the 2006 US survey, predicted co-operation with public health measures involving work restrictions was found to be the lowest. While 57% of respondents maintained that they would comply with requests from public health officials to stay home from work—even if their employers told them to come to work—approximately 35% said they would not comply with such restrictions and would go to work anyway. Unsurprisingly, it was found that the longer public health officials ask individuals to stay away from work the lower the level of compliance because individuals are only able to sustain financial losses for short periods of time. If the state is going to be viewed as fulfilling its reciprocation obligations, there will evidently be a need to provide compensation directly to workers in exchange for staying home, or to provide support (e.g., low-cost loans) for businesses to help pay their workers who are staying home and to keep their doors open or to recover some of their lost revenue.

One final issue to keep in mind is that the role reciprocity may play in increasing support and compliance for restrictive measures need not be complete across the entire population. We should not expect that 100% of the population will voluntarily comply even if the state fulfills its reciprocal obligations; nor is it likely that such a level of compliance is needed to ensure the public health action is successful. What matters is whether reciprocity can contribute to providing individuals with sufficient motivation to comply with restrictive measures at a rate that is adequate to ensure the success of the public health action. For instance, during the SARS outbreak in Toronto in 2003, Toronto Public Health officials reported that only 22 orders for mandatory detainment were necessary amongst the approximately 30,000 people who were voluntary quarantined. While it is impossible to quantify the effect of reciprocity in such situations, it is plausible that the state meeting its reciprocal obligations helped to motivate a majority of people to voluntarily comply with restrictive measures and provided a basis of support for coercion of those who failed to comply voluntarily.

## Conclusion

In some ways, recognizing the importance of reciprocity within public health interventions is reminiscent of the 1791 Poverty Committee of the National Assembly in revolutionary France whereby the notion of the "citizen-patients" was employed, in which individuals undertook the reciprocal obligation of supporting and complying with public health measures because it was morally right and in order to keep themselves healthy (Weiner 2001).

Some individuals assume that the use of restrictive measures will only take place when particular conditions of reciprocity are met. For instance, according to Cetron and Landwirth (2005, 326), "[p]rinciples of modern quarantine and social distancing limit their use to situations involving highly dangerous and contagious diseases and when resources are reliably available to implement and maintain the measures". We know from historical uses of restrictive measures, and even from assessments of current capabilities for dealing with public health emergencies involving highly dangerous and contagious diseases, that the employment of such measures cannot be guaranteed to always occur with adequate resources and facilities in place or administered in an appropriate way (see for instance, Markel 1999; Coker 2000; Batlan 2007).

The specific role of reciprocity as a criterion for adjudicating the morality of public health actions, especially in contexts of public health emergencies, still requires greater discussion and analysis. This paper provides a contribution to this need and posits some philosophical distinctions that should guide this process. We have argued that the morality of restrictive measures depends on ethical, political/legal and scientific considerations. Moreover, we have argued that reciprocity can help assure support and compliance with restrictive measures. Charles Chapin may have been correct that restrictions on individual liberty undertaken in order to protect the public's health may leave some citizens aggrieved; however by ensuring reciprocity is a condition of the restriction's legitimacy we have good reason to believe such restrictions will be more likely viewed as morally permissible and worth complying with.

**Acknowledgements** This research was supported by the Canadian Institutes of Health Research. Dr Upshur is supported by the Canada Research Chair in Primary Care Research.

## References

Ackerman, B. 2006. *Before the next attack: Preserving civil liberties in an age of terrorism*. New Haven: Yale University Press.

Batlan, F.J. 2007. Law in the time of cholera: Disease, state power, and quarantines past and future. *Temple Law Review* 80: 53–122.

Baylis, F., N.P. Kenny, and S. Sherwin. 2008. A relational account of public health ethics. *Public Health Ethics* 1: 196–209. doi:10.1093/phe/phn025.

Bensimon, C.M. 2008. Communicable disease control in the new millennium: A qualitative inquiry on the legitimate use of restrictive measures. (PhD Dissertation, University of Toronto).

Bensimon, C.M., and Ross E.G. Upshur. 2007. Evidence and effectiveness in decision-making for quarantine. *American Journal of Public Health* 97(Supplement 1): 44–8.

Berg, J., J. Dickhaut, and K. McCabe. 1995. Trust, reciprocity, and social history. *Games and Economic Behavior* 10: 122–142. doi:10.1006/game.1995.1027.

Blendon, R.J., J.M. Benson, and K.J.Weldon 2006a. Pandemic influenza and the public: Survey findings. Cambridge, MA: Harvard School of Public Health Project on the Public and Biological Security, available at: http://www.hsph.harvard.edu/panflu/IOM_Avian_flu.ppt. Accessed 17 March 2009.

Blendon, R.J., C.M. DesRoches, M.S. Cetron, J.M. Benson, T. Meinhardt, and W. Pollard. 2006a. Attitudes toward the use of quarantine in a public health emergency in four countries. *Health Affairs* 25: w15–w25. doi:10.1377/hlthaff.25.w15.

Boggio, A., M. Zignol, E. Jaramillo, P. Nunn, G. Pinet, and M. Raviglione. 2008. Limitations on human rights: are they justifiable to reduce the burden of TB in the era of MDR- and XDR-TB? *Health and Human Rights* 10: 1–6.

Cetron, M., and J. Landwirth. 2005. Public health and ethical considerations in planning for quarantine. *The Yale Journal of Biology and Medicine* 78: 329–334.

Chapin, C.V. 1894. Pleasures and hopes of the health officer. In *Papers of Charles V. Chapin, M.D*, ed. F. P. Gorham. New York: The Commonwealth Fund.

Childress, J.F., and R.G. Bernheim. 2003. Beyond the liberal and communitarian impasse: A framework and vision for public health. *Florida Law Review* 55: 1191–1219.

Childress, J.F., R.R. Faden, R.D. Gaare, L.O. Gostin, J. Kahn, R.J. Bonnie, N.E. Kass, A.C. Mastroianni, J.D. Moreno, and P. Nieburg. 2001. Public health ethics: Mapping the terrain. *The Journal of Law, Medicine & Ethics* 30: 170–178. doi:10.1111/j.1748-720X.2002.tb00384.x.

Coker, R. 2000. *From chaos to coercion: Detention and the control of tuberculosis*. New York: St. Martin.

Coker, R., M. Thomas, K. Lock, and R. Martin. 2007. Detention and the evolving threat of tuberculosis: Evidence, ethics, and law. *The Journal of Law, Medicine & Ethics* 35: 609–615.

Department of Health, United Kingdom. 2007. Responding to pandemic influenza: The ethical framework for policy and planning. http://www.dh.gov.uk/en/Publicationsandstatistics/Publications/PublicationsPolicyAndGuidance/DH_080751. Accessed 17 March 2009.

Dyzenhaus, D. 2006. *The constitution of law: Legality in a time of emergency*. Cambridge: Cambridge University Press.

Edmundson, W.A. 1998. Legitimate authority without political obligation. *Law and Philosophy* 17: 43–60.

Enhorn v. Sweden (2005), European Court of Human Rights (application no. 56529/00)

Gostin, L.O. 2003. When terrorism threatens health: How far are limitations on human rights justified? *The Journal of Law, Medicine & Ethics* 31: 524–528. doi:10.1111/j.1748-720X.2003.tb00120.x.

Gouldner, A.W. 1960. The norm of reciprocity: A preliminary statement. *American Sociological Review* 25: 161–178. doi:10.2307/2092623.

Harris, J., and S. Holm. 1993. If only AIDS were different!. *The Hastings Center Report* 23: 6–13. doi:10.2307/3562917.

Harris, J., and S. Holm. 1995. Is there a moral obligation not to infect others? *BMJ (Clinical Research Ed.)* 311: 1215–1217.

Ignatieff, M. 2005. *The lesser evil: Political ethics in an age of terror*. Edinburgh: Edinburgh University Press.

Jacobson v. Massachusetts. 1905, 197 US 11

Jew Ho v. Williamson. (1900), 103 F. 10 (C.C.N.D. Cal.)

Kass, N.E. 2001. An ethics framework for public health. *American Journal of Public Health* 91: 1776–1782. doi:10.2105/AJPH.91.11.1776.

Koller, P. 2007. Law, morality and virtue. In *In Working virtue: Virtue ethics and contemporary moral problems*, ed. R.L. Walker, and P.J. Ivanhoe, 191–206. Oxford: Oxford University Press.

Markel, H. 1999. *Quarantine! East European Jewish immigrants and the New York City epidemics of 1892*. Baltimore: Johns Hopkins University Press.

Meeker, B.F. 1984. Cooperative orientation, trust, and reciprocity. *Human Relations* 37: 225–243. doi:10.1177/001872678403700304.

Millar, M. 2002. Effects of a guilt induction and guilt reduction on door-in-the-face. *Communication Research* 29: 666–680. doi:10.1177/009365002237831.

Nuffield Council on Bioethics. 2007. *Public health: Ethical issues*. London: Nuffield Council on Bioethics.

O'Keefe, D.J., and M. Figgé. 1997. A guilt-based explanation of the door-in-the-face influence strategy. *Human Communication Research* 24: 64–81. doi:10.1111/j.1468-2958.1997.tb00587.x.

Ostrom, E., and J. Walker (Eds.). 2005. *Trust and reciprocity: Interdisciplinary lessons for experimental research*. New York: Russell Sage Foundation.

Parmet, W.E. 2008. J. S. Mill and the American law of quarantine. *Public Health Ethics* 1: 210–222. doi:10.1093/phe/phn029.

Pfaff, D., M. Kavaliers, and E. Choleris. 2008. Mechanisms underlying an ability to behave ethically. *American Journal of Bioethics-Neuroscience* 8: 10–19. doi:10.1080/15265160802179994.

Powers, M., and R. Faden. 2006. *Social justice: The moral foundations of public health and health policy.* Oxford: Oxford University Press.

Selgelid, M. 2008. Ethics, tuberculosis and globalization. *Public Health Ethics* 1: 10–20. doi:10.1093/phe/phn001.

Shah, N. 2001. *Contagious divides: Epidemics and race in San Francisco's Chinatown.* Berkeley: University of California Press.

Singer, P.A., S. R. Benatar, M. Bernstein, A.S. Daar, B. M. Dickens, S.K. MacRae, R.E.G. Upshur, L. Wright, and R. Z. Shaul. 2003. Ethics and SARS: Lessons from Toronto. *BMJ (Clinical Research Ed.)* 327: 1342–1344. doi:10.1136/bmj.327.7427.1342.

Singh, J.A., R. Upshur, and N. Padayatchi. 2007. XDR-TB in South Africa: No time for denial or complacency. *PLoS Medicine* 4: e50. doi:10.1371/journal.pmed.0040050.

Simmons, A.J. 1999. Justification and legitimacy. *Ethics* 109: 739–771. doi:10.1086/233944.

Taylor, C. 1985. Legitimation crisis? In *Philosophy and the Human Sciences: Philosophical Papers 2*, 248–88. Cambridge: Cambridge University Press.

Taylor, C. 1994. Alternative futures: Legitimacy, identity, and alienation in late twentieth century Canada. In *Communitarianism: A new public ethics*, ed. Markate Daly. Belmont, CA: Wadsworth.

Trotter, G. 2007. *The ethics of coercion in mass casualty medicine.* Baltimore: Johns Hopkins University Press.

Tyler, T.R. 2006. *Why people obey the law.* Princeton: Princeton University Press.

University of Toronto Joint Centre for Bioethics Pandemic Ethics Working Group. 2005. *Stand on guard for thee: Ethical considerations in preparedness planning for pandemic influenza.* Toronto: Joint Centre for Bioethics, available at: www.jointcentreforbioethics.ca/people/documents/upshur_stand_guard.pdf. Accessed 17 March 2009.

Upshur, R.E. 2002. Principles for the justification of public health intervention. *Canadian Journal of Public Health* 93: 101–103.

Verma, G., R.E.G. Upshur, E. Rea, and S.R. Benatar. 2004. Critical reflections on evidence, ethics and effectiveness in the management of tuberculosis: public health and global perspectives. *BMC Medical Ethics* 5: 2. doi:10.1186/1472-6939-5-2.

Verweij, M. 2005. Obligatory precautions against infection. *Bioethics* 19: 323–335. doi:10.1111/j.1467-8519.2005.00446.x.

Viens, A.M. *Public health emergencies*, in preparation.

Viens, A.M. 2008. Public health, ethical behaviour and reciprocity. *American Journal of Bioethics–Neuroscience* 8: 1–3. doi:10.1080/15265160802180059.

Viens, A.M., and R.E.G. Upshur. *The concept of reciprocity*, in preparation.

Weiner, D.B. 2001. *The citizen-patient in revolutionary and imperial Paris.* Baltimore: Johns Hopkins University Press.

Wilkinson, T.M. 2007. Contagious disease and self-defence. *Res Publica (Liverpool, England)* 13: 339–359. doi:10.1007/s11158-007-9024-0.

Williamson v. Wong Wai. (1900), 103 F. Rep. 10

# Part V: Opt-Out HIV Testing

Bioethical Inquiry (2009) 6:229–233
DOI 10.1007/s11673-009-9147-4

# Increasing Knowledge of HIV Infection Status through Opt-Out Testing

## Opt-Out HIV Testing

**Harold W. Jaffe**

Received: 6 August 2008 / Accepted: 11 March 2009 / Published online: 2 April 2009


**Abstract** The diagnosis of HIV infection is the point of entry for treatment and prevention services, yet many infected persons in both developed and developing countries remain undiagnosed. To reduce the number of undiagnosed infections, a variety of expanded testing policies have been recommended, including opt-out testing. This testing model assumes that in populations of increased HIV prevalence, voluntary testing should be offered to all patients seen in healthcare settings and performed unless patients specifically decline. While this approach raises ethical issues concerning "voluntariness", access to care, and stigma, the potential benefits of opt-out testing far outweigh its potential adverse effects.

**Keywords** HIV · Diagnosis · Bioethics

### Introduction

In this article, I will outline the case for expanded testing for infection with the human immunodeficiency virus (HIV) as a key strategy for controlling the HIV/AIDS epidemic. I first briefly describe the history of HIV testing policies in the United States, with a focus on recommendations made by the United States Centers for Disease Control and Prevention (CDC), and then examine testing policies in sub-Saharan Africa and in the United Kingdom. In particular, I discuss the "opt-out" approach to HIV testing and the ethical questions that it raises.

H. W. Jaffe (✉)
Department of Public Health, University of Oxford,
Old Road Campus, Headington,
Oxford OX3 7LF, UK
e-mail: harold.jaffe@dphpc.ox.ac.uk

### A Brief History of HIV Testing

In 1985, only 2 years after the discovery of HIV, the U.S. Food and Drug Administration licensed a test to detect antibodies to the virus. The first use of the test was to screen donated blood and plasma to prevent HIV infection in transfusion recipients and persons with hemophilia (Centers for Disease Control 1985). Because of a concern that individuals wishing to know their infection status might seek testing in blood banks, "alternative test sites" were established with provision for confidential or anonymous—that is, with no name identifiers—testing.

Initially, there was strong opposition to the use of the test outside blood and plasma collection settings. This opposition, which came primarily from gay rights advocacy groups, was based on the belief that little benefit and much harm could come from testing. No treatment was available for HIV, and persons at highest risk for infection in the United States, men who have sex with men (MSM), already faced discrimination. Further, the ability of public health agencies to keep test results confidential was questioned. The slogan of the anti-test movement was "No test is best".

In the medical community, these concerns about testing formed the basis of what has been called "AIDS exceptionalism" (Bayer and Fairchild 2006). Whereas consent for routine diagnostic testing was considered to be part of general consent for medical care, specific written informed consent with pre- and post-test counseling was required for HIV testing. In addition, the language of the consent forms often served to discourage testing by emphasizing the negative consequences of a positive test result. The additional requirements of the testing procedure and the negative messages about the test served to discourage providers from offering the test and patients from accepting it.

Attitudes and policies regarding HIV testing remained relatively static for most of the next decade. In 1994, however, a clinical trial showed that the risk of mother-to-child HIV transmission could be reduced by about two-thirds by treating infected pregnant women with zidovudine (Connor et al. 1994). As summarized by Bayer and Fairchild (2006), this finding led several U.S. medical organizations to endorse expanded HIV testing of pregnant women by relaxing some of the most stringent testing requirements. By 2001, the U.S. Public Health Service had recommended that all pregnant women in the United States be tested for HIV infection as a routine part of prenatal care (Centers for Disease Control and Prevention 2001a). Further, either oral or written consent were considered acceptable, and women had the right to refuse testing.

The case for changing testing policy more generally was strengthened later in the 1990s with the increasing availability of highly active antiretroviral therapy, a combination of drugs which dramatically increased the survival of HIV-infected patients. To take advantage of this therapeutic advance, persons needed to know if they were infected. Yet, additional CDC guidelines published in 2001 continued to advocate risk-based testing; that is, they recommended that the offer of testing to persons other than pregnant women should be based upon a judgment of their clinical or behavioral risk for infection (Centers for Disease Control and Prevention 2001b). An underlying assumption of the guidelines was that providers would either know or be able to ascertain if their clients were MSM, had injected drugs, or had multiple heterosexual partners.

Because an estimated 25% of HIV-infected persons in the United States were thought to be undiagnosed, CDC recommendations published in 2003 advocated HIV testing "as part of routine medical care on the same voluntary basis as other diagnostic and screening tests" (Centers for Disease Control and Prevention 2003). Further, pre-test prevention counseling was no longer required. It was not until 2006, however, that CDC modified the guideline for routine screening by recommending an opt-out approach, which was noted to result in higher testing rates in pregnant women than other approaches (Centers for Disease Control and Prevention 2006). Additional support for this modification came from studies showing that high-risk sexual behavior tends to decrease in persons after they become aware of their HIV infection (Marks et al. 2005).

## Opt-Out Testing

The opt-out approach, based on the CDC guideline, meant that patients would be told that HIV testing would be done unless the patient declined. Consent was still required, but it could be obtained either orally or in writing, and no separate consent form for HIV testing was recommended. Prevention counseling was no longer required as part of the testing procedure. The guidelines summarized in Table 1 would apply in all settings unless the prevalence of undiagnosed HIV infection was known to be <0.1%. Once infected persons were diagnosed, they would be referred for appropriate clinical and prevention services.

Because of the much higher prevalence of HIV and the much lower awareness of infection status (estimated to be no more than 10–20%), expanding HIV testing through an opt-out approach could be expected to have a much bigger impact in sub-Saharan Africa than in the United States. Increasing the rate of diagnosis of HIV infection in this region has taken on special importance at a time when major initiatives are leading to the rollout of antiretroviral therapy (ART) in developing countries. By the end of 2007, about 3 million individuals living in low- and middle-

**Table 1** HIV Screening guidelines for the United States

- Opt-out HIV screening is recommended for patients in all healthcare settings
- People at high risk for HIV infection should be screened for HIV at least annually
- Separate written consent for HIV testing is not required; general consent for medical care should be considered sufficient to encompass consent for HIV testing
- Prevention counseling should not be required with HIV diagnostic testing or as part of HIV screening programs in healthcare settings.

Adapted from "Revised recommendations for HIV testing of adults, adolescents, and pregnant women in health-care settings" (Centers for Disease Control and Prevention 2006).

income countries were receiving ART (WHO, UNAIDS, & UNICEF 2008).

Among sub-Saharan Africa countries, Botswana, a country with one of the highest rates of HIV infection in the world, took the lead in recommending routine opt-out HIV testing for all patients accessing medical care (Weiser et al. 2006). Subsequently, the World Health Organization and the Joint United Nations Programme on AIDS published guidelines which also recommended provider-initiated, opt-out HIV testing for all adults and adolescents seen in health care facilities of countries with "generalized epidemics" (defined as an HIV prevalence of >1% in pregnant women) (WHO & UAIDS 2007). A more targeted testing approach was recommended in countries with concentrated and low-level epidemics.

Although an estimated one-third of HIV-infected persons in the U.K. remain undiagnosed (Health Protection Agency 2006), the approach to testing in the U.K. has been somewhat cautious. Opt-out testing is recommended for routine use only in genitourinary medicine clinics and for pregnant women attending antenatal care. My colleagues and I put forward a case to examine the feasibility of expanding opt-out testing in medical facilities that are known to serve people at increased risk for infection (Hamill et al. 2007). In the U.K., those groups would particularly include MSM and recent immigrants from sub-Saharan Africa. The Chief Medical Officer and the Chief Nursing Officer of the U.K. subsequently issued a "Dear Colleague" letter in which they pointed out that late diagnoses accounted for at least 35% of HIV-related deaths in the U.K. The letter concluded with the request to "Please offer your patients an HIV test if they may have been exposed to HIV infection and recommend to them that they should accept testing" (Donaldson and Beasley 2007).

## Ethical Concerns

Given the increasing momentum towards making opt-out HIV testing the standard of practice in many medical settings, what are the arguments against it? One key ethical issue concerns the "voluntariness" of opt-out testing (Rennie and Behets 2006). Although all formal recommendations for opt-out testing emphasize the right of patients to decline the test, some patients will almost certainly not understand that they will be tested or believe that they must accept the test offer (Gostin 2008). Weiser et al. conducted a population-based survey in Botswana following the introduction of national opt-out testing (2006). Although 81% of respondents were in favor of the new testing policy, 68% felt that they could not refuse the test.

Another important testing issue concerns access to care. As previously noted, one of the main drivers towards expanded testing in recent years has been expanded access to ART. Yet despite rapid progress in expanding HIV treatment programs, only about 31% of persons needing treatment in low- and middle-income countries were receiving it by the end of 2007 (WHO, UNAIDS, & UNICEF 2008). Diagnosing HIV infection without being able to provide care creates a serious ethical problem. A more subtle aspect of this problem exists in the U.K, where testing Africans would likely detect previously undiagnosed infection. However, some of these persons may be illegal immigrants or failed asylum seekers and are not entitled to free HIV therapy under the National Health Service.

Although the stigma related to HIV infection has gradually decreased over time, it still exists; and expanding HIV testing may subject newly diagnosed persons to this stigma. In particular, HIV-infected women in low-income countries may experience gender-based discrimination and violence (Rennie and Behets 2006). As noted by Gostin, however, universal HIV testing may also be less stigmatizing than risk-based testing because it does not single out particular individuals or members of particular groups (e.g., MSM) for testing (Gostin 2008).

While all of the aforementioned issues deserve careful consideration in any decision regarding the implementation of an opt-out testing model, the benefits of this approach for most persons far outweigh the risks. Most importantly, modern treatment for HIV saves lives. During the pre-treatment era, almost all HIV-infected persons died as a result of their infection. Median survival from the time of infection to death ranged from about 8–12 years, depending on the age of the individual (Collaborative Group on AIDS Incubation and HIV Survival 2000). With treatment, the excess mortality in infected persons is reduced by more than 90% (Bhaskaran et al. 2008). However, the benefits of treatment for HIV-infected persons cannot be realized unless their infection is diagnosed.

Beyond benefits to the infected individual, early diagnosis and treatment may also serve to reduce HIV transmission. As noted previously, once individuals become aware of their infection, they tend to reduce their high-risk sexual activities. Successful treatment also reduces the concentration of HIV in blood and genital secretions, thus reducing infectiousness. Authors from the WHO have recently suggested that the global impact of HIV/AIDS could be substantially reduced through universal voluntary HIV testing and immediate treatment in countries with generalized epidemics (Granich et al. 2009). If this approach were adopted, the opt-out strategy would certainly facilitate the necessary expansion of HIV testing.

## Conclusion

Ethical issues deserve careful attention in any program designed to expand HIV testing using the opt-out approach. No matter how carefully planned, however, at least some persons will likely be adversely affected by such programs. Nonetheless, that the potential benefits of this approach far outweigh it potential adverse effects. In my view, failure to identify someone whose life is at risk because of undiagnosed HIV infection can no longer be seen as ethical.

## References


Bhaskaran, K., O. Hamouda, S. Sannes, F. Boufassa, A.M. Johnson, P.C. Lambert, et al. 2008. Changes in the risk of death after HIV seroconversion compared with mortality in the general population. *Journal of the American Medical Association* 300: 51–59. doi:10.1001/jama.300.1.51.

Bayer, R., and A.L. Fairchild. 2006. Changing the paradigm for HIV testing—The end of exceptionalism. *The New England Journal of Medicine* 355: 647–649. doi:10.1056/NEJMp068153.

Centers for Disease Control. 1985. Provisional Public Health Service inter-agency recommendations for screening donated blood and plasma for antibody to the virus causing acquired immunodeficiency syndrome. *Morbidity and Mortality Weekly Report* 34: 75–78.

Centers for Disease Control and Prevention. 2001a. Revised recommendations for HIV screening of pregnant women. *MMWR. Recommendations and Reports, 50*(RR19): 59–86.

Centers for Disease Control and Prevention. 2001b. Revised guidelines for HIV counseling, testing, and referral. *MMWR Recommendations and Reports* 50 (RR19): 1–58.

Centers for Disease Control and Prevention. 2003. Advancing HIV prevention: New strategies for a changing epidemic—United States, 2003. *Morbidity and Mortality Weekly Report* 52: 329–332.

Centers for Disease Control and Prevention. 2006. Revised recommendations for HIV testing of adults, adolescents, and pregnant women in health-care settings. *MMWR. Recommendations and Reports, 55*(RR14): 1–17.

Collaborative Group on AIDS Incubation and HIV Survival. 2000. Time from HIV-1 seroconversion to AIDS and death before widespread use of highly-active antiretroviral therapy: A collaborative re-analysis. *Lancet* 355: 1131–1137. doi:10.1016/S0140-6736(00)02061-4.

Connor, E.M., R.S. Sperling, R. Gelber, P. Kiselev, G. Scott, M.J. O'Sullivan, et al. 1994. Reduction of maternal-infant transmission of human immunodeficiency virus type 1 with zidovudine treatment. *The New England Journal of Medicine* 331: 1181–1187. doi:10.1056/NEJM199411033311801.

Donaldson, L., and C. Beasley. 2007. Improving the detection and diagnosis of HIV in non-HIV specialties including primary care. http://www.medfash.org.uk/publications/documents/Improving_the_detection_&_diagnosis_of_HIV_13_09_07.pdf Accessed 1 March 2009.

Gostin, L.O. 2008. HIV screening in health care settings. Public health and civil liberties in conflict. *Journal of the American Medical Association* 296: 2023–2025. doi:10.1001/jama.296.16.2023.

Granich, R.M., C.F. Gilks, C. Dye, K.M. DeCock, and B.G. Williams. 2009. Universal voluntary HIV testing with immediate antiretroviral therapy as a strategy for elimination of HIV transmission: A mathematical model. *Lancet* 373: 48–57. doi:10.1016/S0140-6736(08)61697-9.

Hamill, M., K. Burgoine, F. Farrell, J. Hemelaar, G. Patel, D.E. Welchew, et al. 2007. Time to move towards opt-out testing for HIV in the UK. *British Medical Journal* 334: 1352–1354. doi:10.1136/bmj.39218.404201.94.

Health Protection Agency. 2006. A complex picture - HIV and other sexually transmitted infections in the United Kingdom. http://www.hpa.org.uk/web/HPAwebFile/HPAweb_C/1194947365435 Accessed 1 March 2009.

Marks, G., N. Crepaz, J.W. Senterfitt, and R.S. Janssen. 2005. Meta-analysis of high-risk sexual behaviour in persons aware and unaware they are infected with HIV in the United States. Implications for HIV prevention programs. *Journal of Acquired Immune Deficiency Syndromes* 39: 446–453. doi:10.1097/01.qai.0000151079.33935.79.

Rennie, S., and F. Behets. 2006. Desperately seeking targets: The ethics of routine HIV testing in low-income countries. *Bulletin of the World Health Organization* 84: 52–57. doi:10.2471/BLT.05.025536.

Weiser, S.D., M. Heisler, K. Leiter, F. Percy-de Korte, F. Tlou, S. DeMonner, et al. 2006. Routine HIV testing in Botswana: A population-based study on attitudes, practices, and human rights concerns. *PLoS Medicine* 3(7): 1013–1022. e261.

WHO & UAIDS. 2007. Guidance on provider-initiated HIV testing and counselling in health facilities. http://whqlibdoc.who.int/publications/2007/9789241595568_eng.pdf Accessed 1 March 2009.

WHO, UNAIDS, & UNICEF. 2008. Towards universal access: Scaling up priority HIV/AIDS interventions in the health sector. http://www.who.int/hiv/pub/towards_universal_access_report_2008.pdf Accessed 1 March 2009.

Bioethical Inquiry (2009) 6:235–237
DOI 10.1007/s11673-009-9148-3

# Challenging the Status Quo

**Dominic Wilkinson**

Received: 9 March 2009 / Accepted: 12 March 2009 / Published online: 3 April 2009


**Abstract** Harold Jaffe argues that we should adopt opt-out testing for HIV. There are paternalistic and utilitarian arguments for such an approach. In this commentary I draw attention to some similarities between his arguments and debates about opt-out systems of organ donation. I argue that the status quo bias provides both part of the reason that opt-out approaches work, and an explanation for why such approaches are sometimes resisted.

**Keywords** Organ transplantation/ethics · Ethics, medical · HIV · Tissue and organ procurement/ethics

In this issue, Harold Jaffe argues that the paradigm for human immunodeficiency virus (HIV) testing should change (Jaffe 2009). Instead of offering HIV tests to patients who are suspected to be potentially infected following informed consent, testing would be routine in populations with elevated risk—unless the patient declined.

Such a policy has some precedent. As Jaffe points out, opt-out testing is already the norm for pre-natal testing of pregnant women in the UK. It has recently been embraced as a general approach to testing for HIV by the Centers for Disease Control and Prevention (CDC) in the United States. But lowering the consent requirement for HIV testing could be seen to threaten patient autonomy. After all, the reason to switch to opt-out testing is that more patients will end up being tested. Some of this increase may relate to more patients being offered testing. But there are also likely to be some patients tested under an opt-out system who would have declined consent for testing if offered in the conventional way. Such patients might not understand what testing involves, or may not feel able to refuse the test.

Why, then, should we make the change? Jaffe presents two main arguments in favour of opt-out testing (Jaffe 2009). Identifying patients as being HIV positive enables them to receive anti-retroviral drugs that reduce their risk of HIV-related morbidity and mortality. It would thus be better for patients if they found out their HIV status than if they remained ignorant. This is the *paternalistic* argument for opt-out HIV testing.

Dominic Wilkinson is supported by an Oxford Nuffield Medical Fellowship, Eric Burnard Fellowship, and Royal Australasian College of Physicians Astra-Zeneca Medical Fellowship. The funders had no involvement in this work.

D. Wilkinson (✉)
Oxford Uehiro Centre for Practical Ethics,
The University of Oxford,
Littlegate House, St Ebbes,
Oxford OX1 1PT, UK
e-mail: dominic.wilkinson@gtc.ox.ac.uk

D. Wilkinson
The Ethox Centre, Department of Public Health and Primary Health Care, The University of Oxford,
Oxford, UK

Paternalism in medicine has a bad name. But there are different degrees of paternalism. Opt-out testing is at worst a form of mild paternalism since patients are still given the option of declining to be tested. Those who have strong preferences not to be tested are likely to refuse. The main difference is that individuals who are equivocal about testing, or somewhat fearful of testing, are more likely to end up being tested. And this same degree of paternalism operates for almost all other diagnostic tests (with the exception perhaps of some genetic tests). The doctor identifies and orders investigations or screening tests that are believed to be of benefit. Consent is assumed.

The other argument for opt-out testing is *utilitarian*. This strategy is likely to benefit other individuals in society. Identifying patients as being HIV positive leads to reduction in high-risk sexual behaviour, and anti-retroviral treatment reduces viral load. Both reduce transmission of the virus. The utilitarian argument for opt-out testing is particularly powerful in parts of the world where there are very high rates of HIV. The only way to stop the epidemic of HIV is to reduce the "case reproduction number" to less than one (Granich et al. 2009). Modelling suggests that a policy in sub-Saharan Africa of universal voluntary testing and early treatment would prevent millions of deaths from HIV (Granich et al. 2009).

The question of opt-out testing in HIV has obvious analogies with another debate in public policy—that of organ donation consent. The UK Organ Donation Taskforce has recently considered a move to opt-out consent for organ donation in the UK (Organ Donation Taskforce 2008), and other countries including New Zealand, Australia and the United States continue to debate the issue. There are paternalistic reasons for such a policy: 65–95% of people in the UK are in favour of donating their organs after death, though only 25% sign on to organ donation registries (Organ Donation Taskforce 2008). An opt-out system would respect the wishes of more people about the use of their organs. There are also strong utilitarian arguments in favour of such a policy. An opt-out system of organ donation would be likely to lead to a 25–30% increase in organ donation rates (Rithalia et al. 2009). This could correspond to approximately 650 extra organs in the UK each year.

Given the strong reasons in favour of opt-out systems for HIV testing and for organ donation, why is there so much reluctance to contemplate them? Part of the explanation may be a phenomenon known as the status quo bias, a serious and widespread cognitive bias in decision-making (Samuelson and Zeckhauser 1988; Bostrom and Ord 2006). One way of countering this bias is to imagine that the status quo is reversed (Aberegg et al. 2005). Imagine that the current consent processes for HIV testing were on an opt-out basis. Do the concerns about possible harms from opt-out testing provide sufficient reason to make a change to an opt-in consent given the benefits that would be lost? It is hard to believe that they would.

Ironically, the status quo bias is also part of the reason why opt-out consent leads to higher testing or organ donation rates. Given the same preferences and reasons, patients are more likely to take up an alternative when it is presented as the default than when it is an active choice (Samuelson and Zeckhauser 1988). This bias makes it hard for individuals to do what they have most reason to do. We can reduce the effect of the bias by the way in which choices are presented. Given that there are strong prudential and moral reasons to undertake HIV testing or to agree to donate organs after death, it makes sense to present these as the default position.

Jaffe makes a strong case for rejecting AIDS exceptionalism, and offering HIV testing on the same basis as other diagnostic and screening tests (Jaffe 2009). But he also identifies the potential costs of such a policy. Individuals could be subject to stigma or discrimination as a result of being diagnosed with HIV. Some patients may be diagnosed with HIV, but be unable to access anti-retroviral treatment. These are important concerns, and there are good reasons to mitigate such harms. But they should not stop us from challenging the status quo and moving to an opt-out approach to testing for HIV.

## References


Aberegg, S.K., E.F. Haponik, and P.B. Terry. 2005. Omission bias and decision making in pulmonary and critical care medicine. *Chest* 128: 1497–1505. doi:10.1378/chest.128.3.1497.

Bostrom, N., and T. Ord. 2006. The reversal test: Eliminating status quo bias in applied ethics. *Ethics* 116: 656–679. doi:10.1086/505233.

Granich, R.M., C.F. Gilks, C. Dye, K.M. De Cock, and B.G. Williams. 2009. Universal voluntary HIV testing with immediate antiretroviral therapy as a strategy for elimination of HIV transmission: A mathematical model. *Lancet* 373: 48–57. doi:10.1016/S0140-6736(08) 61697-9.

Jaffe, H. 2009. Increasing knowledge of HIV infection status through opt-out testing. *Journal of Bioethical Inquiry*, 6 (2). doi:10.1007/S11673-009-9147-4

Organ Donation Taskforce. 2008. The potential impact of an opt out system for organ donation in the UK: An independent report from the Organ Donation Taskforce. http://www.dh.gov.uk/en/Publicationsandstatistics/Publications/PublicationsPolicyAndGuidance/DH_090312. Accessed March 7, 2009.

Rithalia, A., C. McDaid, S. Suekarran, L. Myers, and A. Sowden. 2009. Impact of presumed consent for organ donation on donation rates: A systematic review. *BMJ (Clinical Research Ed.)* 338: a3162. doi:10.1136/bmj.a3162.

Samuelson, W., and R. Zeckhauser. 1988. Status quo bias in decision making. *Journal of Risk and Uncertainty* 1: 7–59. doi:10.1007/BF00055564.

# Part VI: Surveillance

Health Care Analysis (2002) 10:19–35
DOI 10.1023/A:1015698411824

# The Limits of Privacy: Surveillance and the Control of Disease

**Ronald Bayer · Amy Fairchild**



**Abstract** What justified the Center for Disease Control's 1999 determination to require HIV case reporting? Why were names necessary? Why did opponents view the reporting of names with such alarm? This paper retells the history of the encounters over HIV reporting that had occurred since the mid 1980s. In placing HIV reporting within a larger context, however, we understand the clash between privacy and public health necessity as a complex issue, both in historical and contemporary practice. By underscoring the similarities and differences with the histories of surveillance for other infectious diseases, vaccination, occupational diseases, cancer, and birth defects, and HIV reporting internationally, we can better understand the implications of the HIV debate for an ethics of surveillance more generally.

**Keywords** Birth defects · Cancer · Ethics · HIV/AIDS · Name-based reporting · Occupational disease · Surveillance · Tuberculosis · Vaccination

On December 10, 1999 the Center for Disease Control made final and formal a policy it had sought to impose for some years. That new policy required of states that they adopt a system of HIV case reporting. While the CDC left open the possibility of using coded unique identifiers, it was clear that the federal health officials favored the use of names (CDC 1999). In adopting this stance the CDC brought to closure a debate that had raged for 15 years, that had pitted advocates of comprehensive public health surveillance against AIDS advocates, gay organizations, civil libertarians, and their allies in some state health departments.

What justified the Center for Disease Control's 1999 determination to require HIV case reporting? In part, it was a reflection of the triumph of tradition over privacy-focused opposition. But more it reflected a growing sense that the surveillance of the AIDS epidemic was no longer adequate to the task. The reporting of AIDS cases—universal in the United States since 1983—represented a picture of the end stage of a disease process that commenced years earlier when HIV infection occurred. If the public health required an understanding of the contours of the epidemic of HIV transmission then something very different was required. Furthermore, with the advent of the era of powerful antiretroviral therapeutics in 1995–1996 the period between infection and an AIDS diagnosis had grown. And so some believed that AIDS case reporting captured the picture of events that had occurred 10 years earlier. Only HIV case reporting could remedy the situation. The availability of powerful new therapies, then, provided

R. Bayer (✉) · A. Fairchild
Center for the History & Ethics of Public Health,
Department of Sociomedical Sciences,
Mailman School of Public Health, Columbia University,
722 West 168th Street, 9th Floor,
New York, NY 10032, USA
e-mail: rb8@columbia.edu

an incentive for testing that might well overcome whatever the putative disincentives of HIV name reporting might be.

But why were names necessary? Why did opponents view the reporting of names with such alarm? To answer these questions requires a retelling of a history of the encounters that had occurred since the mid 1980s. With an appreciation of that history it will then be possible to locate the clash between the claims of privacy and surveillance first, in the context of the history of name based reporting; second, in the context of a range of contemporary surveillance practices; and finally it will be possible to look at the matter from an international perspective.

## AIDS/HIV Reporting: A Brief History

Soon after the first cases of AIDS were reported by the Center for Disease Control in June 1981, state health departments—which bear the primary responsibility for public health activities in the US—began to require physicians and hospitals to report by name each newly diagnosed case (Bayer 1989). In so doing they were pursuing a course understood to be a public health tradition. They shared a common belief that the understanding and control of disease necessitated adequate surveillance data. In the epidemic's early years this entailed not only a matter of enumeration and mapping but of investigating the commonalties among cases for which there was no etiological explanation. If gay men were so prominent among the first cases why were they? If hemophiliacs and blood transfusion recipients fell ill why was that the case? If intravenous drug users seemed at increased risk what could account for that fact? It is remarkable that given the intensity of the opposition that would emerge to HIV reporting just a few short years later that the American Association of Physicians for Human Rights—a gay and lesbian health group—would call upon local health departments to make AIDS cases reportable by name (AAPHR 1983).

Surveillance, in the contexts of most diseases, but not all as we will discuss below, is based on the premise that medical privacy is not an absolute. Both historically and in contemporary practice, reporting the names of those with disease to public health authorities has represented a central example of an acceptable exception to medical privacy and the confidentiality of the clinical relationship. Nevertheless, individuals whose names are placed on disease registries have a right to expect that their identities will be held in confidence, that data reported to registries would not be used in ways that pose a threat to the patient's dignity and well-being. This was done for moral as well as practical reasons. Indeed, to the extent that they do not believe that such confidentiality will prevail, they will tend to resist name-based reporting as an unacceptable intrusion on their privacy.

It was this lack of confidence that confidentiality would be respected that prevailed in the case of HIV. Once the capacity to test for the presence of the antibody to HIV became possible in 1985, it was only a matter of time before some public health official would seek to extend the reporting requirements that were in place for AIDS. The first successful effort to mandate HIV case reporting occurred in Colorado. There the health authorities presented the claims that would be made repeatedly over the next years: Reporting would alert public health officials to the presence of individuals infected with a lethal infection; would allow officials to counsel them about what they needed to do to prevent further transmission; would permit the authorities to monitor the incidence and prevalence of infection. Alert to concerns about privacy and confidentiality, Colorado health officials underscored the existence of administrative, regulatory, and statutory protections for reported names. There was no reason to believe, officials argued, that the state health department would fail to protect the identities of those with HIV when it had protected those with AIDS, tuberculosis, and other reportable infections.

To these propositions the antagonists to name-based reporting retorted that AIDS was different: social hostility and AIDS-related hysteria could lead to changes in policy, legislatively imposed, that would permit for breaches that would never occur with other conditions. And then those in registries would lose their jobs, their housing, and perhaps their liberty. The intensity of the opposition is best captured by the extent to which genocidal images were invoked. In Minnesota, which followed Colorado in making HIV reportable, one opponent declared at a public meeting, "The road to the gas chambers began with a list in Weimar Germany" (Bayer 1989, p 131). A less extreme formulation put the issue this way: "the fear, anger, and mistrust felt by me and many other groups reflects our profound belief that the threat to our fundamental human rights posed by the existence of AIDS is an evil of equal strength to the disease itself. To ignore our feelings will only alienate the gay community thereby impeding [the health department's] often legitimate efforts to arrest this serious health problem" (Bayer 1989).

Here then was the powerful argument against reporting that would impress many health officials in states with relatively large AIDS caseloads. Reporting would be counterproductive; it would drive people away from testing and counseling—essential control measures in the public health campaign against AIDS in the United States. It did not matter that public health departments had an exemplary record in protecting name-based reports (Gostin et al. 1997). If those most at risk for HIV had fears about what would happen to them that was all that mattered.

As therapeutic advances began to emerge in the late 1980s—as public health began to have more to offer than the perceived threat of quarantine or partner notification—fissures began to appear in the relatively broad and solid alliance against named reporting. Thus, in 1989, New York City's Health Commissioner stated that the prospects of early clinical intervention warranted "a shift toward a disease-control approach to HIV infection along the lines of classic tuberculosis practices," including the "reporting of seropositives" (Joseph 1989). Although his proposal met with fierce and effective resistance, it is clear that his call represented part of a national trend.

At the end of November 1990, the CDC declared its support for HIV reporting, which it asserted could "enhance the ability of local, state and national agencies to project the level of required resources" for care and prevention services (MMWR 1990). Within a week, the House of Delegates of the American Medical Association endorsed the reporting of names as well, thus breaking with the traditional resistance of medical practitioners to such intrusions on the physician-patient relationship (Bayer 1991). In 1991, New Jersey became the first high-prevalence state to require HIV-case reporting by name (Intergovernmental AIDS Reports 1989).

In the following years, the CDC continued to press for named reporting of HIV cases, an effort that assumed the dimensions of a campaign. During that period, it was supported by a growing number of public health officials. Indeed, the Council of State and Territorial Epidemiologists adopted resolutions in 1989, 1991, 1993, and 1995 encouraging states to consider the implementation of HIV case surveillance (CSTE, Personal Communication).

Nevertheless, resistance on the part of AIDS activist organizations and their political allies persisted, and as a consequence, HIV cases typically became reportable by name only in states that did not have large cosmopolitan communities with effectively organized gay constituencies or high AIDS case loads. By 1996, although 26 states had adopted HIV-case reporting, they represented jurisdictions with only 24% of reported AIDS cases (CDC 1997). By October 1998, however, it was clear that opposition to name-based reporting was weakening: 32 states now reported cases of HIV by name, though 3 states reported only pediatric cases; Florida, with its large case load, had become a reporting state, and Texas—which together with Maryland, had experimented with a unique identifier system for HIV-case reporting as an alternative to the use of names—had come to the conclusion that such an approach was unworkable and adopted name-based reporting (CDC 1998). This trend must be seen as part of the more general move away from the exceptionalism that had placed such emphasis on the privacy and social rights of people with HIV infection and that had set AIDS policy apart from the response to other communicable conditions (Bayer 1991, 1999).

Nothing more forcefully underscored the changes that occurred than the course of events in New York. In 1997, the state with the largest concentration of AIDS cases began, for the first time, to consider name reporting. Although a state health department task force charged with the responsibility of advising the commissioner of health on the matter remained bitterly divided, the lines of cleavage were stark. It was the representatives of community-based organizations who most adamantly opposed name reporting. Public health officials on the committee and throughout the state supported HIV-case reporting by name. Objections and disagreements notwithstanding, there was significant, broad agreement on the need for HIV surveillance data to track the HIV epidemic and on the need to bring the sexual and needle-sharing contacts of individuals with HIV into testing and treatment. Yet ultimately the deadlock between community and public health officials paved the way for final action in the legislative arena. On June 19, 1998, in the waning hours of the legislative session, the Democratic-controlled assembly voted 112 to 34 for a bill that would mandate case reporting by name and a more aggressive approach to partner notification. In so doing, it joined the Republican-dominated state senate, which had already passed the bill (1998 NY Laws, Chapter 163). For advocates of name reporting, the significance of the New York decision could not be overstated.

The New York decision is best understood in light of therapeutic advances on the national policy debate on name reporting. That impact was made clear in an editorial published in late 1997. Jointly authored by Larry Gostin, a well-known proponent of civil liberties, John Ward, MD, of the CDC, and Cornelius Baker, the African American President of the National Association of People With AIDS, the editorial represented a new alliance. Locating the argument for named reporting in the context of the remarkable therapeutic achievements represented by the protease inhibitors and the advent of triple-combination anti-retroviral therapy, the authors declared:

> We are at a defining moment of the epidemic of HIV infection and AIDS. With therapy that delays the progression to AIDS, mental illnesses, and death, HIV infection or AIDS is becoming a complex clinical disease that does not lend itself to monitoring based on end stage illness. Unless we revise our surveillance system, health authorities will not have reliable information about the prevalence of HIV infection. To correct these deficiencies, we propose that all states require HIV case reporting.

Among the additional advantages of HIV-case reporting, they asserted, was that it would give public health authorities a greater ability to "ensure timely referrals for health and social services" (Gostin et al. 1997, pp 1162–1167).

Although many, if not most, AIDS-service organizations remained adamantly opposed to name reporting, arguing instead for the use of unique identifiers, the public health community, with the CDC in the lead, concluded that such an approach would simply impede the adoption of an effective system of surveillance. Nevertheless, marking the extent to which political factors shape decision-making in public health, the CDC, in its 1999 recommendation, opened the way to the use of unique identifiers in those states that preferred an anonymous reporting course, provided states could radically limit the error rates associated with such an approach.

It was in trying to place HIV reporting within a larger context that we came to understand that the question of public health surveillance is a much more complex issue, both in historical and contemporary practice. Indeed, it was as a result of our ongoing study of this issue that we came to recognize the need for an analysis of the broad history of public health surveillance. Without such an analysis, it becomes impossible to understand that the HIV reporting controversy was radically affected by the circumstances under which it emerged, that is, the existence of a transformed conception of the rights of privacy, constitutional limits on state authority exercised for benevolent purposes, the development of a vigorous debate about medical ethics, and the emergence of patient advocacy as a potent social force. Indeed, without underscoring similarities and differences with the histories of surveillance for other infectious diseases, vaccination, cancer, occupational diseases, and birth defects, the ability to understand the implications of the HIV debate for surveillance more generally becomes impossible.

## Case Reporting in Historical and Contemporary Contexts

Although the quantification of disease and concerns with health statistics have origins in the era of sanitary reform, it was not until the late nineteenth century—in the period in which the new science of bacteriology identified germs that could be transmitted from person to person as the cause of disease—that most nations began systematic reporting of infectious disease among individuals by name, often but not exclusively for the purpose of initiating quarantine, isolation, or vaccination and for epidemiological reasons, as well (Eyler 1979).

The new public health practices that were linked to the bacteriological revolution, however, were also linked to a heightened public and professional concern about such practices. Notification by name for infectious diseases in many western nations followed on the heels of a period of public protest over compulsory or coercive health policies associated with the bacteriological revolution. Physicians, too, on occasion, challenged the scientific authority of public health officials to intervene in the doctor-patient relationship. In New York City for example, physician outrage over mandatory tuberculosis reporting beginning in 1897 resulted in the development of an essentially voluntary reporting system in which physicians withheld the names of their private patients and reported the names of their poor, dispensary cases (Fox 1975, 1986).

Despite such opposition and some anticipation of what might follow the extension of the reporting requirement, public health officials began to argue in the second decade of the twentieth century that "All the general arguments for complete reporting of other communicable diseases apply with equal force to venereal disease" (Snow 1917). But they appreciated the various factors influencing the potential for venereal disease reporting. They most often opted to forego name-based notification—remaining content with an inadequate surveillance system focused on public clinics. Although it was ultimately unsuccessful, public health officials in New York requested that physicians report cases of venereal disease by code beginning in 1912. A 1911 California system, which required physicians to report cases of venereal disease by code to protect patient confidentiality, served as their model (Brandt 1987). Similarly, although it ultimately opted for name reporting, Massachusetts also considered adopting a laboratory-based coded system for tracking syphilis cases in 1916. Allan Brandt has underscored the point: "Although anonymous reporting precluded rigorous case-tracing, officials hoped it would deflate the possible objections of practitioners." How opposition to name-based reporting could vary and how such opposition was often linked to the way in which reports could trigger public health interventions that could be coercive is demonstrated by the early history of polio reporting.

The New York City Department of Health declared polio a communicable disease and made it mandatory for physicians to report all cases in 1910. During 1916 the epidemic became a public affair. Newspapers reported cases amongst the most prominent in the City. The City's health commissioner published a daily tally of new cases and deaths by name and street address in local newspapers. Homes with a sick child displayed a placard warning of the presence of disease (Emerson 1917).

What is astonishing is that while polio primarily struck the middle class, in sharp contrast to the history of reaction to tuberculosis reporting discussed above, reporting elicited no objection from physicians or the private patients they served in large measure due to the differential nature of departmental intervention, particularly in the case of quarantine. Families with a private toilet for the patient, separate dining facilities, and a private nurse could maintain a domestic quarantine. Children of those who lived in tenements or other types of multi-family dwellings were taken, sometimes by force, to public hospitals. Similarly, tenement homes and the children living in them were subject to unannounced inspections. As a consequence resistance to reporting and the interventions that followed has been documented only amongst poor, working class, or immigrant families. An analysis of the period recounts that during the epidemic of 1916 one mother warned that she and her child would disappear by morning if her doctor reported the case to health authorities. The Department of Health nurse assigned to inspect tenement houses received a letter promising, "If you report any more of our babies to the Board of Health we will kill you and nobody will know what happened to you. Keep off our streets and don't report our homes and we will do you no harm" (Rogers 1992, p. 54).

The point here is to underscore the fact that opposition to name based reporting is not new. Although it is important to note that as part of the tradition of public health practice it had gone largely unquestioned in recent years—until AIDS. While infectious disease reporting represents the oldest example of public health surveillance, the creation of vaccine registries—designed to prevent infectious disease by tracking the vaccination history of children by name of the child and parents and following them across states and over time—represents the most recent effort. Development of vaccine registries began in the 1970s, but only recently have federal efforts to coordinate and link these registries begun. On January 12, 1999, in response to sporadic disease outbreaks, poor coverage in urban, inner-city communities, increasingly complex vaccine schedules, family mobility, and poor provider and patient awareness of immunization coverage levels, the National Vaccine Advisory Committee (NVAC), as part of the federal Initiative on Immunization Registries, recommended creation of a nationwide network of state and community immunization registries (NVAC, http://www.cdc.gov/nip/registry/i_recs.htm).

The federal initiative to register immunization coverage put a premium on community participation and cooperation, principally because of the fears of immigrant communities (worried that registry information would be a means of alerting the Immigration and Naturalization Service to their status), parents (those who opposed vaccination for their children feared that they would be harassed and discriminated against), and providers (those with low immunization rates were concerned that they would be "punished" in some fashion).

Central to the recommendations of the National Vaccine Advisory Committee was the protection of patient confidentiality. Registry developers were to give careful consideration to privacy and confidentiality issues in a way that reflected the values and special needs of the communities they served. The committee's analysis of confidentiality highlighted the fact that a tension existed between a need for the completeness of data and risks of unacceptable disclosure. The committee thus adopted as a guiding principle a commitment to direct, active parental notification that the registry exists and to parental choice in participation: "Parents," said NVAC, "must be given the option to decide whether or not their children will participate in a registry." Remarkably, despite these recommendations, the most recent survey of immunization registries has found that 35 rely on implied consent to participation in registries and that 12 states did not notify parents of their child's participation.

Cancer registries in the United States provide the primary example of a surveillance regime that has not produced ethical or political controversy (Von Tigerstrom et al. 2000; Cavoukian 1992). Nevertheless such registries, by their very definition, represent an ongoing intrusion on privacy and confidentiality. Proposals to make cancer reportable date back more than 70 years (Wood 1930). Cancer registries have been in existence for 60 years and, outside of infectious disease reporting, represent one of the most substantial efforts of the public health and medical communities to trace patterns of morbidity and mortality and evaluate therapeutic interventions. In 1971 the National Cancer Act mandated that collection and analysis of data on cancer be undertaken to assist in the prevention, treatment, and diagnosis of cancer. The Surveillance, Epidemiology, and End Results program at the National Cancer Institute was organized to take advantage of cancer data already being collected at several population-based tumor registries. Some 20 years later, Congress enacted the Cancer Registries Amendment Act (1992), which authorized the CDC to establish a national program in support of cancer registries. The goal of the program was to enhance existing registries and to help establish new ones so that all states would have registries that met minimum standards for completeness, timeliness, and quality.

Despite the wide array of medical information to which cancer registries are linked or linkable and the duration of surveillance for each case—from the first pathology report through death—few patients are ever told that they will be reported and followed over time.

Although cancer is historically a highly stigmatized disease and registration of cases in Western Europe has in recent years been the subject of strict regulation, the necessity for reporting and tracking those with cancer without consent has almost never been challenged in the United States. For example, in Rhode Island there is an exception to the confidentiality statute, which permits reporting of health care information on an individual to the state's central cancer registry (R.I. GEN. LAWS 1987). While professionals often note the importance of preserving patient confidentiality, the focus of their concern has been on enhancing the reliability and usability of the registries as part of follow-up research (Hermeren 1988).

When issues of privacy and confidentiality have been addressed, those most committed to cancer registries have argued strongly for the necessity of using names as the basis for linking records, grounding their arguments in the demands of surveillance accuracy. For example, researchers assert, "The incontrovertible fact is that linkage of individual records is essential if cancer is to be measured accurately, the causes ascertained at minimum expense, and the effect of control measures assessed. This is an issue that has to be faced squarely: one cannot have both absolute secrecy and rational cancer control" (Muir et al. 1985, p. 21). The North American Association of Central Cancer Registries has declared, "The public health surveillance system must be exempted from restrictions on collection and retention of personal identifying information in medical privacy legislation. Personal identifiers ... must be collected ...without individual consent" (North American Association of Central Cancer Registries 1999).

In a climate where privacy and confidentiality concerns have become so salient, the status and function of cancer registries has become a matter of consternation. In 1999 the National Cancer Institute (NCI) noted, "Unfortunately, in the current concern about confidentiality protections, the needs of clinical research are not often explicitly addressed. Some of the contemplated or actual legal remedies, or their interpretation, seriously threaten the conduct of important medical research." The NCI explained, "One of the difficulties in the formation of policy to cover a broad and complex area like health care is that laws or regulations designed to protect against worst-case scenarios may exert unintended and highly adverse consequences on the conduct of medical research, which depends on access to and exchange of information" (National Cancer Institute, http://www.nci.nih.gov/confidentiality.html).

It was not however only public health agencies that were concerned with how privacy standards could effect registries. In sharp contrast to the events that surrounded AIDS, breast cancer advocates urged the maintenance of reporting requirements. The National Breast Cancer Coalition, in their February 2001 "Position Statement on Medical Privacy" (NBCC, http://www.natlbcc.org/bin/index.htm) stressed, "The fundamental right to privacy must include the right to keep one's health information confidential and control the flow of and access to this information," but noted, "Privacy protections should ensure that health information remains private but should not impede the progress of medical research." The statement continued, "Specific authorization to disclose health care information should be required for uses that are not directly related to treatment, payment, or health care operations. A trustworthy system with a proper informed consent process should create an environment where most people would not object to sharing health care information for the purpose of research. With large studies," the NBCC noted, "there are legitimate and serious questions about the feasibility of seeking individual authorizations, because sometimes the research involves thousands of individuals. In cases where it is not possible or feasible to obtain individual consent, there should be clear, consistent and transparent criteria for determining when individual authorization should be waived." The statement acknowledged, "While data can be encrypted, researchers need to link this data back to individuals in order to generate meaningful conclusions." This commitment to research was put to the test in Massachusetts, where an effort to make cancer registration voluntary was opposed by breast cancer advocates who declared: "To have that kind of requirement would certainly undermine 100% ascertainment" (NBCC 2001, http://www.natlbcc.org/bin/index.htm). This encounter underscores the fact that there are occasions when those whose privacy will be compromised view such limits not as a burden but as serving their interests. This pattern could also be seen in the context of occupational disease reporting.

Although sixty thousand people die each year of occupational diseases and the federal government has borne primary responsibility for the surveillance of occupational diseases and injuries, advocates of workers' health argue that such diseases and injuries are under-recognized (Rosenman et al. 1997). Advocates have accordingly urged that occupational diseases be made reportable for purposes of epidemiological surveillance and, significantly, intervention to protect workers' health.

It was the relative inadequacy of existing reporting mechanisms that ultimately led the National Institute for Occupational Safety and Health (NIOSH) to develop the Sentinel Event Notification System for Occupational Risks in 1987 (SENSOR). SENSOR helps 20 state programs expand their reporting capacity and develop standardized case definitions. The program initially focused on six targeted conditions (silicosis, occupational asthma, pesticide poisoning, lead poisoning, carpal tunnel syndrome, and noise-induced hearing loss) and has since expanded to include accidental amputation, work-related dermatitis, and injuries to minors. But the full range of occupational disease surveillance supported by NIOSH is much broader.

Infectious disease surveillance and its role in guiding public health efforts have also served as a model for those concerned about birth defects. In 2000, the Pew Environmental Health Commission declared, "The United States has an adequate network to capture data on infectious disease in order to spot dangerous outbreaks before they spread. Certainly, we know how to build an effective mechanism that provides the consistency of reporting data and privacy protections." What is needed, however, "is a national policy to guide state implementation of a comprehensive, modern tracking program that will help identify environmental and other preventable factors that contribute to birth defects and other disabilities and chronic diseases" (Pew Environmental Health Commission 2000).

Although New Jersey required the reporting of birth defects in 1928, the modern era of birth defects registries did not begin until the 1960s, when the Thalidomide disaster and growing concern over addressing environmental and teratogenic hazards to the fetus in utero sparked new interest in surveillance (Hogan 1994). The Metropolitan Atlanta Congenital Defects Program was the first new state-based registry, established in 1967. The pace of development was slow, however. The CDC began its own Birth Defects Monitoring Program using hospital discharge data in 1974 and became the largest source of birth defects information in the nation. But by 1978, only two states (Nebraska and Florida) had established registries. As of the mid-1980s, 14 additional states had developed registries. By the year 2000, 42 states had done so. In 1999, following a congressional mandate to develop a clearing house of birth defects surveillance, the CDC was given appropriations to establish or improve state-based surveillance.

Advocates for birth defects reporting note the importance of using names. For instance, CDC states, "the use of personal identifiers facilitates follow-up studies and allows investigators to link infant, maternal, and paternal records" (Lynberg and Edmonds 1992).

This brief historical and contemporary review has sought to demonstrate that the move toward HIV name-based reporting must be viewed as entailing an effort to integrate HIV/AIDS into the broad system of public health surveillance in the United States, to end the exceptionalism that had characterized AIDS policy in the epidemic's formative period.

Nonetheless it is instructive to note that with its emphasis on name reporting, the United States sets itself apart from the practice common in Europe. In February 1998, a meeting of European experts convened under the auspices of the European Centre for the Epidemiological Monitoring of AIDS concluded:

> At the European level AIDS case reporting, introduced in 1984, has been the principal means of monitoring the epidemic. ...However, in the changing epidemiological context [AIDS case reporting] is no longer sufficient. HIV case reporting is a key element for HIV surveillance. ...It should be continued where it exists and, where necessary, developed. At a country level, confidentiality should be guaranteed and elimination of duplicate reports should be ensured. HIV case reports should be linkable with AIDS case reports (Hammers 1998, p. 51).

All of this, the experts concluded, could be achieved without the use of names. The commitment to linkable records without the use of names reflected the professional concerns of epidemiologists troubled by the existence of reporting systems that failed to meet the highest statistical standards or accurate surveillance.

These recommendations reflected current practice regarding HIV reporting in Europe. A 1998 study found that 36 countries, including 9 European Union countries, had nationwide HIV reporting systems. Reporting was mandatory in 27. Notification was by name in 10 countries, by code in 20, and without unique identifiers in 6. Strikingly, the use of names was almost exclusively restricted to the former Communist nations. As in the United States, AIDS-related organizations in Europe have tended to support coded HIV reporting but oppose the use of names as a threat to privacy and human rights. Thus, in Spain, which approved a national anonymous registry of people with HIV using a 15-digit code, the Movimiento Cuidado Antisida supported the new registry, but expressed its opposition to the name-based approach adopted in the region of Asturias. "We do not agree with a [name-containing] registry since names of persons have nothing to do with the epidemiologic knowledge of the infection and, in addition, may seriously harm the confidentiality of a given person" (Bosch 1999, p. 977).

## Conclusion

The central ethical question posed by HIV name reporting indeed of all disease reporting is: When do the claims of public health legitimately trump the claims of privacy and confidentiality in the context of disease surveillance? A subsidiary question is: Do the claims of privacy carry sufficient weight to make reporting systems that are less accurate, but that are nevertheless adequate more compatible with ethical standards?

While these questions have, in some way, been at the heart of disease reporting for more than a century, with the exception of HIV/AIDS, despite almost three decades of systematic discussion of the ethics of human subjects research, no sustained discussion of the ethics of public health reporting has been undertaken. In the 1970s, Leon Gordis, Alexander Capron, and others began to discuss whether the emerging rules and regulations for human subjects research would apply to epidemiological studies, whether the principle of informed consent for the use of records was necessary, and whether such requirements would render epidemiological research virtually impossible (Gordis et al. 1977; Gordis and Gold 1980; Gostin 1991; Capron 1991; Cann and Rothman 1984; Hershey 1985; Rothman 1981).

Yet that discussion has not extended to public health surveillance. While research, including epidemiological research, has been the subject of IRB review, public health surveillance has not been subject to similar oversight. Indeed, dispute exists over the boundary distinguishing research—that must be subject to review—from public health practice—such as case identification and treatment (Snider and Stroup 1997; Mariner 1997).

Surveillance stands at the boundary of public health practice and research. Surveillance data is not collected toward the end of research, though it is clear that it serves those ends. Austin, for example, refers to cancer registries as "a tool in epidemiology" (Austin 1983, pp. 119–140). And while Meriwether argues that research should not be confused with surveillance, she does acknowledge its critical role in the generation of research hypotheses (Meriwether 1996). Finally, in the one chapter dealing with ethical issues in Teutsch and Churchill's *Principles and Practice of Public Health Surveillance*, Hahn states, "although several features may distinguish surveillance related ethical issues from ethical issues in other areas of epidemiology and public health, many of the ethical issues confronting public health surveillance are similar to those of epidemiology" (Hahn 1994, pp. 175–189).

Surveillance, undertaken for public health purposes rather than epidemiological research, carries the risk, however small, that information might be inadvertently disclosed despite the best efforts to keep it confidential. It also may trigger public health intrusions, such as, in the case of HIV/AIDS, partner notification. Notifying the sexual partners of people with HIV may place them at risk of domestic violence, of losing housing, or of losing employment. Yet the consequences and risks change over time. As we have seen in the prior discussion, they vary by both the nature of the disease in question and the social perception of it. They also vary in terms of those who bear the burden of disease and their own sense of social vulnerability. Thus, as we noted, breast cancer advocates have proven adamantly opposed to the notion of requiring informed consent for registration of cases.

The case of HIV dramatically underscores the limits of considering ethical questions regarding surveillance out of political and social context, in a way that does not account for the characteristics of the people affected by disease including their agency and vulnerability, the cultural perception of the disease in question, and the public health consequences of disease. Fairness requires that equals be treated equally. It also requires that where morally relevant differences exist, they be taken into account. In short, we must begin to account for those factors—such as race, gender, and class that clinical medical ethics needed to elide to prevent researchers from capitalizing on social or political vulnerability in designing and conducting studies—in a systematic yet not rigid fashion.

What then can be said about how the confrontation over the limits of privacy and confidentiality should have gone forward in the case of HIV and should go forward in other instances of surveillance? What standards should govern decision-making? The following might serve as principles worthy of consideration.

1 Wherever the state seeks to breach confidentiality for purposes of the surveillance it bears the burden of demonstrating that such an intrusion on privacy is critical for the ends of protecting the public health.
2 When the state breaches confidentiality in the name of surveillance it must demonstrate that it has taken all necessary steps to protect the

confidentiality of the names it will collect; that it has in place mechanisms that will preclude the possibility or unwarranted intrusions upon its records; that it has promulgated regulations and laws that will penalize unwarranted intrusions.

3 When those whose names are to be reported express fears about how they will suffer as a consequence of notification the state must seek to address their concerns directly and respectfully in a process of an open consultation.

But, though officials and even some advocates may prize the demands of public health over those of privacy, in the end it is clear that there is an inherent tension between public health and the claims of privacy, though the response to the tension may vary over time and place. What we have a right to expect is that the balance struck will be fair, judicious, and carefully wrought. To believe, however, that we can escape the tension is a dangerous illusion.

## References


Austin, D. 1983. Cancer registries: A tool in epidemiology. *Reviews in Cancer Research* 2: 119–140.

Bayer, R. 1989. *Private acts social consequences: Aids and the politics of public health.* New Brunswick: Rutgers University Press.

Bayer, R. 1991. Public health policy and the AIDS epidemic: An end to HIV exceptionalism? *New England Journal of Medicine* 324: 1500–1504.

Bayer, R. 1999. Clinical progress and the future of HIV exceptionalism. *Archives of Internal Medicine* 159: 1042–1048.

Bosch. 1999. Confidential Spanish registry of HIV-infected individuals. *Journal of the American Medical Association* 281: 977.

Brandt, A. 1987. *No magic bullet.* New York: Oxford University Press.

Cann, C., and K. Rothman. 1984. IRBs and epidemiologic research: How inappropriate restrictions hamper studies. *IRB: A Review of Human Subjects Research*, July/August: 5–7.

Capron, A. 1991. Protection of research subjects: Do special rules apply in epidemiology? *Law, Medicine & Health Care* 19: 184–190.

CDC. 1990. Update: Public health surveillance for HIV infection—United States, 1989 and 1990. *Morbidity and Mortality Weekly Report* 39: 861.

CDC. 1997. *HIV/AIDS surveillance report.* Atlanta: CDC 8.

CDC. 1998. Evaluation of HIV case surveillance through the use of non-name unique identifiers: Maryland and Texas, 1994–1996. *Morbidity and Mortality Weekly Report* 46: 1254–1258.

CDC. 1999. *Guidelines for national human immunodeficiency virus case surveillance*, 1–28. Atlanta: CDC.

Emerson, H. 1917. *A monograph on the epidemic of poliomyelitis [infantile paralysis] in New York City in 1916. Based on the official reports of the Bureaus of the Department of Health.* New York: Department of Health.

Eyler, J. 1979. *Victorian social medicine: The ideas and methods of William Farr.* Baltimore: Johns Hopkins University Press.

Fox, D. 1975. Social policy and city politics: Tuberculosis reporting in New York, 1889–1900. *Bulletin of the History of Medicine* 49: 169–195.

Fox, D. 1986. From TB to AIDS: Value conflicts in reporting disease. *Hastings Center Report*, December, 11–17.

Gordis, L., and E. Gold. 1980. Privacy, confidentiality and the use of medical records in research. *Science* 207: 153–156.

Gordis, L., E. Gold, and R. Seltzer. 1977. Privacy protection in epidemiologic and medical research: A challenge and a responsibility. *American Journal of Epidemiology* 105: 163–168.

Gostin, L. 1991. Ethical principles for the conduct of human subject research: Population-based research and ethics. *Law, Medicine & Health Care* 19: 191–201.

Gostin, L., J. Ward, and C. Baker. 1997. National HIV case reporting for the United States: A defining moment in the history of the epidemic. *The New England Journal of Medicine* 337: 1162–1167.

Hahn, R. 1994. Ethical issues. In *Principles and practice of public health surveillance*, ed. S. Teutsch and R. Elliott, 175–189. New York: Oxford University Press.

Hammers, F. 1998. Recommendations for HIV surveillance in Europe. *Eurosurveillance* 3(5): 51.

Hermeren, G. 1988. Ethical problems in register based medical research. *Theoretical Medicine* 9: 105–116.

Hershey, N. 1985. IRB jurisdiction and limits on IRB actions. *IRB: A Review of Human Subjects Research*, March/April, 7–9.

Hogan, J. 1994. The Michigan birth defects registry: Development and operation. *Journal of AHIMA* 65(6): 38–40.

Intergovernmental Health Policy Project. 1989. HIV reporting in the states. *Intergovern-mental AIDS Reports*, November–December.

Joseph, S. 1989. Remarks at the 5th International Conference on AIDS, mimeo, June 5.

Lynberg, M., and L. Edmonds. 1992. Surveillance of birth defects. In *Public health surveillance*, ed. W. Halperin and E.L. Baker, 157–177. New York: Nostrand Reinhold.

Mariner, W. 1997. Public confidence in public health research ethics. *Public Health Reports* 112: 33–36.

Meriwether, R. 1996. Blueprint for a national public health surveillance system for the 21st century. *Journal of Public Health Management and Practice* 2(4): 16–23.

Muir, C., E. Demaret, and P. Boyle. 1985. The cancer registry in cancer control: An overview. *The Role of the Registry in Cancer Control.* IARC Scientific Publications, 21.

National Breast Cancer Coalition. www.natlbcc.org/bin/index.htm. National Cancer Institute. Confidentiality, Data Security, and Cancer Research: "Perspectives from the National Cancer Institute," http://www.nci.nih.gov/confidentiality.html.

National Vaccine Advisory Committee Report of the National Vaccine Advisory Committee (NVAC). Development of Community-and State-Based Immunization Registries. http://www.cdc.gov/nip/reistry/i_recs.htm.

North American Association of Central Cancer Registries. 1999. Policy statement 99–01: Confidentiality, November 17.

Pew Environmental Health Commission. 2000. Healthy from the start: Why America needs a better system to track and understand birth defects and the environment. *Rhode Island General Laws* 5–37, 3–4(b) (18) 1987.

Rogers, N. 1992. *Dirt and disease: Polio before FDR*, 54. New Brunswick: Rutgers University Press.

Rosenman, K., M. Reilly, and D. Kalinowski. 1997. A state-based surveillance system for work-related asthma. *Journal of Occupational and Environmental Medicine* 39(5): 415–425.

Rothman, K. 1981. The rise and fall of epidemiology, 1950–2000 A.D. *New England Journal of Medicine* 600–602, March 5.

Snider, D., and D. Stroup. 1997. Defining research when it comes to public health. *Public Health Reports* 112: 29–32.

Snow, W. 1917. Public health measures in "Relation to venereal diseases". *Proceedings of the Second Pan American Scientific Congress, 1915–1916, Section 8, Part I. Washington, D.C.* 9: 491.

Von Tigerstrom, B., M. Deschenes, B. Knoppers, and T. Caulfield. 2000. Legal regulation of cancer surviellance: Canadian and international perspectives. *Health Law Journal* 8: 1.

Wood F. (1930) Need for cancer morbidity statistics. *American Journal of Public Health* 11–19.

Bioethical Inquiry (2009) 6:187–195
DOI 10.1007/s11673-009-9163-4

# Syndromic Surveillance and Patients as Victims and Vectors

**Leslie P. Francis · Margaret P. Battin ·
Jay Jacobson · Charles Smith**

Received: 24 December 2008 / Accepted: 10 May 2009 / Published online: 9 June 2009


**Abstract** Syndromic surveillance uses new ways of gathering data to identify possible disease outbreaks. Because syndromic surveillance can be implemented to detect patterns before diseases are even identified, it poses novel problems for informed consent, patient privacy and confidentiality, and risks of stigmatization. This paper analyzes these ethical issues from the viewpoint of the patient as victim and vector. It concludes by pointing out that the new International Health Regulations fail to take full account of the ethical challenges raised by syndromic surveillance.

**Keywords** Surveillance · Syndromic surveillance · International Health Regulations · Confidentiality · Privacy

Protection of populations from infectious disease requires effective surveillance to identify diseases and disease trends. The better the surveillance, the more quickly outbreaks can be identified and contained. This is especially important for a rapidly spreading condition with high levels of mortality and morbidity, as human-to-human pandemic influenza is thought likely to be. Yet there are many barriers to effective surveillance, including inadequate public health systems, limited resources, reluctant population groups, and ethical objections. In this contribution, we discuss how an ethical perspective we have developed—what we call "the patient as victim and vector", or "PVV" for short (Battin et al. 2009)—can help in analyzing ethical concerns about a new and important form of surveillance: so-called "syndromic surveillance", that employs a variety of innovative information technologies to monitor for clusters of symptoms or complaints.

Several ethical concerns have been thought to apply to syndromic surveillance. These include the possibility that access to individuals and collection of information from them may occur without their consent; the potential for loss of privacy and confidentiality; and, the risk that individuals or groups may be stigmatized, physically harmed, or otherwise victimized by the information collected. There are political concerns as well: the establishment of novel data-gathering means without public knowledge, decision-making or oversight. On our PVV perspective, we conclude that robust surveillance regimes of the type envisioned by syndromic surveillance can only be ethically justified, despite their anticipated benefits, if they are accompanied by attention to the victim-needs of those about whom data are obtained. These victim-needs include transparency and oversight, protection from harm, and access to preventives or treatment to the extent possible, but do not extend to informed consent or protection of privacy in every instance. In considering the ethical issues raised by syndromic surveillance, moreover, it is especially

L. P. Francis (✉) · M. P. Battin · J. Jacobson · C. Smith
University of Utah,
Salt Lake City, UT, USA
e-mail: francisl@law.utah.edu

important to distinguish privacy as access to individuals in the initial information-gathering encounter, and confidentiality as protection of the transfer of identifying or identifiable information about them.

## Traditional Surveillance and Syndromic Surveillance

Surveillance has been called the "backbone" of public health efforts in disease prevention and control (Gostin and Berkman 2007, 155). Individual case surveillance identifies people with particular diseases (such as tuberculosis or syphilis) and provides the option to intervene to treat and to stop spread. In its traditional form, such case surveillance involves specification of a list of "reportable" diseases to an entity such as a department of health, followed by treatment and/or contact tracing as deemed necessary. It also involves reporting or monitoring of laboratory testing results for identified organisms, toxins, or other suspected agents of disease. In complement, statistical surveillance identifies disease trends in populations: incidence, prevalence, distribution, and the like (Stoto 2008).

These traditional surveillance methods begin with a determination of the diagnoses, or agents of disease, that are thought to be of public health interest. For example, the World Health Regulations in effect until 2007 required reporting of cholera, yellow fever, and plague—but only these three diseases (Chretien et al. 2008). In the United States, under the National Notifiable Diseases Surveillance System (NNDSS), disease surveillance at the federal level has been voluntary, and based on case reports under reporting systems mandated at the state level and alerts from clinicians and laboratories about disease clusters (Centers for Disease Control, National Notifiable Diseases Surveillance System). At the state level, public health statutes typically require reporting of specified infectious diseases (NY CLS Pub Health § 2130 2008), cancer diagnoses (e.g., California Health & Safety Code [Deering's] § 103885 2008), workplace toxins (Minn. Stat. § 175.33 2008), and more recently agents associated with bioterrorism (Ariz. Rev. Stat. § 36–782 2008). Other recent proposals have extended surveillance beyond contagious disease and environmental toxins, the traditional domains of public health, to identify incidence and prevalence of diseases such as diabetes—an expansion that has come under criticism (Mariner 2007).

However, with emerging contagious diseases such as HIV or SARS, new strains of influenza, or as-yet-to-be-imagined agents of bioterrorism, illness may reach pandemic proportions if effective surveillance must wait upon identification of a diagnosis or disease-causing agent that is the object of interest. Instead, observation and subsequent investigation of behavioral or symptom patterns of potential significance is an important way of ascertaining a developing public health threat. The basic idea of such "syndromic surveillance" is to collect real-time data about disease indicators in order to detect possible outbreaks of diseases even before the diseases themselves have been identified (Buehler et al. 2004; Mandl et al. 2004). Syndromic surveillance thus relies on a wide variety of data available in electronic or other forms beyond those used in traditional surveillance (Chretien et al. 2008; Heffernan et al. 2004). This includes information such as data about chief complaints, symptoms, medication sales; grocery store purchases such as pediatric electrolyte formulas or even orange juice; absenteeism from work or school; or internet queries for topics such as "influenza" or "fever."[1] For example, an important data source in syndromic surveillance is emergency room visits. One of the measures of disaster preparedness employed in the American College of Emergency Physicians' report card on the status of emergency medicine in the United States is the presence of real-time surveillance systems for common emergency department presentations (American College of Emergency Physicians 2009). As an illustration, North Dakota receives daily electronic feeds of chief complaint data from eight large emergency rooms in the state (North Dakota Health Department). Such feeds can alert public health officials about unusual clusters or increased rates of symptoms such as diarrhea, respiratory illness, or joint pain—and trigger further investigation about what might be causing the observed phenomena. In Europe, syndromic surveillance has been developed quite extensively (Smith et al. 2006; Josseran et al. 2006).

[1] Google health claims to be able to predict flu trends more quickly than CDC (Ginsburg 2008; Google 2008).

Syndromic surveillance, as thus understood, is based on novel data sources and data-mining techniques: emergency department data in electronic form, electronic medical records, electronic prescription data, pharmacy purchases, reported absenteeism, and traffic on the web in particular (Sengupta et al. 2008; Mandl et al. 2004). Such surveillance presents new possibilities and new challenges. One difficulty in the construction of syndromic surveillance techniques is validation: for example, is an increase in certain pharmacy purchases indicative of a rise in respiratory disease? (One study concludes that it is (van den Wijngaard et al. 2008).) Other studies have concluded that reports of respiratory symptoms in pediatric emergency rooms are indicative of a rise in respiratory syncytial virus (Bourgeois et al. 2006). On the other hand, purchases of antivirals may be generated by individual decisions to stockpile after publicity about influenza, rather than with any increased rates of influenza itself (Centers for Disease Control 2006). Concerns have also been raised about the accuracy of syndromic surveillance at single institutions; however, the problem may be limited data rather than methodological difficulties with syndromic surveillance per se (Weber and Pitrak 2003). Even when measures are validated, sensitivity and specificity pose additional problems. It is desirable to have highly sensitive measures to avoid missing detection of potentially serious outbreaks, but this raises concerns about false positives and attendant costs and risks (Buehler et al. 2004).

Several features of syndromic surveillance are particularly noteworthy for ethical purposes. With traditional reporting systems, conditions of interest are identified in advance. This identification is typically codified by legislative action or administrative rule-making. There has thus been a degree of public oversight of the decision to make a disease reportable. However, as we detail below, even recent and proposed reforms of public health law have not anticipated the full range of possibilities syndromic surveillance may present. Thus, as it has developed to date, syndromic surveillance has not been subject to the level of public scrutiny that has attended traditional public health surveillance. Legally-established reporting regimes typically also implement mechanisms for protecting the confidentiality of any reported data, but comparable regimes have not been fully developed for protecting the data obtained for purposes of syndromic surveillance.

Moreover, because in traditional surveillance the need for reporting is identified in advance, informed consent discussions of health care providers with their patients can include any relevant reporting requirements. A physician recommending testing to a patient for HIV or syphilis can explain the significance of a positive test result before the patient agrees to the test. With new methods of syndromic surveillance, by contrast, issues of informed consent and data use are far less well analyzed and understood. As it involves the identification of patterns of interest, patients and providers may not know in advance that a particular symptomatic report entered into an electronic medical record will be of any significance whatsoever: whether *this* fever triggers interest may only be known after a pattern of fevers is observed in an interoperable set of electronic records. Moreover, no informed consent process at all is involved in such activities as purchase of an over-the-counter anti-diarrheal or a search of the web for information about managing fever.

Some syndromic surveillance collects electronically-stored data that includes identifying information about individual patients, allowing for possible investigation if patterns of concern are identified (Nordin et al. 2008). Such data collection practices pose risks to patient confidentiality if data security is imperfectly protected (Myers et al. 2008). To be sure, some syndromic surveillance in the United States involves "de-identified" electronic health data, health records from which a defined list of identifying information has been removed as set out in the federal privacy rule for medical information transmitted in electronic form (HIPAA 2008).[2] However, increasingly concerns have been raised about whether de-identified data can be readily re-identified, especially when data sets are combined (Porter 2008), as data sets are likely to be under robust syndromic surveillance regimes. Consider, for example, combining electronic medical records, pharmacy purchase data, and grocery store purchases of over-the-counter remedies using a frequent-shopper discount card that contains purchaser identifying

[2] HIPAA defines "de-identified data" as data from which 18 identifiers (such as date of birth, social security number, medical record number, telephone number, and so on) have been removed, 45 C.F.R.§164.514(b)(2) (2008). Under HIPAA, data may also be de-identified if statistical analysis determines that the probability of re-identification is very small.

information. Moreover, entities issuing de-identified data sets may keep coded identifiers to permit re-identification in case of public health need (Sengupta et al. 2008). Thus there may be risks to patient confidentiality even when de-identified data sets are employed for syndromic surveillance. These very real risks to confidentiality highlight the importance of careful consideration of regimes for data protection if syndromic surveillance is to be employed.

Even when re-identification of individual patients is unlikely, syndromic surveillance may pose risks of stigmatization of both groups and individuals whose group membership is known (National Committee on Vital and Health Statistics 2008, 4). This is of particular concern given the imperfect validation of syndromic surveillance techniques, as well as the risks of false positives when the emphasis is placed on detection methods with high sensitivity (Stoto et al. 2004). Syndromic surveillance may identify suspected higher rates of illness or disease risk in particular populations. One quite recent example of group stigmatization involved an HIV exposure alarm among students at a particular school (whose school population happened to be 99% African-American) (Gay 2008).[3] Stigmatization has also been alleged concerning minority patients with diabetes in New York City (Goldman et al. 2008). The untoward result may be prejudicial to everyone who meets the given description, without regard to the accuracy of the initial suspicions and without concern for them as people, too.

But there is surely more to come than the syndromic surveillance methods we have seen to date. The data collection in syndromic surveillance, as it has developed so far, is just the beginning. Surely, as more robust systems of electronic health records are put into play, more extensive data mining for public health purposes will come into play. But there is more. Consider the thought experiment—or perhaps realistic proposal—that we developed elsewhere: universal rapid testing for infectious disease in airports, on public transit, at schools, workplaces, movies and sporting events (Battin et al. 2009, Ch. 15). Or suppose that it were possible to detect overall temperature levels in a population by means of remote thermal imaging. Suppose this could be done in such a way that no one was aware that data were being collected and no information about particular individuals was included in the data collection. All that was ascertained was the occurrence of shifts in the amount of heat emitted by bodies of a given size in a particular area. Such sensing is a technologically possible method for determining whether there has been an increase in bodily temperatures in a population—and a possible method for determining whether a corresponding rise in infection rates has been occurring in a population. Although remote thermal sensing of people while they are in their homes would likely be an unreasonable search and seizure under United States law, this use of thermal imaging could be a very effective way of ascertaining increased rates of infectious disease in a population, perhaps even more effective than monitoring data about purchases of aspirin or acetaminophen in local pharmacies.[4]

## Syndromic Surveillance and the Patient as Victim and Vector

A central goal of surveillance is to identify threats to the public health so that effective intervention can take place. With transmissible disease, surveillance focuses on the individual as a source of illness to be identified and contained, or as a source of information about transmission. In the language of the analysis we have developed elsewhere, that of the patient as "victim and vector", an aspect of surveillance is to regard everyone as potential vectors from whom

[3] For a description of the racial stereotyping that occurred to students at the school, see Brown (2008). Initial indications are that the scare was a false alarm (Bernhard and Giegerich 2008).

[0] In *Kyllo v. United States*, 533 U.S. 27 (2006), the Supreme Court held that it was a violation of reasonable expectations of privacy to use a remote thermal sensing device to measure differences in the exterior temperature of a dwelling, and thus an unreasonable search and seizure without a warrant. In thus ruling, the Court attempted to fashion doctrine that would apply well beyond the crude sensing device employed by the police to ascertain from differential outside temperatures of the house whether Kyllo was using the high-temperature lamps to cultivate marijuana within. Justice Stevens, in dissent, argued that the case was just a garden-variety use of external observation, albeit enhanced—just like the visual observation that snow was melting differentially in areas of the home's roof. This analysis would not apply, however to measurements obtained when someone is outside of the home. Also worthy of note, the new International Health Regulations specifically exclude thermal imaging from the definition of invasive procedure (International Health Regulations, art. 1 (definitions)).

society is to be protected. Syndromic surveillance is no exception to this generalization.

As we have argued, however, the field of bioethics has been impoverished by the failure to attend to persons as *both* victims and vectors (Battin et al. 2009). As human animals, we are way stations for microbial transmission, biologically interrelated in networks of organism interchange. Seen from the perspective of our ordinary lives, we are more-or-less susceptible to infection: some are immune-compromised, some already ill, some in conditions of poverty where disease transmission is especially high and susceptibility is great, and some protected by living in conditions of apparent relative safety. However, there is a sense in which no one is immune: we are all potentially victims and vectors to each other, unknown and unknowingly. As victims, we are concerned that vectors may transmit illness to us; but as vectors, we are victims too. We exist behind what might be thought of as an infectious-disease veil of ignorance; our ethical judgments must come to terms with this feature of our human condition. This is not a matter of mere self-interest, requiring us to calculate from our own particular circumstances how likely infection is to occur. It is a deeper metaphysical point: both the victim and vector perspectives belong to everyone, all of the time.

To the extent that it is effective in detecting potentially dangerous disease—an improvement on other surveillance techniques—syndromic surveillance would be defensible from the perspective in which we do not know whether we are victims or vectors. It should be emphasized that this justification is contingent on the efficacy of syndromic surveillance: if syndromic surveillance raises insurmountable technical difficulties, cannot be validated, is less sensitive or specific than other surveillance methods, or even poses greater risks than these other methods for limited or no improvement, it would not be justified out of concern to protect ourselves from potential vectors. But even if syndromic surveillance is justified as a means for preventing disease spread, this is not the end of the ethical story; any such justification would also warrant attention to ourselves as victims, in a number of respects.

First of all, as victims we would want to be sure that surveillance is not more extensive than apparently needed to detect outbreaks of potentially serious disease. Widespread "fishing" expeditions of uncertain validity would be unacceptable to us as victims. Otherwise, the risks to ourselves as victims who are affected by surveillance might be greater than the gains to ourselves in being protected from potential vectors. But this requirement of narrow tailoring is just a beginning.

Additionally, as vectors who are also potential victims we would want assurance that we are protected to the extent possible in the course of whatever surveillance takes place. Such protection starts by subjecting surveillance methods to public oversight. At a minimum, there must be transparency about what is happening with respect to surveillance: public knowledge of what surveillance is taking place and how it is being conducted. Without such transparency, immense amounts of data may be collected about people, combined and recombined, without any public knowledge of what is happening whatsoever. There should as well be some kind of public decision making process—legislation or administrative rule-making, for example—to scrutinize and accept the surveillance process. Finally, there should be public oversight of surveillance: a mechanism for assessing whether methods being employed are appropriately limited to need, and that people are informed if there are breaches of guarantees such as confidentiality.

Arguably, such public knowledge and oversight is the best available substitute for an informed consent process on the individual patient level. If there is full public information about what surveillance is being done, as well as oversight through the political process, then the political process might be viewed as analogous to community consent of the form utilized in research when subjects cannot be identified in advance (McClure et al. 2003). However, it is important to note that so-called "community consent" models as they are currently implemented may fail to communicate adequately with community members about planned research. As victims, we would want to insist that syndromic surveillance be fully vetted at the political level, and that there be ongoing public oversight to ensure that safeguards are employed as promised.

One of the most serious objections to any surveillance is patient privacy and confidentiality. As we have already indicated, the novel uses of data in syndromic surveillance may place serious pressures on confidentiality. To take just one example, if a novel influenza strain appears as it apparently did in the spring of 2009, intense efforts may be devoted to identifying and detaining air travelers with potential exposures (Centers for Disease Control 2008). Although these two concepts are often used interchangeably, privacy refers to the initial intrusion—the contact from which data are obtained—and confidentiality refers to individual control over the information thus obtained. From the victim/vector perspective, it is not clear that privacy is the more important value. Protection from each other as vectors may be significantly inadequate without the initial access that allows data to be gathered. At the same time, if confidentiality is not protected and people are identified, then risks of harm may be significant. These risks stem from the information becoming known, not from its being gathered in the first place; the only likely harm, for example, from a grocery store keeping an electronic record of an aspirin purchase, even a purchase linked to a particular individual, might be identification of that individual as being ill. The reason for protecting privacy is not the harm involved in the moment of data gathering; it is instead the concern that, once gathered, the data will inevitably come to light. To put the point succinctly, confidentiality is the reason for protecting privacy, not the reverse (Francis 2008).

Because of the more extensive threats to confidentiality involved in syndromic surveillance, reconsideration of what data confidentiality and security require in this context is especially urgent. As victims, we would like to be assured that we will not be publicly identified as disease threats—and that if we are identified at all, it will be for our own protection. This requires assurance that when a disease threat is determined and individuals must be contacted, as when codes are broken with de-identified data sets to all for individual contact, the contact will include offers of treatment—or if treatment is not yet a possibility, with assurances of protection from harm to the extent possible. It also requires assurance that we will be told if confidentiality is ever breached in this or other ways, so that we may know about the need for protection and be able to take steps to avoid harm from the confidentiality breach.

Finally, as victims we will also be concerned about risks of stigmatization. To some extent, transparency and political oversight can help to modulate these risks. But the risks remain, at least in a world in which fear and prejudice have not been forgotten. One critic of New York City's surveillance for diabetes argued that these risks of harm demand that surveillance be coupled with the availability of resources for prevention and treatment.

> These initiatives do not balance heightened surveillance and intervention with the provision of meaningful safeguards or resources for prevention and treatment. The programs intrude on the doctor-patient relationship and may alienate the very patients and health professionals they aim to serve. (Goldman et al. 2008)

One way to blunt or mitigate the risks of stigmatization is to make prevention and treatment available as a complement to surveillance activities—to everyone, to the extent possible. If prevention and treatment are available, people will have less reason to fear and to regard others as ones-to-be-feared. Moreover, prevention and treatment are what people have to gain from the risks of having data about them be used in efforts to identify disease early on.

Nonetheless, the most difficult cases are those in which prevention and treatment are not available, because supplies are scarce, treatment is very expensive, or treatment has yet to be developed. With pandemic H5N1 influenza, this is exactly the fear: that it will be highly lethal and that anti-virals will prove ineffective. As victim-selves, the best we can do in such circumstances is to cooperate in efforts to stop disease at the earliest point. Thus we would support syndromic surveillance if it seems likely to be effective. But we would want the oversight to be very careful indeed—with ongoing attention paid to what surveillance techniques are being employed and whether they continue to be needed or effective. And we would want society to continue to be engaged in the project of considering how to respect people who are victims of disease, even if their conditions cannot be ameliorated.

## Syndromic Surveillance and the New International Health Regulations

Although the need for reform of public health laws has been widely recognized, especially in the wake of fears of pandemic influenza and the realities of SARS and 9–11, reforms that have been enacted may not have caught up fully with the possibilities of syndromic surveillance. Legal regimes governing surveillance function at many different levels, from the World Health Organization to the very local. Here we give a snapshot of recent reforms in the WHO International Health Regulations that are important but that may not grapple with the full ethical implications of syndromic surveillance. Although these reforms contemplate more extensive and effective surveillance, they are non-specific about whether what is contemplated is a wider range of traditional disease surveillance or shifts to syndromic surveillance.

In June of 2007, the new International Health Regulations went into effect. These Regulations require states parties to meet specified functional requirements for surveillance. "Surveillance" in the Regulations is defined as "the systematic ongoing collection, collation, and analysis of data for public health purposes" (International Health Regulations, art. 1). The Regulations thus represent an enormous advance over the prior regulations, which only required reporting of three identified diseases: cholera, yellow fever, and plague. At the local level, functional requirements include the capacity to detect events involving disease or death above expected levels in all areas of the territory (International Health Regulations, Annex I). They also include the ability to report available information to the relevant response level—information including clinical descriptions, laboratory results, sources and types of risk, numbers of human cases and deaths, conditions affecting spread, and health measures taken. Local authorities are also expected to be able to implement preliminary control measures immediately. At the intermediate level, requirements include confirmation of the status of events and the ability to support or augment control measures. They include, in addition, assessment of the urgency of the situation and the ability to transmit information about any urgent situations to national authorities. National authorities, in turn, must be able to assess events reported as urgent and to report as necessary to the WHO. They must also be able to provide adequate public health responses on a 24-hour basis.

These are clearly extensive requirements and may be difficult to meet in economically challenged areas of the world. In recognition, the Regulations also commit more affluent states parties to help the less affluent to comply with the requirements. They also permit a two-year grace period for implementation generally, and longer periods for compliance with requirements such as adequate response capability. As of February 2008, all 194 nations were states parties to the IHR (http://www.who.int/csr/ihr/states_parties/en/index.html). Notably, the United States has become a state party under a reservation: the insistence on implementing the regulations consistently with federalism. Three limiting "understandings" were also submitted by the United States: that the notification requirements apply whether the emergency is natural or human-caused in origin; that the requirement to report if "practicable" known emergencies outside the country's territory does not apply in cases that would jeopardize the effective operation of U.S. armed forces; and that the IHR do not create enforceable private rights of action (http://www.who.int/csr/ihr/states_parties/en/index.html).

Although the new Regulations are widely regarded as a major step forward, concerns remain. These include the lack of technical capacity to implement the regulations, issues of resource allocation, concerns about privacy, and questions about overall governance (PLoS Medicine Editors 2007; Baker and Fidler 2006). The editors of *PLoS Medicine*, for example, point out that most of the investment in preparing for pandemic influenza has involved stockpiling resource in developed countries (PLoS Medicine Editors 2007). Other discussions praise the wider reach of the regulations about what are regarded as events of public health significance, but also express concern about whether the investment will be there to build the technical capacity for the required surveillance (Sturtevant et al. 2007).

Despite the advances they represent, it is controversial whether the Regulations in their final form are meant to include the capacity for syndromic surveillance. Baker and Fidler (2006) contend that although syndromic surveillance was discussed, the decision was not to include it in the Regulations because of concerns about validity. However, in fashioning the requirements for surveillance and reporting, the Regulations define a public health emergency of international concern as "an extraordinary event which is determined . . . to constitute a public health risk to other states through the international spread of disease and to potentially require a coordinated international response" (International Health Regulations, art. 1). This definition elides whether the reference is only to identified diagnoses or agents or includes syndromic identification as well. Although the definition of "surveillance" quoted above is surely broad enough to include syndromic surveillance, nothing more specific is stated about the possibilities. In discussing the resource issues raised by the Regulations, Chretien et al. (2008) give illustrations of successful establishment of syndromic surveillance capacity in Indonesia and Peru. It seems increasingly likely, moreover, that as syndromic surveillance techniques become better developed, pressures will increase for their use in detecting emerging disease before spread becomes likely—especially, we might hypothesize, spread to more affluent areas of the world.

Thus if the Regulations encompass syndromic surveillance, they are insufficiently attentive to the ethical issues we have raised. The Regulations state that all measures should be implemented in a transparent and non-discriminatory manner (International Health Regulations, art. 42), but do not set out any specific requirements for what this might involve. With respect to privacy, Article 45 states both that data should be processed anonymously and that personal information may be used when needed, so long as they are processed fairly and not kept longer than necessary (International Health Regulations, art. 45). These provisions are quite vague, however, and do not attend specifically to the privacy and confidentiality issues that may be raised by increasing use of non-traditional forms of surveillance. Although the Regulations commit more affluent countries to helping others in developing surveillance capacities (International Health Regulations, art. 44), they do not include commitments to more extensive development of the health infrastructure needed to ensure that treatment is available to the extent possible for those who are identified as disease threats.

## Conclusion

So-called "syndromic surveillance" poses novel and unexplored possibilities for protection from disease, protection that as victims we would find especially important when diseases are severe and treatments are unknown or inadequately distributed. However, because of the risks to confidentiality and concerns about stigmatization, data use in syndromic surveillance may pose more extensive risks to perceived vectors than more traditional forms of surveillance. As attempts to monitor for emerging pandemic infections continue to develop, the ethical problems raised by syndromic surveillance will need much further attention.

## References


American College of Emergency Physicians. 2009. National report card on the state of emergency medicine. http://www.emreportcard.org/uploadedFiles/ACEP-ReportCard-10-22-08.pdf.pdf.

ARIZ. REV. STAT. § 36–782 (2008).

Baker, M.G. and D.P. Fidler. 2006. Global public health surveillance under New International Health Regulations. *Emerging Infectious Diseases* 12(7): 1058–1065.

Battin, M.P., L.P. Francis, J.A. Jacobson, and C.B. Smith. 2009. *The patient as victim and vector: Ethics and infectious disease*. New York: Oxford University Press.

Bernhard, B., and S. Giegerich. 2008. State finds no HIV outbreak at Normandy High; County Health Department continues its own investigation. *St. Louis Post Dispatch* 4 (December), C1.

Bourgeois, F.T., et al. 2006. Validation of syndromic surveillance for respiratory infections. *Annals of Emergency Medicine* 47(3): 265.e1.

Brown, S., Jr. 2008. Normandy High problem quickly became a racial issue. *St. Louis Post Dispatch* 26(October), D1.

Buehler, J.W., et al. 2004. Framework for evaluating public health surveillance systems for early detection of outbreaks. *MMWR* 53(RR05): 1–11. http://www.cdc.gov/mmwr/preview/mmwrhtml/rr5305a1.htm (accessed April 22, 2009).

CALIFORNIA HEALTH & SAFETY CODE [DEERING'S] § 103885 (2008).

Centers for Disease Control. 2006. Increased antiviral medication sales before the 2005–06 influenza season–New York City. *MMWR* 55(10): 277–279.

Centers for Disease Control. 2008. Federal air travel restrictions for public health purposes—United States June 2007–May 2008. *MMWR* 57: 1009–1012.

Centers for Disease Control. National Notifiable Diseases Surveillance System, http://www.cdc.gov/ncphi/disss/nndss/nndsshis.htm.

Chretien, J.-P., et al. 2008. Syndromic surveillance: Adapting innovations to developing settings. *PLoS Medicine* 5(3): e72. doi:10.1371/journal.pmed.0050072 (accessed April 22, 2009).

Francis, L.P. 2008. Privacy and confidentiality: The importance of context. *The Monist* 91(1): 52–67.

Gay, M. 2008. H.I.V. scare unnerves a St. Louis high school. *New York Times*, 9 November 9, A30.

Ginsburg, J. 2008. Detecting influenza epidemics using search engine query data. *Nature*, accessed April 22, 2009. doi:10.1038/nature07634.

Goldman, J., et al. 2008. New York city's initiatives on diabetes and HIV/AIDS: Implications for patient care, public health, and medical professionalism. *American Journal of Public Health* 98(5): 807–813. doi:10.2105/AJPH.2007.121152.

Google.org.Flu trends. 2008. http://www.google.org/about/flutrends/how.html.

Gostin, L.O. and B.E. Berkman. 2007. Pandemic influenza: Ethics, law, and the public's health. *Administrative Law Review* 59: 121–175.

Heffernan, R., et al. 2004. Syndromic surveillance in public health practice, New York City. *Emerging Infectious Diseases* 10(5): 858–864.

HIPAA. 45 C.F.R.§164.514(b)(2) (2008).

International Health Regulations. http://whqlibdoc.who.int/publications/2008/9789241580410_eng.pdf (accessed April 22, 2009).

Josseran, L., et al. 2006. Syndromic surveillance based on emergency department activity and crude mortality: Two examples. *Eurosurveillance* 11(12): 1.

*Kyllo v. United States*, 533 U.S. 27 (2006).

Mandl, K.D., et al. 2004. Implementing syndromic surveillance: A practical guide informed by the early experience. *Journal of the American Medical Informatics Association* 11(2): 141–150.

Mariner, W.K. 2007. Mission creep: Public health surveillance and medical privacy. *Boston University Law Review. Boston University. School of Law* 87: 347–395.

McClure, K.B., et al. 2003. Attitudes of emergency department patients and visitors regarding emergency exception from informed consent in resuscitation research, community consultation, and public notification. *Academic Emergency Medicine* 10(4): 352–359. doi:10.1111/j.1553-2712.2003.tb01348.x.

MINN. STAT. § 175.33 (2008).

Myers, J., et al. 2008. Ethics in public health research: Privacy and public health at risk: Public health confidentiality in the digital age. *American Journal of Public Health* 98(5): 793–801.

National Committee on Vital and Health Statistics. 2008. Enhancing protection for uses of health data: A stewardship framework. http://www.ncvhs.hhs.gov/080424rpt.pdf (accessed December 13, 2008).

Nordin, J.D., et al. 2008. Bioterrorism surveillance and privacy: Intersection of HIPAA, the common rule, and public health law. *American Journal of Public Health* 98(5): 802–807.

North Dakota Health Department. http://www.ndhealth.gov/Disease/Surveillance/syndromicsurveillance.htm.

NY CLS PUB HEALTH § 2130 (2008).

PLoS Medicine Editors. 2007. How is WHO responding to global public health threats? *PLoS Med* 4(5): e197. doi:10.1371/journal.pmed.0040197.

Porter, C.C. 2008. De-identified data and third party data mining: The risk of re-identication of personal information. *Shidler J.L. Com. & Tech.* 5 (Sep. 23). http://www.lctjournal.washington.edu/Vol5/a03Porter.html (accessed December 12, 2008).

Sengupta, S., N.S. Calman, and G. Hripcsak. 2008. A model for expanded public health reporting in the context of HIPAA. *Journal of the American Medical Informatics Association* 15: 569–574.

Smith, G.E., et al. 2006. A national syndromic surveillance system for England and Wales using calls to a telephone helpline. *Eurosurveillance* 11(12): 1.

Stoto, M.A. 2008. Public health surveillance in the twenty—first century: Achieving population health goals while protecting individuals' privacy and confidentiality. *Georgetown Law Journal* 96: 703–719.

Stoto, M.A., M. Schonlau, and L.T. Mariano. 2004. Syndromic surveillance: Is it worth the effort? *Chance* 17(1): 19–24.

Sturtevant, J.L., A. Anema, and J.S. Brownstein. 2007. The new International Health Regulations: Considerations for global public health surveillance. *Disaster Medicine and Public Health Preparedness* 1(2): 117–121.

van den Wijngaard, C., et al. 2008. Validation of syndromic surveillance for respiratory pathogen activity. *Emerging Infectious Diseases* 14(6): 917–925.

Weber, S.G. and D. Pitrak. 2003. Accuracy of a Local Surveillance System for Early Detection of Emerging Infectious Disease. *JAMA* 290(5): 596–598.

# Part VII: Dual-Use Research

Nanoethics (2009) 3:175–183
DOI 10.1007/s11569-009-0074-y

ORIGINAL PAPER

# Dual-Use Research Codes of Conduct: Lessons from the Life Sciences

**Michael J. Selgelid**

Received: 21 October 2009 / Accepted: 4 November 2009 / Published online: 20 November 2009


**Abstract** This paper considers multiple meanings of the expression 'dual use' and examines lessons to be learned from the life sciences when considering ethical and policy issues associated with the dual-use nature of nanotechnology (and converging technologies). After examining recent controversial dual-use experiments in the life sciences, it considers the potential roles and limitations of science codes of conduct for addressing concerns associated with dual-use science and technology. It concludes that, rather than being essentially associated with voluntary self-governance of the scientific community, codes of conduct should arguably be part of a broader regulatory oversight system.

**Keywords** Ethics · Nanoethics · Dual use · Biological weapons · Chemical weapons · Mousepox · Polio · Influenza · Codes of conduct · Responsibility · Science policy · Regulation

M. J. Selgelid (✉)
Centre for Applied Philosophy and Public Ethics (CAPPE), The Australian National University,
LPO Box 8260, Canberra ACT 2601, Australia
e-mail: michael.selgelid@anu.edu.au
URL: http://www.cappe.edu.au/staff/michael-selgelid.htm

M. J. Selgelid
World Health Organization (WHO) Collaborating Centre for Bioethics, The Australian National University, Canberra, Australia

M. J. Selgelid
National Centre for Biosecurity, The Australian National University, Canberra, Australia

## 'Dual Use'—Multiple Meanings

The expression 'dual-use technology' was originally used to refer to technology that could be used for both civilian and military purposes. This was a non-normative use of the expression 'dual use'. Conceived this way, "dual-use" technology was not necessarily considered to be problematic (except, perhaps, by those who think that military activity is inherently evil). From the perspective of policymakers, *this kind* of dual-use technology could sometimes be considered a good thing—i.e., a way of killing two birds with one stone by promoting a particular path of technological development. There are obvious economic advantages to developing technologies that will simultaneously meet both a country's civilian and its military needs. Although dual-use technologies, as traditionally conceived, could thus in some contexts be considered desirable, they could also give cause for concern. A country might be reluctant, that is, to export dual-use technologies (as traditionally conceived) to adversary countries to which it would not ordinarily want to export weapons.

In recent years, the expression 'dual use' has most commonly been used in an explicitly normative fashion. The expression 'dual use' is now usually meant to refer to research, knowledge, technology, or materials that can be used for both beneficial and harmful purposes. Current debates about "dual-use" science and technology refer to science and technology that has legitimate uses (e.g., in medicine) but that might also be used by malevolent actors for nefarious purposes (e.g., in bioterrorism) [14]. Though the expression 'dual use' could be used to apply broadly to things that might be used for both good and bad purposes, when characterized this way almost everything could count as "dual use". Machetes are used for farming, but they were also used in the Rwandan genocide as tools of murder. Paper has obvious good uses, but a piece of paper could also be used to (intentionally) set fire to a building. Contemporary debates about dual-use science and technology, however, have usually been more narrowly circumscribed. Most of the current debate has focused on research/knowledge/technologies/materials with implications for weapons, and usually weapons of mass destruction in particular—i.e., where the consequences of malevolent use would be especially severe.

There are thus at least three plausible definitions of 'dual-use science and technology':

1. that which has both civilian and military applications
2. that which can be used for both beneficial/good and harmful/bad purposes, and
3. that which has both beneficial/good and harmful/bad purposes—where the harmful/bad purposes involve weapons, and usually weapons of mass destruction in particular.

In what follows I will be operating with the third definition of 'dual use' (which falls at the intersection of the first two definitions), because this is the way 'dual use' is (implicitly) most commonly used in contemporary debates about the "dual use dilemma".

The dual use dilemma arises, then, because it is sometimes the case that the very same scientific research that can be used to benefit humankind can also be used to cause grave harm (e.g., via biochemical weapons). The dual use phenomenon poses a dilemma for well-intentioned individual scientists who must decide what projects to work on. Responsible scientists want to generate scientific knowledge that will benefit humankind; but, at the same time, they presumably want to avoid generation of scientific knowledge that would ultimately do more harm than good. The dual use phenomenon also poses a dilemma for policymakers, who aim to make policies that promote and/or avoid the same kinds of outcomes—and who are responsible to citizens for making policies that do so.

The dual use dilemma is not altogether new. When atomic physicists made key discoveries regarding atomic fission and the chain reaction early in the 20th century, they realized that these discoveries might have beneficial applications in medicine and the generation of energy, but they also realized that the same discoveries might lead to the development of new, monstrously devastating weapons [18]. The production and use of the first atomic bombs revealed that these concerns were justified. Since the dawn of the 21st century, the dual-use potential of the life sciences has become especially salient. In many ways, the situation of life sciences at present is similar to that of physics when atomic weapons first became possible. This is partly revealed by a recent unclassified CIA document titled "Our Darker Bioweapons Future" which claims, among other things, that recent advances in biotechnology enable the production of "biological agents... worse than any disease known to man" [4]. It has also been recognized that nanotechnology and other converging technologies associated with life sciences are increasingly raising dual use dangers. A recent US National Research Council (NRC) report on *Globalization, Biosecurity, and the Future of the Life Sciences* notes that

> other fields not traditionally viewed as biotechnologies—such as materials science, information technology, and nanotechnology—are becoming integrated and synergistic with traditional biotechnologies in extraordinary ways enabling the development of previously unimaginable technological applications. It is undeniable that this new knowledge and these advancing technologies hold enormous potential to improve public health and agriculture, strengthen national economies, and close the development gap between resource-rich and resource-poor countries. However, as with all scientific revolutions, there is a potential dark side to the advancing power and global spread of these and other technologies. For millennia, every major new technology has been used for hostile purposes, and most experts believe it naive to think that the extraordinary growth in

the life sciences and its associated technologies might not similarly be exploited for destructive purposes [15: 1–2].

The dual-use potential of nanotechnology is partly revealed by its association with (i.e., as a constituent technology of) "synthetic biology", which is commonly considered to be a paradigm example of an emerging dual-use science/technology [17]. In what follows, I aim to show that those concerned with ethical issues associated with the dual-use potential of nanotechnology have much to learn from recent history regarding dual-use research in the life sciences and associated debates regarding the role of science codes of conduct in particular.

## Lessons from Life Sciences

There are numerous reasons why the dual use dilemma has been a centre of attention in life science policy debates in recent years. One explanation is the elevation in fear of bioterrorism following the events of 11 September 2001 and the subsequent anthrax attacks in the US. Recent developments in the biological sciences—and three controversial experiments in particular—have also drawn attention to the problem. Australian scientists, for example, genetically engineered the mousepox virus with the aim to develop an immunocontraceptive that would serve as a means of (rodent) pest control. To their surprise they discovered that they had accidentally produced a superstrain of mousepox that killed both mice that were naturally resistant to, and mice that had been vaccinated against, ordinary mousepox. They published their findings, along with description of materials and methods, in 2001 [7]. In a second study, American researchers at SUNY, Stony Brook artificially synthesised a "live" polio virus from scratch [3]. Following the map of the polio RNA genome, which is published on the Internet, they stitched together corresponding DNA sequences purchased via mail order. The addition of the synthesised genome to "cell juice" containing key proteins resulted in a virus that paralysed and killed mice. They published their results, including description of materials and methods, in 2002.

Both of these studies have implications for smallpox in particular. The former study might enable production of vaccine resistant smallpox (which is closely related to mousepox), and the latter might enable artificial synthesis of smallpox by those that would not have access to the natural virus. Smallpox, meanwhile, is one of the worst diseases known to humankind—and it usually tops lists of feared biological weapons agents. Because routine smallpox vaccination ended with eradication of smallpox in 1980, a large proportion of the world population now lacks immunity to the disease. Modelling has shown that a smallpox attack (e.g., by bioterrorists) could lead to the devastation expected from (a series of) nuclear attack(s). The significance of the mousepox study partly relates to the fact that there is no known treatment for smallpox; vaccination is our only protection against it.

In a more recent study the 1918 flu virus—which killed 20 to 100 million people—was reconstructed in 2005 via synthetic genomic techniques similar to those used in the polio study [21]. Again, the (US) researchers published their findings along with description of materials and methods. This study has important implications for medicine, especially given current concerns about pandemic influenza; but it may also facilitate bioterrorism.

Given obvious implications for biological weapons making, critics complained that these studies, and others like them, should not have been conducted and/or that their results (and/or description of materials and methods) should not have been published. Publishing such studies, according to critics, alerted would-be bioterrorists to new possible ways of making weapons and (worse) provided them with explicit instructions—"recipes", "road-maps", or "blueprints"—for doing so. Many in the scientific community, on the other hand, defended what was done. All of this research was conducted by well-intentioned researchers and, it was argued, there were good reasons for publication. Many claimed, for example, that publication was important to inform the scientific community about new dangers we need to develop protections against. In response to objections that materials and methods should have been omitted from the published articles, it was argued that publishing description of materials and methods is essential to scientific methodology (e.g., for purposes of replication and verification).

Whether or not these studies should have been published, we can imagine some that probably should not be. If a scientist (perhaps accidentally) discovered an easy way to produce a pathogen as deadly, contagious, and untreatable as smallpox, for example, then details about how to do so should presumably be kept out of the public domain—at least until appropriate protections are developed [19]. Hypothetical examples from nanotechnology and other areas of science and technology could also be imagined. If censorship of the life sciences or nanotechnology might sometimes be appropriate, then the important question of who should have ultimate decision making authority arises. Should we rely on voluntary self-governance of scientists (perhaps guided by codes of conduct) in matters of censorship—or might censorship by government sometimes be legitimate? Government censorship of nuclear science with weapons implications has been the norm for decades [14].

Recent history of dual-use life science research is relevant to nanotechnology partly because synthetic biology[1] lies at the intersection of biology and nanotechnology and partly because a majority of contemporary debate and policy making regarding dual-use research has thus far focused on the life sciences in particular, and especially the three studies described above.

In the aftermath of the mousepox and polio studies, for example, a number of important science journals announced that they would screen submitted articles for security implications and that they would modify, or refrain from publishing, studies in cases where harms would otherwise outweigh benefits [10]. In 2004 the NRC published the "Fink Report"—a landmark study of the dual use dilemma in the context of biotechnology [14]. Among other things, it called for voluntary self-governance of the life science community in matters of censorship, increased education of scientists about the dual use phenomenon, and the development of relevant codes of conduct for scientists.

## Codes of Conduct—Roles

In the context of dual-use science and technology, be it biology or nanotechnology, there are numerous reasons why science codes of conduct might be important; and there are various roles they might be expected to play. Even the best codes of conduct, however, will have important limitations that must be kept in mind.

### Raising Awareness of the Dual Use Phenomenon and Relevant Weapons Conventions

One of the primary roles envisioned for science codes of conduct in the context of dual-use science is that they would promote much needed awareness-raising among scientists [20]. It has been shown, for example, that life scientists generally lack awareness of the ways in which their well-intentioned research might be abused by malevolent actors and, indeed, that they lack awareness of the dual use phenomenon in general. There is likewise remarkably little awareness, among life scientists, of the 1972 Biological and Toxin Weapons Convention (BTWC) and/or its implications [5]. Codes of conduct which both draw attention to (the importance of adherence to) BTWC prohibitions and ways in which research permitted by the BTWC could be used (in prohibited ways) by malevolent actors is thus essential. Similar things can be presumably said about nanotechnology. Given what has been shown about the lack of awareness regarding these issues in the life sciences, it is not unlikely that those working in nanotechnology likewise lack awareness of the dual use phenomenon and details about what is prohibited by relevant biological and chemical weapons conventions.

### Raising Awareness Regarding Social Responsibility

A related role for codes of conduct is to raise awareness regarding scientists' social responsibilities more generally. This is especially important when we bear in mind the history of scientific culture [8]. At various times in history, to a greater or lesser degree, science has been characterized as neutral, apolitical, and/or value free. Common ideas among scientists have been that science involves an impartial pursuit of knowledge and/or that (scientific) knowledge is inherently good [11]. Another idea, which was heard especially often in debates about social responsibility in the context of nuclear weapons, is that knowledge, technology, and other fruits of science are neither good nor bad—and that, to the contrary, it is *the uses*

[1] which might, like the polio and 1918 flu studies, involve synthesis of pathogens.

*to which they are applied* (by others) that are good or bad. Similar things (relevant to nanotechnology) have recently been said about chemistry: "There are no bad molecules, only evil human beings" [2]. If this were so, then some might be tempted to think that well-intentioned scientists should not be considered responsible for any bad consequences that result from knowledge gained or technologies made possible by scientific research. If scientists do not produce anything that is inherently bad, one might think that scientists are not responsible for any bad outcomes that result from their morally neutral scientific pursuits and products. Those who employed scientific knowledge in a malign manner—and/or policy makers who failed to prevent them from doing so—would be responsible for bad outcomes, and scientists would remain innocent.

The idea that scientists should be (fully) divorced from responsibility for the consequences of their well-intentioned research, however, is not all that tenable. If one foresees that his work is likely to be used in ways that cause more harm than good and proceeds regardless, then he will be implicated in the bad consequences that ensue. If I knowingly enable a malevolent actor to cause harm, then I am partly responsible for harm that results. We should go farther by saying that scientists have a responsibility to consider the uses to which their work will be applied—and that they bear significant responsibility for bad outcomes that are foreseeable whether or not they are actually foreseen by the scientists in question. The point here is that scientists (within reason) have a responsibility to be aware and/or to reflect on the ways in which their work will be used. The failure to reflect—or to foresee the foreseeable—should be considered negligence. In the context of weapons of mass destruction, such negligence could cause grave harm.

Related ideas are eloquently stated in one of the earlier formal guidelines concerned with dual-use science in particular—the American Medical Association's 2005 "Guidelines to Prevent the Malevolent Use of Biomedical Research":

> Biomedical research may generate knowledge with potential for both beneficial and harmful application. Before participating in research, physician-researchers should assess foreseeable ramifications of their research in an effort to balance the promise of benefit from biomedical innovation against potential harms from corrupt application of the findings.
>
> In exceptional cases, assessment of the balance of future harms and benefits of research may preclude participation in the research; for instance, when the goals of research are antithetical to the foundations of the medical profession, as with the development of biological or chemical weapons [6].

I would argue that a similar statement can and should be adopted in codes of conduct for nanotechnology.

The importance of drawing attention to the weapons conventions, and their requirements, is often emphasised by those advocating scientific codes of conduct in the context of dual-use research. This is crucial, but it is also important to draw attention to responsibilities regarding well-intentioned dual-use research permitted by the weapons conventions. In addition to being familiar with, and acting in accordance with, international law, scientists should assess—and take (at least some) responsibility for—the harms and benefits of research that is legal. Neither the BTWC nor the 1993 Chemical Weapons Convention (CWC) was designed to address the dual use dilemma as defined earlier in this paper (e.g., according to the third, stipulated definition). As revealed by "general provisions clauses" in both the BTWC and CWC, the conventions' prohibitions largely turn on the *intentions* of researchers and/or research programs. Well-intentioned dual-use research falls outside the domain of these two weapons conventions' prohibitions. No one, so far as I am aware, has argued that the mousepox, polio, or flu studies contravened the biological or chemical weapons conventions. The point of critics was that these were dangerous experiments/publications—not that they were (already) prohibited ones. Even if these studies were (by hypothesis) too dangerous to be conducted or published, they were not illegal according to the relevant weapons conventions.

## Winning Trust

An additional role for codes of conduct, from the perspective of the scientific community, lies in the fact that their adoption may help win public trust in the scientific enterprise. Consider the history of nuclear weapons and current controversy surrounding the biotechnology revolution—especially things like cloning and genetically modified organisms—and growing concerns about the implications of nanotechnology. Despite the undeniable enormous benefits that scientific progress has made possible, the public is often (and sometimes rightly) fearful of scientific progress. Science, according to many, is driven by a technological imperative, where anything goes. People are afraid that, rather than being driven by what is best for society and humankind and/or the environment, science is driven by what is technically feasible—or, perhaps worse, by what will maximize industry profits. The public wants science to make the world a better place; and it funds scientific research with the expectation that it will do so. Commitment, via codes of conduct, to a value oriented approach to science—i.e., science explicitly aimed at the promotion of human flourishing and the avoidance of harm—may be instrumental in alleviating public anxiety about science. Insofar as the public funds science, the public holds the scientific enterprise accountable, the expectation being that science will promote the good of society. This is a social contract. A code of conduct with suitable content would partly amount to a scientists' pledge to hold up their end of the bargain. If codes are convincing—and followed—then trust will be gained.

### Avoiding Over-Regulation

A related role for science codes of conduct, and one that may be especially important from the perspective of the scientific community, is that endorsement of (appropriate) codes would partly amount to a statement that "we scientists will regulate our conduct, and these are the values and rules that we will live and work by." If science is potentially dangerous and if the scientific community does not acknowledge this and proactively (e.g., via the adoption of codes of conduct) take measures to govern its own conduct in a manner that the public is comfortable with, then more governmental regulation can be expected. The autonomy of science—i.e., scientific freedom—within limits anyway, is important. The Lysenko affair [9] in the former Soviet Union (which involved a thoroughgoing politicisation of biology), though an extreme example, illustrates reasons why this is so.

My point here is not that implementation of self-regulatory measures (such as the adoption of codes) by the science community would or should make governmental regulation of dual-use science unnecessary. The point is that proactive self-governance via codes of conduct, among other things, may help avoid a situation of overregulation. Some members of the synthetic biology community have explicitly advocated proactive self-regulation on the grounds that this would help avoid imposition of restrictions from above [12].

Though self-regulation via codes of conduct may reduce government interference with science, the government may, nevertheless, still have an important role to play in the regulation of dual-use science in particular (even if apt codes are adopted) for reasons I will explain later. For now I will merely suggest that completely autonomous self-governed science would likely be incompatible with democracy. Science affects society in innumerable ways, and so society should surely have at least some control over science [11].

### "Process Benefits"

A final potentially beneficial role of science codes of conduct, according to Brian Rappert, relates to "process benefits" that accrue from deliberation about them or other activities related to their development and/or adoption. The perceived need for (and resultant activities surrounding) codes of conduct to address the dual use dilemma in the life sciences, according to Rappert, has lead to a fruitful "furthering [of] communication, consultation, coordination, and collaboration between organisations" and/or key stake holders that previously had relatively little to do with each other [16]. Another benefit that may arise from the development of codes of conduct is that sustained rigorous debate and deliberation about their content may lead to greater clarity regarding the ethical principles that should govern scientific activity.

## Codes of Conduct—Limits

While codes of conduct may, as described above, play valuable roles in dealing with problems posed by dual-use science and technology, they also have limitations. Codes of conduct may be important, but they are not magic bullets. One common critique of codes of conduct points to challenges regarding their level of specificity. While people such as Joseph Rotblat (in the 1990s) have championed the idea of a "Hippocratic Oath for Scientists"—i.e., a universal code of conduct for scientists—others have argued that a universal science code of conduct would inevitably lack substance and/or be too general to be action guiding. One point is that any science code of conduct that would be generally acceptable to all sciences and scientists would presumably be one which merely listed uncontroversial commonsense precepts that conscientious people would presumably seek to follow whether or not they were enshrined in codes of conduct. A second point is that any science code of conduct that was general enough to apply to all sciences may lack sufficient detail to clearly prescribe action in the specific contexts of particular sciences. While a response to the second concern may be the idea that different sciences need their own codes of conduct, a proliferation of potentially conflicting codes may then arise and raise questions about which has ultimate authority. In any case, according to critics, the more specific detail that is put into codes (for any particular sciences) to make them more clearly prescriptive about who should do what under what circumstances, the more controversial and less widely accepted they would be.

A second major critique of science codes of conduct holds that, unless they are enforced, codes of conduct will not be effective. The point here is simply that those who would do the kinds of things ruled out by codes of conduct are precisely the kinds of people that would not follow (voluntary) codes of conduct to begin with. To be truly effective, according to critics, codes of conduct must be enforced by sanctions.

## Enforcement

In response to this last objection, it should be noted that there are various mechanisms by which science codes of conduct could be enforced in practice. While codes of conduct are often advocated as a form of "bottom-up" voluntary self-governance by scientists and/or the scientific community, this does not mean that no enforcement of science codes of conduct is possible. One idea is that the scientific community could itself enforce codes on its members. This would be possible, for example, via the *professionalisation* of sciences [22]. If sciences were professionalised (like medicine), then adherence to codes of conduct could be required as a condition of official membership within, or licensing by, the professional society.

Enforcement of codes of conduct is also possible via funding bodies. One commonly proposed mechanism for addressing problems posed by dual-use research would involve including review of dual use dangers associated with proposed research as part of the research oversight process. For such a mechanism to work most effectively, we would want scientists to (reflect upon and) report dual use issues arising with the research being proposed to the ethics and/ or biosafety committee reviewing the research proposal. Codes of conduct could mandate that scientists do this, and funding bodies could make adherence with such a mandate a condition of funding eligibility. This is how clinical research ethics guidelines are currently enforced in countries like the US: rather than being required by law, adherence to clinical research ethics guidelines is a condition of (e.g., NIH) funding. Given the importance of funding to research, this kind of enforcement has proven to be highly effective.

Last but not least, science codes of conduct could also potentially be enforced by law. Governments, that is, could impose legislation requiring that scientists adhere to codes requiring them to, among other things, (reflect upon and) report dual use issues arising with research (and/or potential publications) being proposed to relevant institutional review committees. This could be part of a broader set of regulations that also mandate the establishment of appropriate committees and specify procedures to be followed by committees reviewing studies (and/or potential publications) posing dual use dangers [13]. Such regulations might require that review committees at the level of research institutions eventually refer studies (and/or potential publications) to a governmental body or a nongovernmental regulatory authority for "higher-level review" in the most difficult cases. Just as regulations might require individual scientists to refer studies to a local institutional review board, regulations could require local institutional review boards to refer them to higher-level review boards (e.g., with greater expertise and/or decision making authority) under specified circumstances.

In response to the idea that at least some parts of science codes of conduct should be legally enforced, one might be tempted to think that if particular actions are required by law then their inclusion in codes of conduct would be redundant. This objection, like many of the other objections to codes of conduct considered above, fails to recall the role of codes of conduct with regard to awareness-raising. Though prohibitions of the weapons conventions are already written into law (in signatory countries), a benefit of including clauses regarding the weapons conventions in codes of conduct is that this would increase scientists' awareness of what the law actually is.

## Regulation

While codes of conduct are often advocated by those who favour voluntary self-governance of the scientific community, it is dubious that (with or without codes of conduct) we should rely entirely on scientists to govern themselves in the context of dual-use science and technology. A consensus has emerged in debates over the dual use dilemma in the life sciences that we need to strike a balance between the promotion of scientific progress, on the one hand, and the promotion of security, on the other [14]. Both of these legitimate values are at stake, and neither should have absolute priority over the other. Heavy regulation of science may come at too high a cost in terms of scientific progress; but we need adequate governance/oversight for the protection of security.

Scientists are right to be worried about too much governmental interference with science. If decisions about what research is done and what papers are published are left in the hands of bureaucrats, then (based on what they do for a living) the decision makers will likely be biased in favour of security over science values, and they might often lack expertise for judging the scientific importance of research they might want to vet or papers they might want to censor [19].

Leaving decision making in the hands of scientists, on the other hand, poses similar risks. Scientists (based on what they do for a living) are likely to be biased in favour of science values over security values, and (lacking background in security studies) they will usually lack expertise for assessing the security dangers of their research. The danger of relying on voluntary self-governance of scientists is perhaps best illustrated by further reflection on the mousepox study. This case reveals that scientists are sometimes systematically denied access to information required for assessment of the risks of research and/or publication [19]. The primary risk associated with the mousepox study is that the genetic engineering technique they used might enable production of vaccine resistant smallpox. For bioterrorists (or state sponsored biological weapons programs) to employ this technique on smallpox, however, they would need to have access to the smallpox virus to begin with. Because all of the world's remaining smallpox samples are officially supposed to be safe and secure at only two facilities worldwide (i.e., the Centers for Disease Control and Prevention in the US, and a similar facility in Russia), the primary danger is that there has been proliferation from the former Soviet Union's biological weapons program's stockpiles of the virus. Any detailed information about likely/possible smallpox proliferation, however, is classified information [1] that scientists (lacking security clearance) would not have access to. Assessing the dangers of publishing the mousepox study, therefore, is beyond the expertise of ordinary scientists.

If we want decision making that strikes a balance between the promotion of science and the protection of security—by decision makers that have adequate expertise for assessing the extent to which both kinds of values are threatened—it may thus be imprudent to allow scientists to govern themselves (via voluntary codes of conduct). The ultimate decision making authority (in difficult cases) should embody sufficient expertise regarding both science and security, and should not be biased in favour of either science or security values. A mixed panel of experts comprised of scientists, security experts, ethicists, civilians, and members of government could arguably provide the right combination of expertise and values [19]. Retrospective analysis of the mousepox study reveals that we would have wanted the scientists involved to have their paper reviewed/approved by such a panel prior to publication. An enforceable code of conduct that required them to refer the paper to such a panel would have helped make that happen. A code of conduct would have played a role, but it would have been part of a broader regulatory oversight system.

## Conclusion

Those concerned with ethical issues associated with the dual use potential of nanotechnology have much to learn from recent experience regarding dual-use life science research—which has been the focus of attention regarding dual-use science and technology in recent years. Science codes of conduct may play important roles in raising awareness about the dual use phenomenon, the requirements of weapons conventions, and the social responsibilities of scientists. Implementation of codes of conduct might also help win trust in the scientific enterprise and prevent over-regulation of science by government. Nevertheless, there are challenges regarding the level of generality/specificity that science codes of conduct should have; and unenforced codes of conduct may not effectively govern behaviour of scientists. In response to criticisms that codes of conduct are ineffective if they are unenforceable, it should be noted that there are various mechanisms by which codes of conduct can be enforced. Rather than being essentially associated with voluntary self-governance of scientists, (at least some parts of) codes of conduct should arguably be part of a broader regulatory oversight system.

**Acknowledgment** An earlier version of this paper was presented at the "Gordon Cain Conference: The Dilemmas of Dual Use", Chemical Heritage Foundation, Philadelphia, March 2008. The production of this article was partly supported by a Wellcome Trust Enhancement Award in Biomedical Ethics—"Building a Sustainable Capacity in Dual-Use Bioethics" (Chief Investigators: Malcolm Dando, Simon Whitby, Jim Whitman, Brian Rappert, Judi Sture, and Michael Selgelid). I am grateful to an anonymous reviewer for numerous astute editorial suggestions.

## References

1. Annas GJ (2005) American bioethics. Oxford University Press, New York
2. Cardellini L (2007) Ronald Hoffmann's *Should've*: Ethics and science on stage. Chemistry international, 29. Retreived March 9, 2008 from http://www.iupac.org/publications/ci/2007/2903/1_cardellini.html
3. Cello J, Paul AV, Wimmer E (2002) Chemical synthesis of poliovirus cDNA: generation of infectious virus in the absence of natural template. Science 297:1016–1018
4. Central Intelligence Agency (2003) The darker bioweapons future. Retreived June 19, 2009 from http://www.fas.org/irp/cia/product/bw1103.pdf
5. Dando MR, Rappert B (2005) Codes of conduct for the life sciences: Some insights from UK academia. Briefing Paper No. 16, Department of Peace Studies, University of Bradford. Retreived 18 October 2009 from http://www.brad.ac.uk/acad/sbtwc/briefing/BP_16_2ndseries.pdf
6. Green SK, Taub S, Morin K, Higginson D et al (2006) Guidelines to prevent malevolent use of biomedical research. Camb Q Healthc Ethics 15:432–447
7. Jackson RJ, Ramsay AJ, Christensen CD, Beaton S, Hall DF, Ramshaw IA (2001) Expression of mouse interleukin-4 by a recombinant ectromelia virus suppresses cytolytic lymphocyte responses and overcomes genetic resistance to mousepox. J Virol 75:1205–1210
8. Jones N (2007) A code of ethics for the life sciences. Sci Eng Ethics 13:25–43
9. Joravsky D (1970) The Lysenko affair. Harvard University Press, Cambridge
10. Journal Editors and Authors Group (2003) Uncensored exchange of scientific results. Proc Natl Acad Sci 100:1464
11. Kitcher P (2001) Science, truth and democracy. Oxford University Press, New York
12. Maurer SM, Lucas KV, Terrell S (2006) From understanding to action: Community-based options for improving safety and security in synthetic biology. University of California, Berkeley Retrieved June 1, 2007 from http://gspp.berkeley.edu/iths/UC%20White%20Paper.pdf
13. Miller S, Selgelid MJ (2008) Ethical and philosophical consideration of the dual-use dilemma in the biological sciences. Springer, Dordrecht
14. National Research Council (2004) Biotechnology research in an age of terrorism. National Academies, Washington DC
15. National Research Council (2006) Globalization, biosecurity, and the future of the life sciences. National Academies, Washington DC
16. Rappert B (2007) Codes of conduct and biological weapons: an in-process assessment. Biosecurity and Bioterrorism 5:145–154
17. Samuel GN, Selgelid MJ, Kerridge I (2009) Managing the unimaginable: regulatory responses to the challenges posed by synthetic biology and synthetic genomics. EMBO Reports 10:7–11
18. Schweber S (2000) In the shadow of the bomb: Bethe, Oppenheimer, and the moral responsibility of the scientist. Princeton University Press, Princeton
19. Selgelid MJ (2007) A tale of two studies. Hastings Cent Rep 37:35–43
20. Somerville MA, Atlas RM (2005) Ethics: a weapon to counter bioterrorism. Science 307:1881–1882
21. Tumpey TM, Basler CF, Aguilar PV, Zeng H, Solorzano A, Swayne DE et al (2005) Characterization of the reconstructed 1918 Spanish Influenza pandemic virus. Science 310:77–80
22. Weir L, Selgelid MJ (2009) Professionalization as a governance strategy for synthetic biology. Syst Synth Biol 3:91–97

Arch. Immunol. Ther. Exp. (2008) 56:147–152
DOI 10.1007/s00005-008-0020-7

VARIA – ETHICS IN SCIENCE

# Dual Use and the Ethical Responsibility of Scientists

**Hans-Jörg Ehni**

Received: 19 February 2008 / Accepted: 8 May 2008 / Published online: 30 May 2008


**Abstract** The main normative problem in the context of dual use is to determine the ethical responsibility of scientists especially in the case of unintended, harmful, and criminal dual use of new technological applications of scientific results. This article starts from an analysis of the concepts of responsibility and complicity, examining alternative options regarding the responsibility of scientists. Within the context of the basic conflict between the freedom of science and the duty to avoid causing harm, two positions are discussed: moral skepticism and the ethics of responsibility by Hans Jonas. According to these reflections, four duties are suggested and evaluated: stopping research, systematically carrying out research for dual-use applications, informing public authorities, and not publishing results. In the conclusion it is argued that these duties should be considered as imperfect duties in a Kantian sense and that the individual scientist should be discharged as much as possible from obligations which follow from them by the scientific community and institutions created for this purpose.

**Keywords** Research ethics · Dual use · Responsibility · Complicity

H.-J. Ehni (✉)
Institute of Ethics and History of Medicine,
University of Tübingen,
Tübingen, Germany
e-mail: hans-joerg.ehni@uni-tuebingen.de

## Introduction

"Dual use" is a concept which is basically related to the possibility to use goods or technologies for either civilian or military purposes. This is especially relevant in the context of export, where an international agreement, "The Wassenaar Arrangement on Export Controls for Conventional Arms and Dual-Use Goods and Technologies" of May 12, 1996, has now been signed by 40 nations. The European Union issued directive EC 1334/2000, which contains a list of dual-use goods and technologies which should not be exported. Very often it is just the intention of an actor which determines whether something could be considered a weapon or not. The phenomenon is obviously not new, also in the context of science and technology, as such legends as the use of mirrors invented by Archimedes to burn ships show. But the existence of weapons of mass destruction and the increase in international terrorism contribute to a very critical situation.

The results of scientific research, especially if it concerns fundamental natural processes, can have a wide range of desirable and undesirable technological applications. It might be difficult, and only possible in the long run, to decide which are desirable and which are not. The "classical" dual-use case from the beginning of the 20th century is the discovery of chain reactions and the like in physics and its dual use for atomic bombs and nuclear energy. In the beginning of the 21th century, the technology which raises the most concern is the genetic construction and reconstruction of pathogenic organisms and viruses by biotechnological means. The most discussed recent cases have been the description of a procedure to increase the pathogenic character of mousepox, which could be used for smallpox as well, the synthesis of a polio genome, and the reconstruction of the virus which caused the fatal Spanish flu in 1918 (Selgelid 2007; Van Aken 2007). What raises special concern is that bioweapons are much cheaper to construct with these technologies and that, once the necessary procedures are published, they are available via the internet. While the dual use of technologies, scientific results, and goods which are well known requires juridical regulation on the national and international level, the possible dual use of new technologies and new scientific results creates ethical problems for the scientist and the scientific community, especially with regard to how to define the responsibility to prevent such dual use. As a first step towards such a definition, the concept of dual use has to be further analyzed to show where these problems are most acute.

In principle, the concept of dual use can be related to several different pairs of oppositions. The following are relevant in this context: intended or unintended, beneficial or harmful, and legal or criminal. Basic research can of course be carried out without having any application in mind. A researcher may also try to develop a certain application for a technology, discover a second possibility for a future use, and also follow up on this possibility. From this point it would be considered "intended dual use". Even if the research was dedicated to achieve a certain purpose and to develop a certain technology, this technology may be used by others for purposes other than those originally intended. Depending on the technology and on the newly intended purpose, this can be beneficial or harmful, in some cases extremely harmful, as for instance in the case of the use of nuclear energy and the construction of nuclear weapons. However, even harmful technologies might be used by states for legal purposes, such as wars justified by international law, which at least for some scientists may not create specific ethical problems. Therefore, the further distinction of legal or criminal has to be introduced. Applications can be legal or criminal, such as doping in sports or possible terrorist attacks with modified pathogenic organisms. The latter is the kind of dual use that calls for strict juridical regulation. From the perspective of the scientist and the scientific community, all these types of dual use generate different normative problems, but also the last case is the most difficult to solve.

However, it is not the normative evaluation of dual use in such acts and their contexts (actors, victims, ideologies, etc.) which creates any specific problems in itself. A terrorist attack in which people are killed will be considered murder, and if a new technology was abused to carry out this action, this adds nothing to this basic qualification. Of course, the sophisticated application of a technology in a crime or the high degree of cruelty which is needed to apply a certain technology for such a purpose will qualify a crime as especially malicious and detestable, but this is related to the kind of technology which is used and precisely how it is used. The simple fact that a new technology or scientific knowledge is applied for a criminal purpose for which it was not originally conceived is not an ethical problem in itself. Also, national and international regulation in reaction to potentially harmful and dangerous research results, their application, or dissemination does not create an ethical problem in itself, as it is a legitimate aim to protect citizens from harmful technologies in an international context.

The ethical problem is the specific responsibility of the scientist who created these results and of science as a social institution. Here the freedom of science conflicts with other values. There is no basic difference between direct involvement of research dedicated to the development of a dual-use application and direct involvement in any other action. Consequently, this kind of responsibility will not be the main concern in this context. Analyzing the responsibility of the individual scientist and of the scientific community becomes more difficult if dual use is unintended, harmful, and criminal.

## Responsibility in Dual Use

Responsibility is often analyzed as a predicate with four variables: *Who* is responsible for *what* to *whom* and *why*? Or more formally: "X is responsible for Y to W because of Z", where X is the actor, Y the object of that action, W the person or institution which has a claim on that responsibility, and Z is defined by the relevant moral duties in the respective context. Additionally, prospective responsibility is distinguished from retrospective responsibility. Prospective responsibility can be illustrated by the responsibility to care for somebody founded on a duty resulting from the role the responsible person has, e.g. the responsibility parents have for their children. In the case of harmful unintended dual use it is crucial to define the duties of the scientist and of the scientific community from which the prospective responsibility of both result. Retrospective responsibility is that which is related to imputation, e.g. for the result of an action which is imputed to the actor who contributed actively to this action or who could have prevented it. Both forms of responsibility are interconnected: because somebody has had a certain prospective responsibility, he can be held responsible for a certain action. The question here is not how far a scientist is responsible for the intended effects of his action, but how far he is responsible for the foreseen effects of his research, for their prevention and also for the effort to predict certain effects. The answer will depend on how the prospective responsibility related to the duties corresponding to the role of the scientist and the scientific community will be defined in the given case (Duff 1998).

## The Freedom of Science, Moral Skepticism, and Responsibility

But is a scientist really responsible in this case? Does not the freedom of science allow someone to carry out research however undesirable its results may be, and is it not the task of legislation and the executive powers of the state to control its application? In unintended, harmful, and criminal dual use, the scientist could be considered not to have any responsibility regarding the application of the results of his research. As the freedom of science and research are considered important values in our societies, an unclear, indirect responsibility might not provide sufficient arguments for a limitation of this freedom. On the other hand, a scientist could still believe himself to have far-reaching prospective and retrospective responsibility for such an application, even if he only provided the necessary basic knowledge. A scientist could very well feel guilty because of foreseeable effects of dual-use applications and for his omission to prevent harmful effects. There is a basic conflict between the freedom of the researcher and the duty to prevent harm which is difficult to solve because it is unclear what the contribution to the relevant action is and to what degree this is controllable. As we are only responsible for something we can control, the point is to what degree the scientific community and the individual scientist can be considered to be able to control such effects. For both options, i.e. a high degree of responsibility and no responsibility, further arguments can be provided.

The scientist could be considered to have no responsibility at all for the application of the results of his research work in dual use. A possible foundation for this position could be general skepticism directed against the relevance of ethical principles to science. For instance, the German sociologist Niklas Luhmann considered science to be a self-organizing social system which follows a binary code, with the options true or false. Moral reflections can have no influence in the quest for truth. Luhmann believes that the autopoiesis of knowledge, as he calls the generation of knowledge in the self-organizing social system of science, cannot be controlled by research ethics and by the interdiction of certain types of research. The social system of science will produce any truth in the long run, no matter how undesirable knowing this truth might be. Of course, other social systems, such as the juridical system, could apply their own binary codes, such as legal or illegal, to science and research. But Luhmann thinks that the effectiveness of prohibiting research and the publication of results is very low. Distinctions like beneficence or maleficence run across to the basic code of science, i.e. true or false. Even if there is agreement that in some cases ignorance would be better, this can hardly be achieved by prohibitions, because they are too easy to break and can be too easily avoided in an international context. For Luhmann, science is confronted with two impositions: to consider the quest for truth as risky and to assume responsibility if the true knowledge generated by scientific research triggers causal chains. Both impositions are inconsistent with truth as the positive ideal of science (Luhmann 1990). While at least the sociologist might accept that there is a problem, as there are important risks, he offers no solution and also confirms that there can be none. A social institution would be needed to decide what would be right or wrong in the quest for scientific truth. But such an institution, in his opinion, is impossible because there cannot be an institution representing the whole society within society itself. This raises important questions in the context of dual use: Can the production of knowledge which is considered dangerous because of dual-use applications be controlled? Can the dissemination of this knowledge be controlled? And how can an institution which controls dual use be conceived and what can the role of science in such an institution be? Skeptics like Luhmann provide no positive answers to these questions, but they show that there will be no easy solution.

Surprisingly, Hans Jonas, one of the most widely read philosophers in the ethics of science in Germany and still influential in the international bioethics community, shares some of the basic assumptions of Luhmann's moral skepticism: It will be extremely difficult or even impossible to ban a certain type of research completely because of the global dimension of scientific research. And it is also hardly possible to keep scientific results secret (Jonas 1987). But Jonas offers a different analysis of the basic situation of science. Scientific freedom which includes the claim to be free of restrictions can only be justified by the contemplative character of science, without any involvement in the sphere of actions. However, Jonas shows that this contemplative character is lost in most scientific disciplines apart from mathematics and cosmology. The reason for this is the inseparable unity which links modern science with technology. Technological demands, interests, and input in the form of results of applications direct scientific endeavor in which technological instruments are themselves indispensable tools for further progress, for example in measurement. Science is no longer pure theory and therefore scientists and the scientific community are accountable for the consequences of their research. From these possible consequences of potentially apocalyptical, global dimension results a very high degree of responsibility for scientists. In the long run it is also extremely difficult to distinguish legitimate use from misuse of technologies and scientific results, which is directly relevant in the case of dual use. In his main work, "The Imperative of Responsibility", Jonas therefore, as a reaction to this situation, formulates an ethics of responsibility. The internal dynamics and immense power of modern science require an increased awareness of individual and social responsibility, which is expressed by Jonas in a modification of Kant's categorical imperative: "Act so that the effects of your action are compatible with the permanence of genuine human life" (Jonas 1984). This imperative demands foresight and precaution from each scientist and the scientific community. It is clear from his above skepticism that this responsibility cannot be borne alone by individual scientists, and that it also cannot be guaranteed by political or social institutions alone, which according to Jonas are difficult to conceive and are only in their early beginnings. Part of this responsibility certainly has to be assumed by institutions created by the scientific community itself and by their recommendations, as in the case of the ethics of research involving human subjects. Jonas also offers an example of concrete measures: a moratorium on a certain type of research. While these are all general recommendations based on his conception of responsibility, he offers no detailed analysis of the responsibility of the scientist or the scientific community which could provide a model for prospective responsibility and the related duties in the case of unintended, harmful, and criminal dual use.

## Duties and Complicity

The general duty of the scientist and the scientific community in this case is not to contribute to this type of dual use, as far as this is controllable, and to help to prevent it. This results not only from the duty to prevent harm, but also from the scientific competence to support or foresee such dual-use applications with scientific knowledge. Without the contribution of scientists it will not be possible to predict and regulate dual use. Some more concrete and possible duties which might fall under this general duty and which need further discussion have already been mentioned above, and others can be easily added. The first two duties are related to limitations of research, while 3 and 4 require a certain handling of results:

1) do not carry out a certain type of research;
2) systematically anticipate dual-use applications in order to warn of dangers generated by them;
3) inform public authorities about such dangers;
4) do not disseminate results publicly, but keep danger ous scientific knowledge secret.

The scope of these duties and the degree of the related prospective responsibility is difficult to determine from a general point of view. However, an analysis of the retrospective responsibility in a concrete case will contribute to further clarification. A helpful instrument in such an analysis is the concept of complicity, which is used in other bioethical debates (Birnbacher 2006).

The concept of complicity is used to distinguish different degrees of contribution to the success of an action. These degrees correspond to decreasing involvement in the action: "direct causality", "indirect causality", "causality by normative evaluation", and "expressive dissonance". In particular, this means that an actor, K, contributes to an action in the following ways:

1) K contributes consciously to the success of an immoral action h (direct causality);
2) K causes or encourages another actor to h (indirect causality);
3) K encourages third parties to a more tolerant attitude to h (causality by normative evaluation);
4) K disagrees with the moral condemnation of h (expressive dissonance).

All types of complicity generate a corresponding degree of retrospective responsibility. How could they be applied in a concrete case of unintended, harmful, and criminal dual use? As an example, let us assume a scientist has carried out basic research on the modification of cells. As a possible application of his new discoveries, he postulates a technology to increase the pathogenic character of a certain kind of bacteria. He publishes a scientific article about his research, including a detailed description of the technological application, and some months later there is an assault, obviously based on his findings. This might be an unrealistic scenario as the awareness of such possible dangers is already increased, but this does not necessarily have to be the case in the future, so even if the example is unrealistic at the moment, it is not impossible that something comparable might happen.

In such a case, the scientist might possibly feel responsible, and even guilty. Is this justified in relation to the different degrees of complicity? Expressive dissonance (4) and causality by normative evaluation (3) can be excluded in this case, although they might be relevant in other dual-use contexts, for instance if a medical doctor generally describes the advantages of a certain therapy and possible other uses in a way that encourages doping in sports. Direct causality (1) can also be excluded, as by definition the scientist did not contribute consciously to the unintended dual use. What remains is indirect causality (2). Did the scientist in our case cause or encourage another actor to carry out an assault? Clearly this was not the case, as the scientist was not involved in the planning or in the proceedings of the action. But there might be a lower degree of indirect causality in the present case to which the scientist has contributed. He did not cause another actor to act, but he created one of the necessary preconditions to this action. The scientist did not give a stone to somebody and tell him: "If you throw this stone in that window, I will make you a rich man", but he may have left a pile of stones somewhere or described how stones could be made. He did not encourage the actor to act, but he described how such an action could be carried out. The scientist not tell anyone, "It would be a good thing to throw a stone through this window", but he stated: "This is a stone which can be found in this place and it could be thrown through windows". How should we evaluate the degree of responsibility which would result from comparable statements? In certain contexts it would be morally neutral, but if people are around who are searching for stones to throw through windows and the scientist should have known that, it may be considered negligent behavior with a low degree of indirect causality and, therefore, a certain corresponding moral responsibility, probably without legal consequences, but perhaps not in the juridical system of the U.S., which tends to generous compensation for damages of all sorts. Whether the scientist feels guilty or not in the present case may be a question of character and moral sensibility, but it could hardly be said that it is totally unjustified.

## Perfect and Imperfect Duties

According to these reflections it is possible to assume a low degree of responsibility of the scientist involved in the present case of dual use resulting from a variant of indirect causality. However, to have a low degree of responsibility for a fatal outcome could still be the foundation for strict duties. Which of the duties mentioned above does the scientist have in the present case? Should he have stopped his research before the results which were used in the assault could be produced? Or did he even have the duty to systematically continue his research in the new direction in order to discover possible dangers and counter-measures? A principle or maxim in the Kantian sense would be, for instance, "Stop research if there is a danger of unintended, harmful, criminal dual use", on which such duties could be considered imperfect duties. The contrary "Never stop research..." would not be universally applicable, as rational beings would not want the possibility that they might be harmed by the respective research, and this cannot be excluded. But the maxim still corresponds to an imperfect duty. This means that it is possible to think of it as a universal law, but it is not desirable for rational beings. It is not a perfect duty because a universal law according to which research should never be stopped does not lead to a contradiction which makes it unthinkable, and it is also not a perfect duty because it depends on contexts and further practical judgments, like other imperfect duties according to Kantian examples, for instance the duty to help. On the other hand, continuing the respective research to explore dangers and counter-measures, together with informing public authorities, could contribute to the prevention of fatal incidents of dual use. The same arguments could be provided for the duty not to publish results.

## Conclusion

I have tried to show that the involvement of a scientist in a fatal case of unintended, harmful, and criminal dual use can be considered complicity in the sense of a weak indirect causality. From this results a retrospective responsibility and, possibly, the feeling of guilt, which cannot be easily refuted. Furthermore, four basic duties can be formulated to define the prospective responsibility of scientists: 1) stopping research in some cases, 2) systematically exploring dangers of dual use in some cases, 3) informing public authorities about possible dangers resulting from research and the application of its result, and 4) not publishing results and descriptions of research results and possible dual-use applications.

All these duties can be considered imperfect duties, and the precise obligations which result from them in the context of concrete cases can be very difficult to determine. Also, moral skepticism and the ethics of responsibility share doubts on the effectiveness of measures taken by the individual researcher or scientist. These doubts refer to both possible measures: banning research and the publication of results. This difficult situation for the individual researcher can only be solved by the scientific community and their institutions. A heated debate has especially resulted from the mousepox and polio studies around the problem whether in that case the benefits of publication outweighed the risks. But who will be able to determine the long-term risk of a fatal bioterrorist attack? In February 2003 a "Statement on Scientific Publication and Security" was published by the "Journal Editors and Authors Group" (Atlas et al. 2003). Concerned by a possible limitation of the integrity of the scientific process, including adequate publication of results, the statement acknowledges that "on occasion an editor may conclude that the potential harm of publication outweighs the potential societal benefits" (Atlas et al. 2003). Of course the argument of public security to limit civil freedom may be easily abused and the censorship of scientific results is a severe problem for academic freedom and freedom in our societies in general. But Jonas' imperative of responsibility, the difficulty to predict long-term effects, and the difficulty to know the context of a publication can render the weight of responsibility far too great for a single editor and a single scientist. It is no solution to the "dual-use" problem to transfer total responsibility to individuals in these cases. Miller and Selgelid (Miller and Selgelid 2007) discuss different options of how to organize this responsibility in a long recommendation on how to handle the dual-use dilemma. These options range from the autonomy of the single scientist to complete governmental control. According to the moral requirements formulated above, only a mixed authority which is constituted by the scientific community together with governmental bodies, but with the participation of scientists meeting their responsibility so far as possible, can solve the problem. Scientists should identify with the purposes of such institutions because these assume the greatest part of their personal responsibility.

Scientific knowledge and the awareness of individual scientists are indispensable, but not sufficient. As it would be ineffective if only applied by individuals, it can only be the scientific community which should arrange committees to fulfill the necessary tasks resulting from the four duties above. Authorities like the US National Research Council can and should formulate lists of "experiments of concern", as has been done in the NRC "Report on Biotechnology in an Age of Terrorism" (National Research Council 2004). Public authorities alone will not be sufficiently competent and individual scientists will need colleagues who are familiar with dual-use problems to consult in cases where their responsibilities are hard to define. But the wider context of the relevant research and the necessary knowledge to meet the "imperfect duties", for instance possible security threats, can only be provided by public authorities. As the reflections of Miller and Selgelid (Miller and Selgelid 2007) show, the task of organizing such an authority is complex and difficult and cannot be discussed in the context of the present article. However, the analysis of the possible retrospective responsibility of the individual scientist and the corresponding duties shows that it is necessary to create such authorities, not at least to discharge scientists from a responsibility which might be of low degree, but have far too heavy a weight for individuals.

## References


Atlas, R., P. Campbell, N.R. Cozzarelli, G. Curfman, L. Engquist, G. Fink, A. Flanagin, J. Fletcher, E. George, G. Hammes, D. Heyman, T. Inglesby, S. Kaplan, D. Kennedy, J. Krug, R.E. Levinson, E. Marcus, H. Metzger, S.S. Morse, A. O'Brien, A. Onderdonk, G. Poste, B. Renault, R. Rich, A. Rosengard, S. Salzburg, M. Scanlan, T. Shenk, H. Tabor, H. Varmus, E. Wimmer, K. Ymamoto, and Journal Editors and Authors Group. 2003. Uncensored exchange of scientific results. *Proceedings of the National academy of Sciences of the United States of America* 100: 1464.

Birnbacher, D. 2006. *Bioethik zwischen Natur und Interesse*, 357–360. Frankfurt am Main: Suhrkamp.

Duff, R.A. 1998. Responsibility. In *Routledge encyclopedia of philosophy*, 8, 290–294. London-New York: Routledge.

Jonas, H. 1984. *The imperative of responsibility*, 11. Chicago: The University of Chicago Press.

Jonas, H. 1987. *Technik, Medizin und Ethik*, 78. Frankfurt am Main: Suhrkamp.

Luhmann, N. 1990. *Die Wissenschaft der Gesellschaft*, 663–664. Frankfurt am Main: Suhrkamp.

Miller, S., and M.J. Selgelid. 2007. Ethical and philosophical consideration of the dual-use dilemma in the biological sciences. *Science and Engineering Ethics* 13: 563–580.

National Research Council. 2004. *Biotechnology research in an age of terrorism*. Washington, D.C: National Academies of Science.

Selgelid, M.J. 2007. A tale of two studies. ethics, bioterrorism, and the censorship of science. *The Hastings Center Report* 37: 35–43.

Van Aken, J. 2007. Ethics of reconstructing Spanish flu: Is it wise to resurrect a deadly virus? *Heredity* 98: 1–2.

# Keyword Index

MIX
Papier aus verantwortungsvollen Quellen
Paper from responsible sources
FSC® C105338

If you have any concerns about our products,
you can contact us on
**ProductSafety@springernature.com**

In case Publisher is established outside the EU,
the EU authorized representative is:
**Springer Nature Customer Service Center GmbH**
**Europaplatz 3, 69115 Heidelberg, Germany**

Printed by Libri Plureos GmbH
in Hamburg, Germany